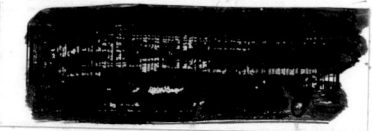
THE ART OF
BRYAN TALBOT

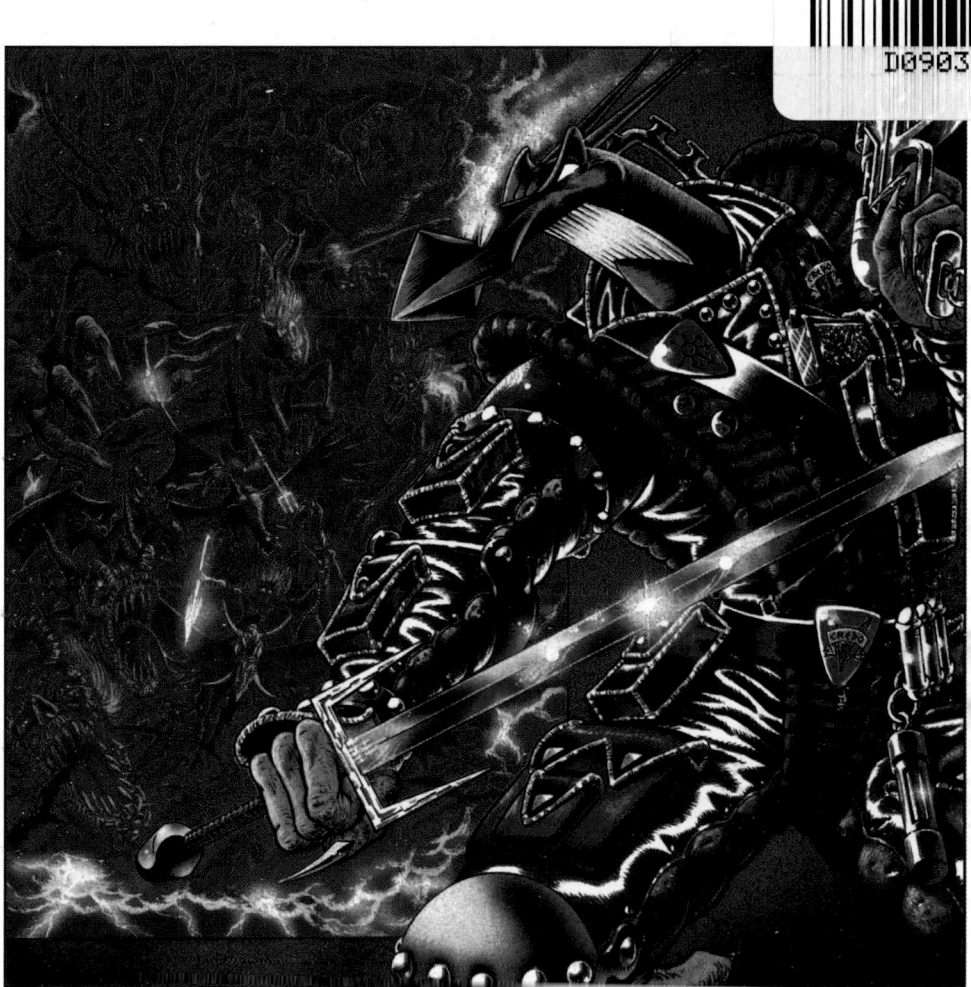

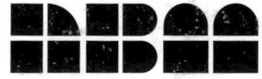

NANTIER · BEALL · MINOUSTCHINE
Publishing inc.
new york

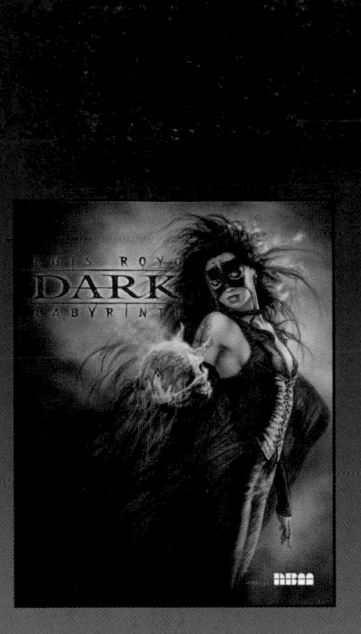

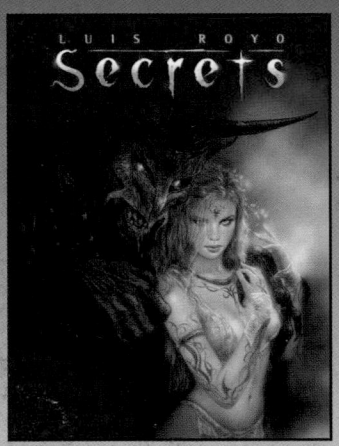

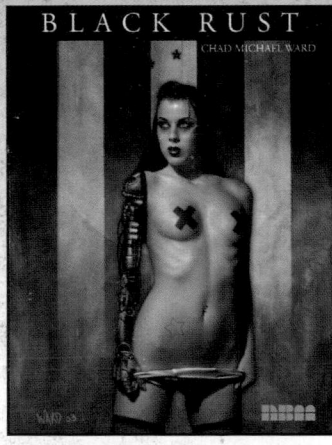

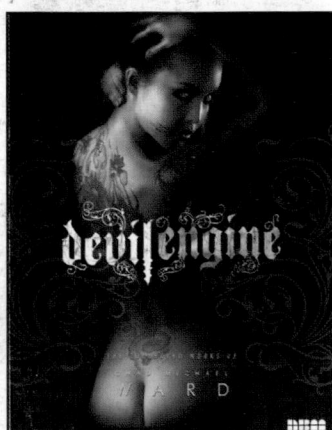

Add $3 P&H first item $1 each additional.

Write for our complete catalog
of over 200 graphic novels:
NBM
40 Exchange Pl., Suite 1308
New York, NY 10005
www.nbmpublishing.com

ISBN 10: 1-56163-512-X
ISBN 13: 978-1-56163-512-2
©2007 Bryan Talbot
Printed in China
3 2 1

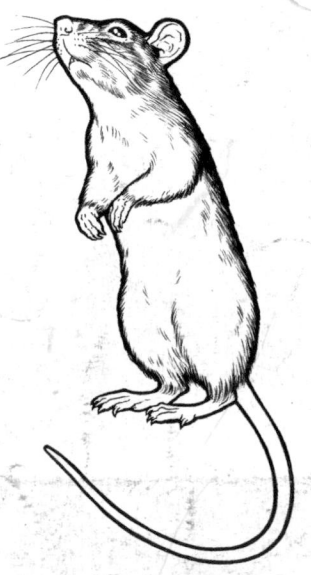

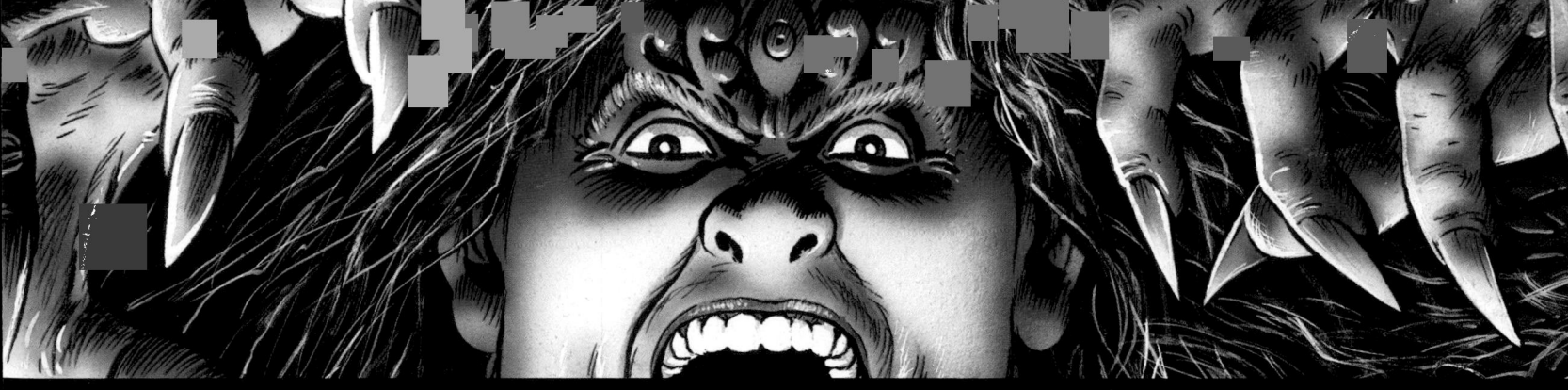

INTRODUCTION

Bryan Talbot,

I was there at the beginning, or almost. I was fourteen, and my cousin Adam, almost a year older than I was, into music and hippie stuff and not really into comics at all, handed me Brainstorm number one. I read the stories of Chester P. Hackenbush, cosmic alchemist, seeing influences from the Underground and the Overground, from comics and SF, and finding it fresher and more interesting than most psychedelic comics. The drawing I thought, in that snotty way that 14 year olds do better than anyone, had potential.

Over the next few years Bryan Talbot stayed on my radar – I loved his early Luther Arkwright work, was happy to see him cropping up in SOUNDS, and was impressed when I met him for the first time, stylish and flame-haired (the hair-colour was henna-assisted), at a Benefit for Knockabout Comics, who were in, I think, 1983, being persecuted by the police and UK Customs.

Our paths kept crossing. My second short story was published in a magazine with a Bryan Talbot cover and feature. I started writing things, and found myself invited to talk to the Preston SF group, of which Bryan was a pillar and organiser, and discovered to my terrified surprise that I could talk to groups of people and rather enjoyed it.

Our first collaboration was on, I think, a story called "From Homogenous to Honey", for Alan and Phyllis Moore and Debbie Delano's Artists Against Rampant Government Homophobia anthology. Then we did SLOTH for Knockabout Comics and I found myself hooked on working with that man Talbot. Bryan is a craftsman. If you write comics, you want Bryan to draw your scripts, it's as simple as that. I did it again and again in Sandman, when I wanted someone sane who would draw the script and bring something else to it as well. The way the shadows in the market place move with the sun in our story about the emperor Augustus – it was small, and brilliant, and it made the story real.

Personally, Bryan is kind, funny, sensible, quizzical and generous. That's not why people like his art, though, nor why they buy his comics.

There's a point where artists stop growing, stop changing, stop learning. Bryan isn't there yet. The point of a book like this is that it charts his progress.

We love artists because they give us their eyes, they give us a new way of seeing.

The point of a book like this is it shows us the world through Bryan's eyes (I love his figure drawings – at the same time both figure drawings and unmistakably Bryan Talbot people.) The point of a book like this is that it shows us how that world has changed.

When you watch someone grow and change over thirty years, sometimes the changes are imperceptible. They are always themselves. It's rarely a one-day-you-look-different shock (Bryan had one of those the day he stopped hennaing his hair and discovered he had amazing grey streaks no-one had known about, not even him). A book like this – and it's merely the tip of the iceberg that is Bryan Talbot's work – gives a sense of rapid change and growth, as a young man learns his craft in public, and blossoms, like a flower in speeded-up film.

Enjoy.

Neil Gaiman

October 5, 2007

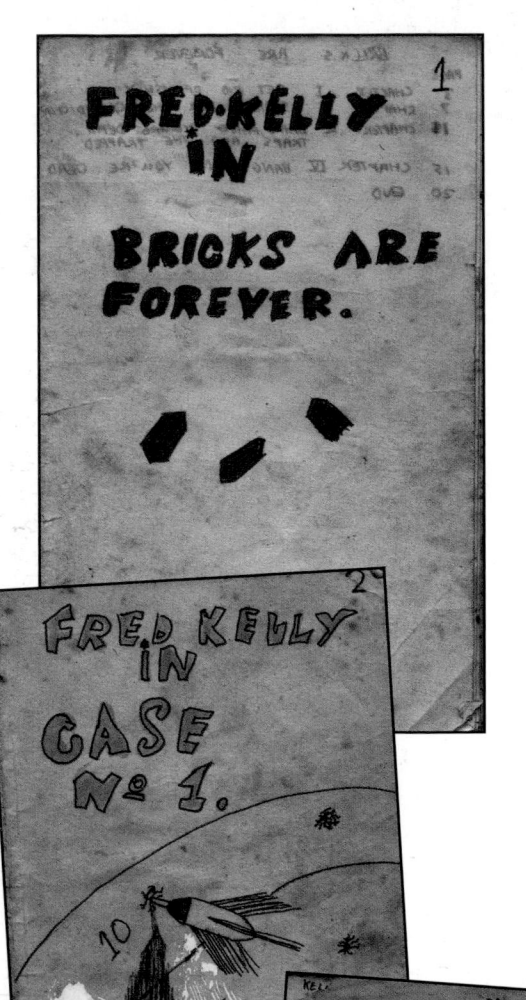

When it comes to art, I usually claim that I'm self-taught. That is to say, I was taught by a very ignorant person indeed. My art education was, in fact, a cock-up of monumental proportions. At grammar school my art teacher was a loveable old duffer but his technique involved handing out sheets of paper and instructing us to "draw something". He read the newspaper for the duration of the lesson and collected the completed work with mutters of "very nice". Unsurprisingly, I barely scraped through my art exams.

Attending a one-year art foundation course at Wigan School of Art was even worse. I was taught by three exhibiting abstract artists. To be blunt, they were fine art fascists who wouldn't allow students to do any figurative work which, at the time, was way out of vogue. I learnt nothing about drawing or painting there, so went on to do a graphic design course, rather than the fine art one I'd envisaged taking.

Unfortunately, the course I took at the Harris College in Preston was strongly typographically-based: no illustration was taught, though I did learn layout, photography, the use of technical pens and so forth. It was only after the course, when I was unemployed and went to the local library once a week to take out books on anatomy, perspective and composition, that I finally began to learn about the fundamental principles of drawing. I'm learning them still.

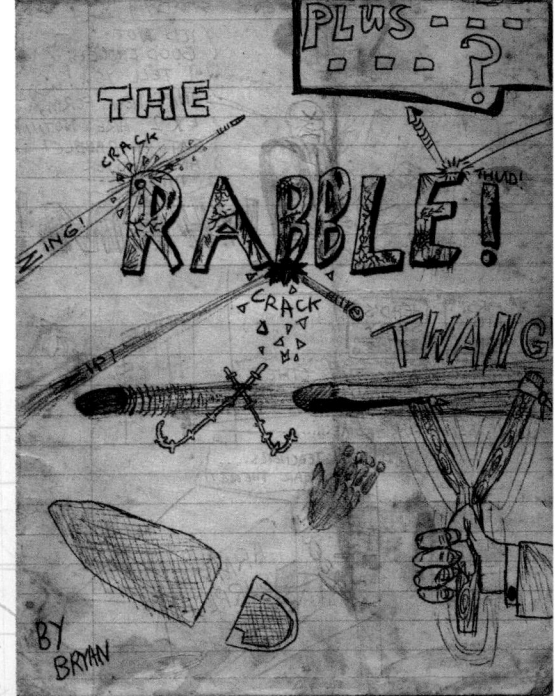

I'm a slow learner. Some artists seem to spring fully-formed into print at a young age. I have a long and painful evolution, which you are about to witness.

Here are the covers ome of the comics I produc or my ow usement when I was ten welve years . 1962-64.

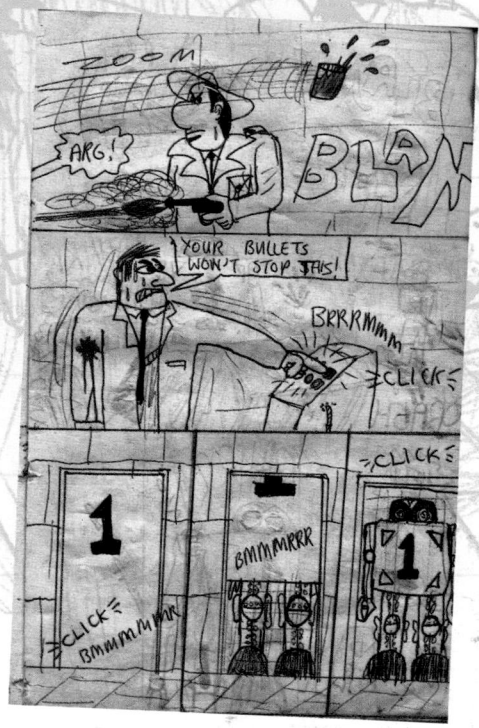

As you can see from these sample pages, these comics were crap.

From around thirteen to sixteen, I made 8mm home movies with Geoff Sim, a friend who was two years older. He taught me a lot about editing and visual storytelling in general, something that I took with me into my comic work. One of our films won Best Film of the Year 1966 at the Wigan Cine Club!

By seventeen, I was a science fiction and fantasy nut and my illustrations were first published *in* fanzines such as The Mallorn, the journal of the British Tolkien Society, and the first issues of the British Fantasy Society magazine, circa 1971.

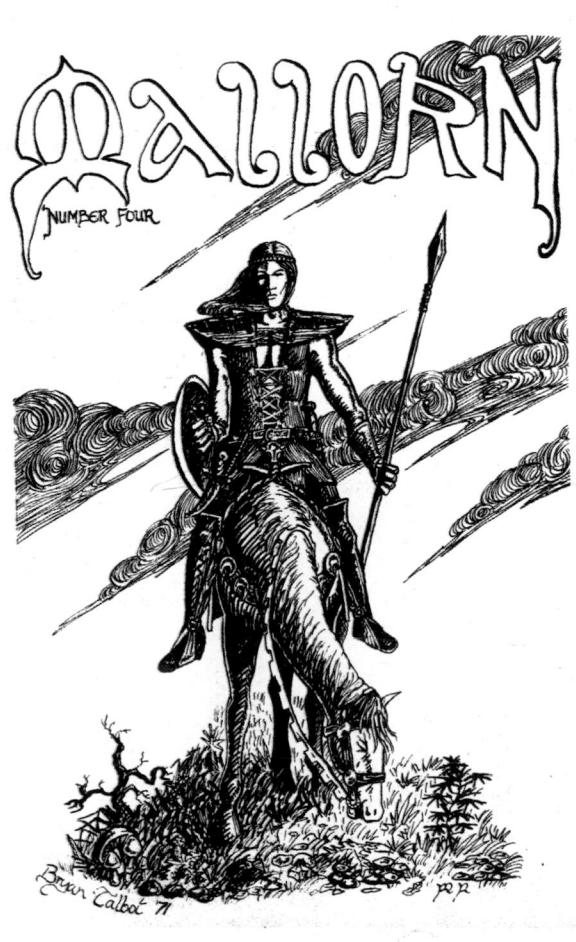

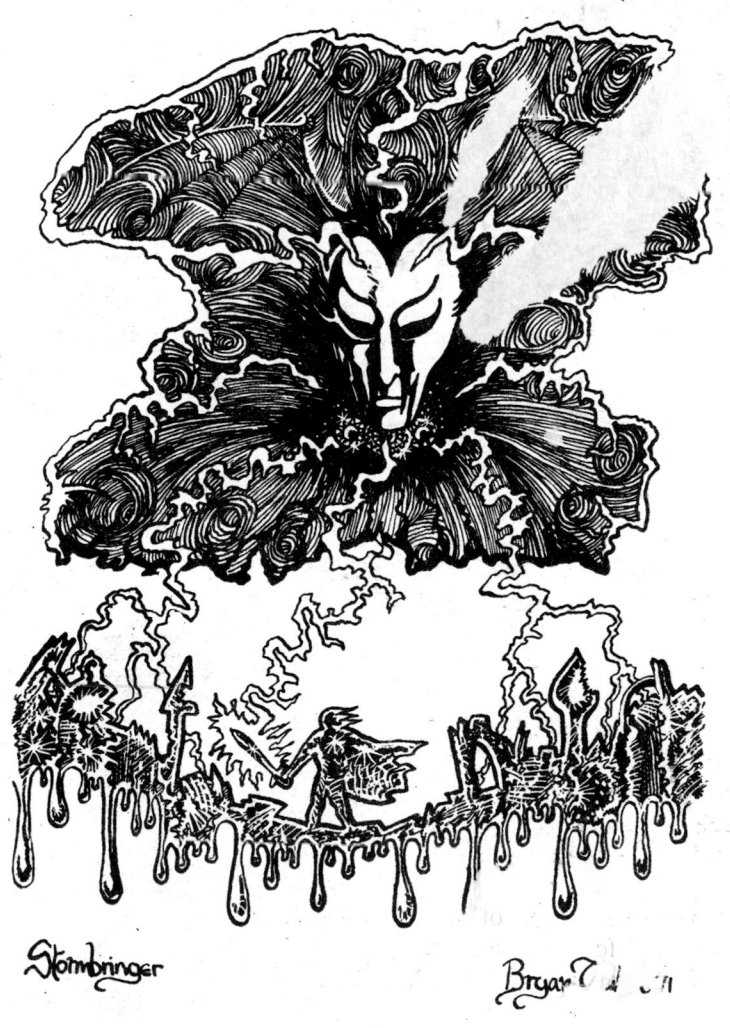

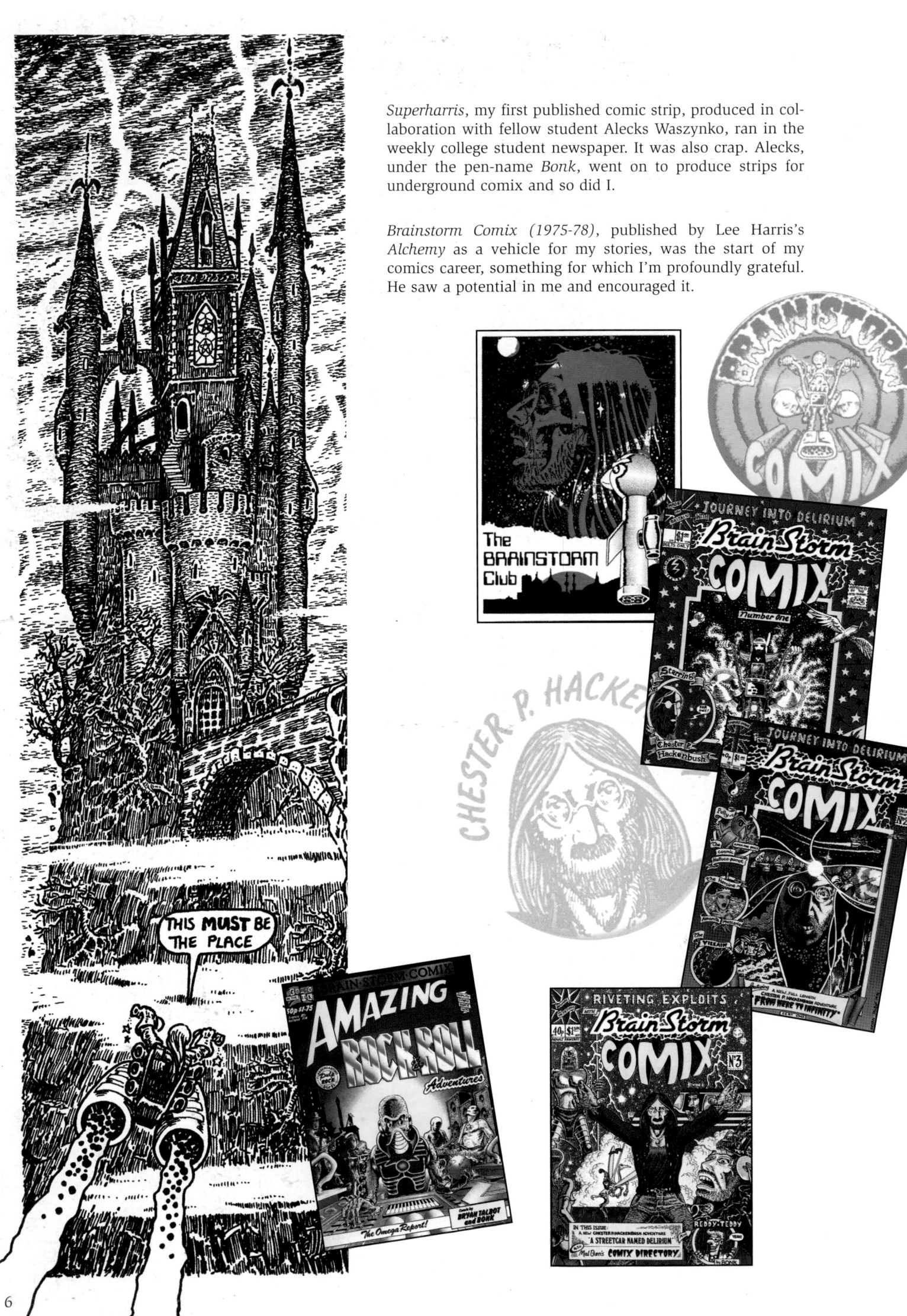

Superharris, my first published comic strip, produced in collaboration with fellow student Alecks Waszynko, ran in the weekly college student newspaper. It was also crap. Alecks, under the pen-name *Bonk*, went on to produce strips for underground comix and so did I.

Brainstorm Comix (1975-78), published by Lee Harris's *Alchemy* as a vehicle for my stories, was the start of my comics career, something for which I'm profoundly grateful. He saw a potential in me and encouraged it.

THIS MUST BE THE PLACE

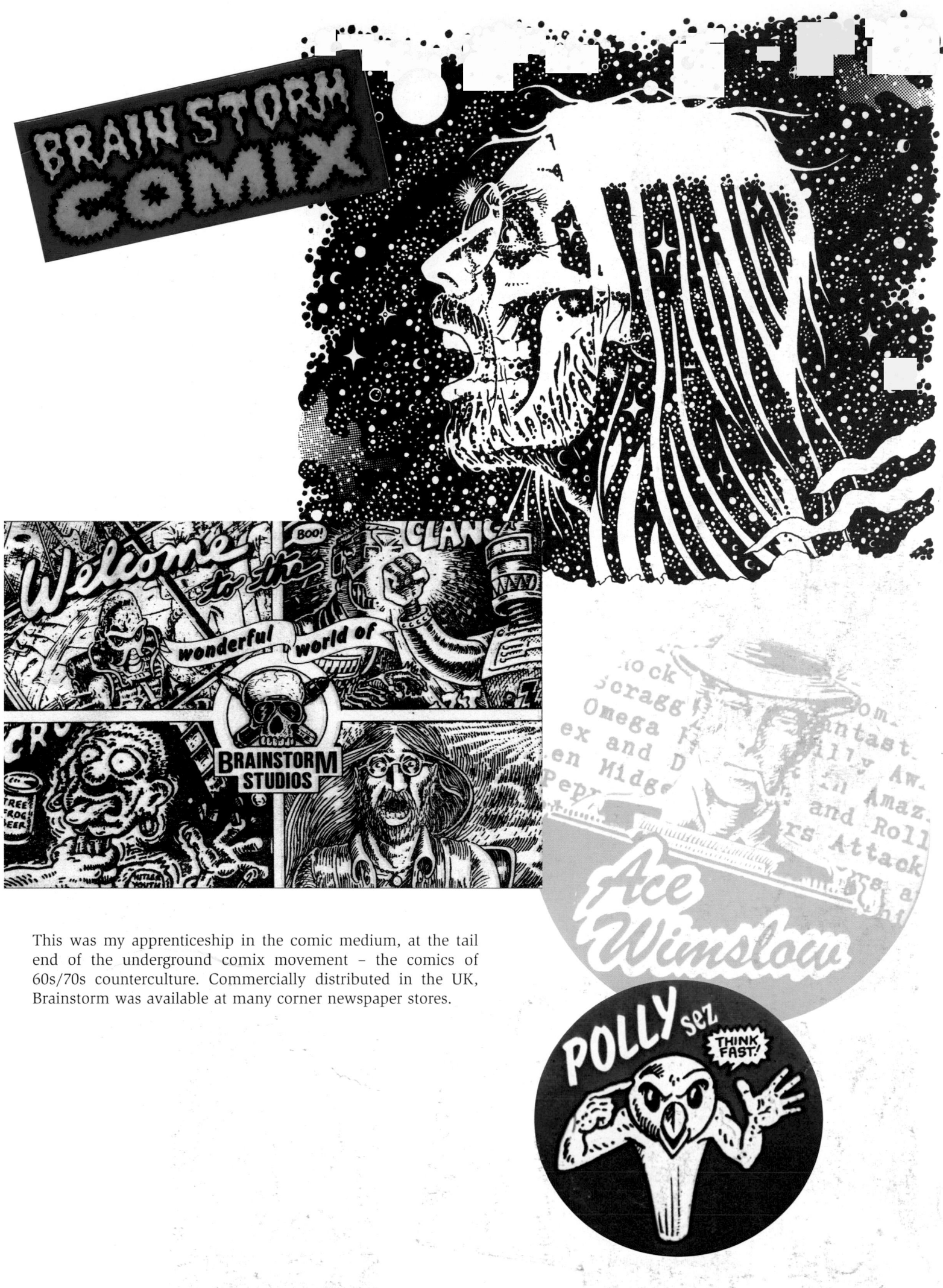

This was my apprenticeship in the comic medium, at the tail end of the underground comix movement – the comics of 60s/70s counterculture. Commercially distributed in the UK, Brainstorm was available at many corner newspaper stores.

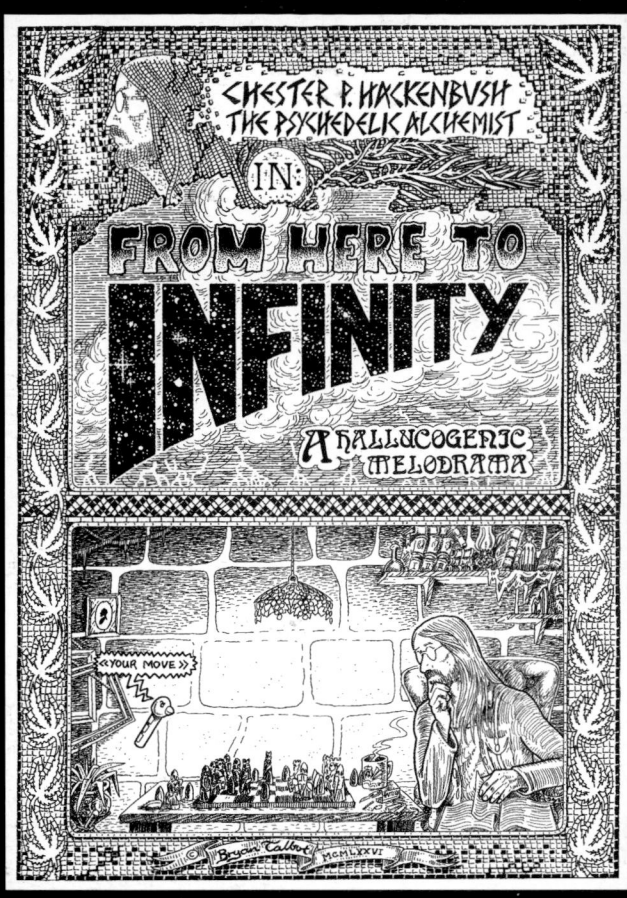

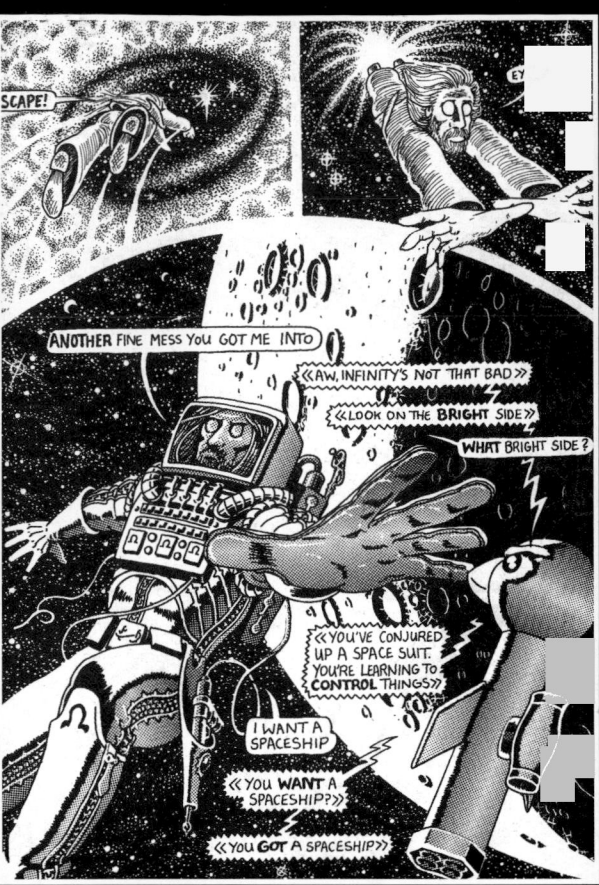

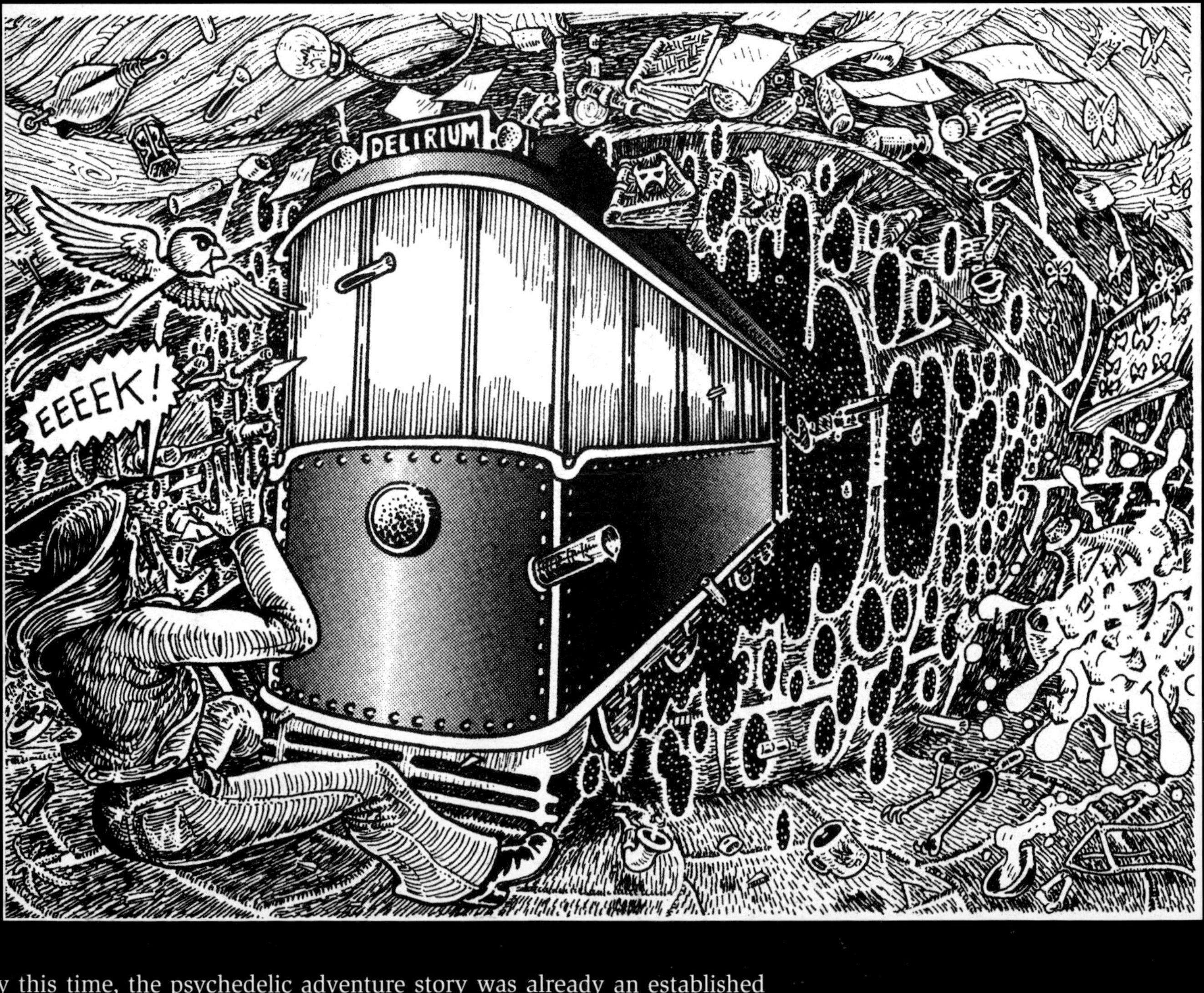

By this time, the psychedelic adventure story was already an established genre in underground comix. My protagonist, *Chester P. Hackenbush* was later homaged as *Chester Williams* in Alan Moore's run on *Swamp Thing*.

Facing: cover illustration for Alchemy reprint of Chester's adventures. Inks. 1982.

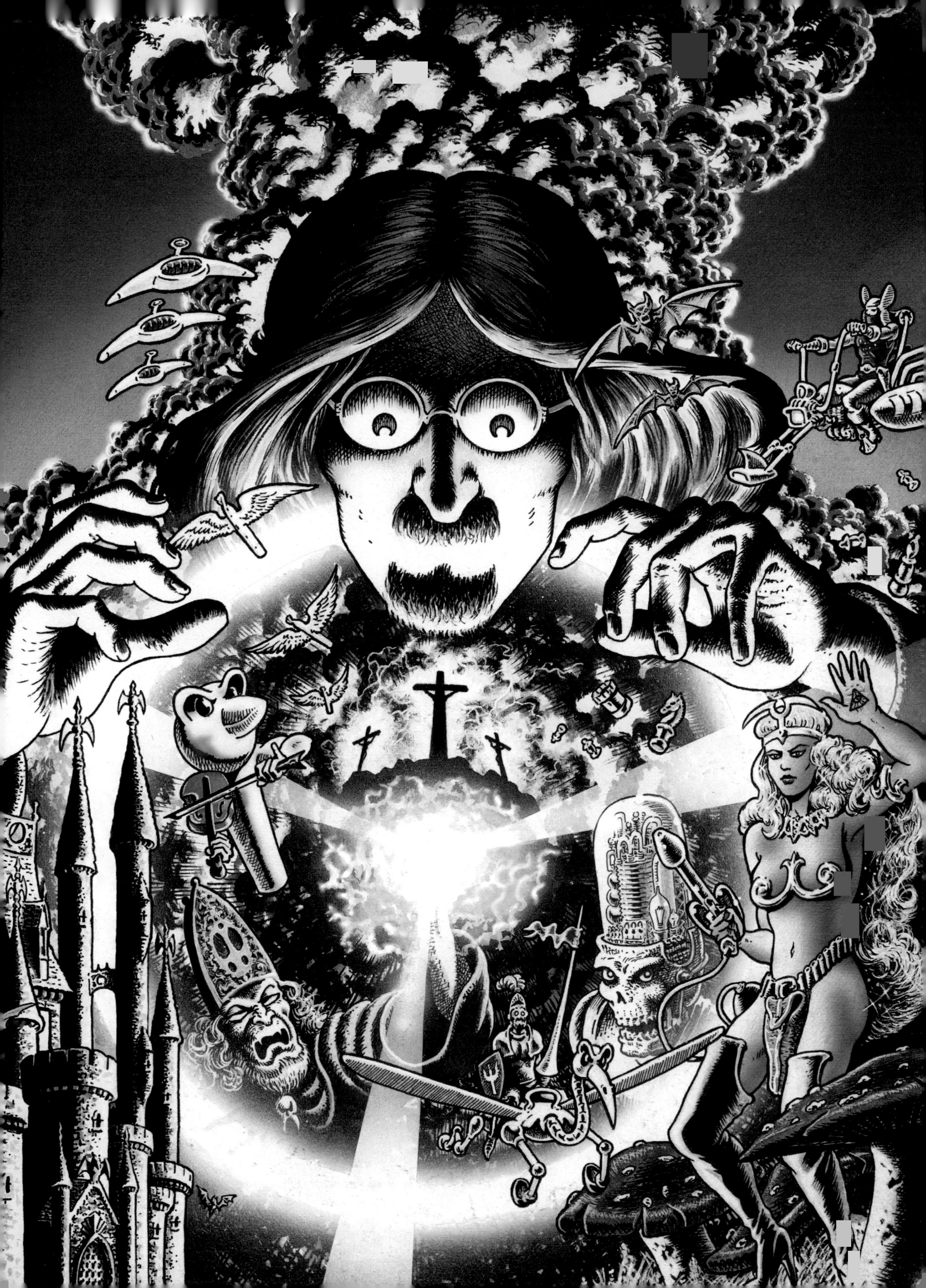

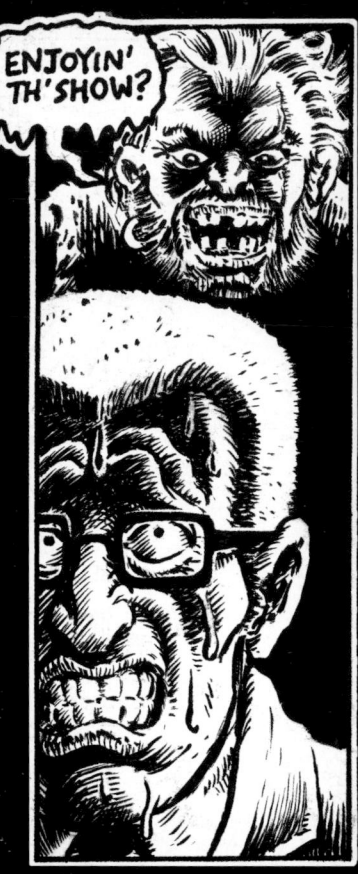

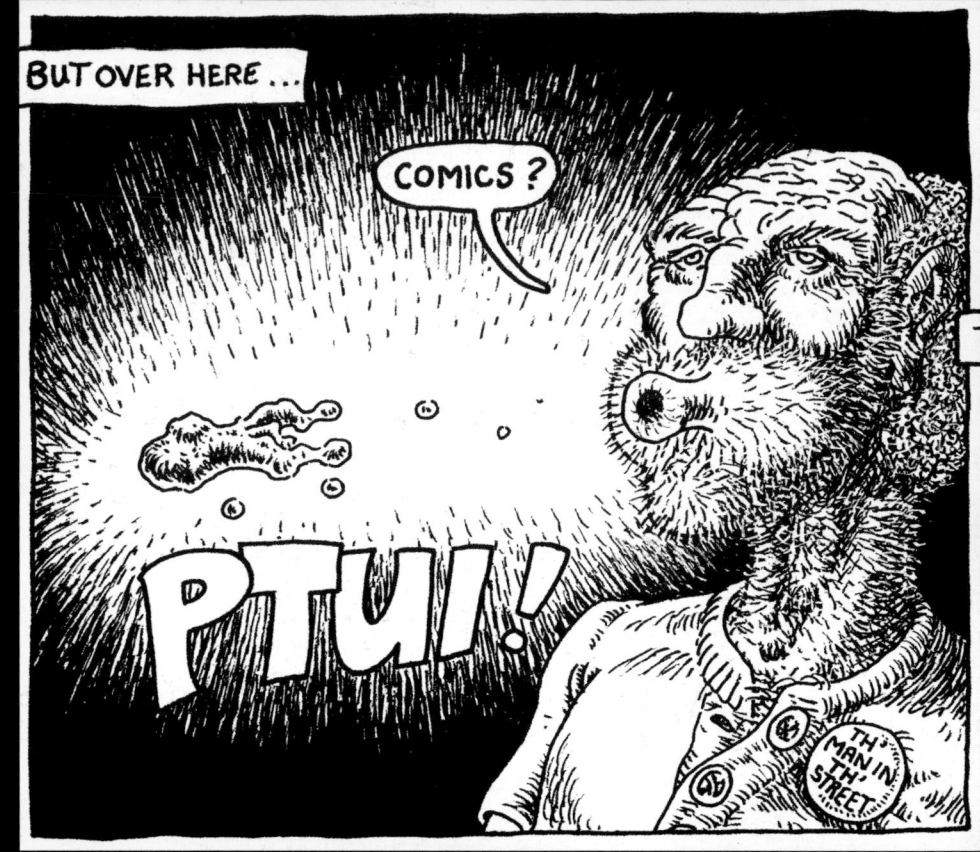

I produced strips for other UK UGs, including *Komix Comics* for Hunt Emerson's *Streetcomix* (1977, above right) and *Arnold Gets Cross* for Tony and Carol Bennett's *Knockabout Comics* (1981, above left) plus assorted ephemera. Rob King, owner of the *Edinburgh Science Fiction Shop* published the Xmas card right in 1978, Alchemy the one below in 1975.

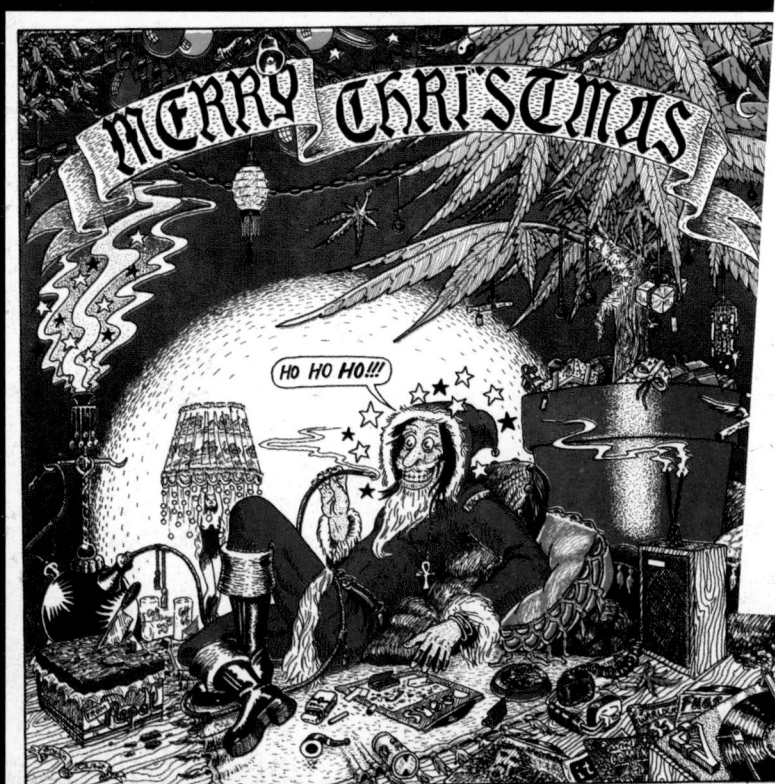

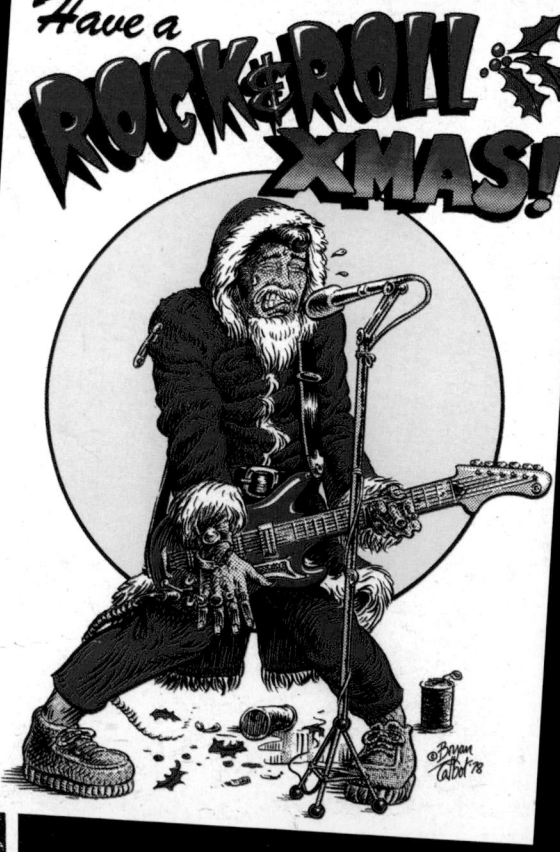

Facing: poster for my first one-man exhibition - at the Harris Museum, Library and Art Gallery, Preston (visible in the background). 1981.

BRAINSTORM!

AN EXHIBITION OF COMIC WORK & FANTASY ILLUSTRATION BY BRYAN TALBOT

5th Sept - 3rd Oct

THE
HARRIS
MUSEUM·AND·ART·GALLERY
MARKET SQUARE, PRESTON, LANCASHIRE.

BRYAN TALBOT 1981

In the late 70s I did the monthly one-page comedy-adventure series *Frank Fazakerly, Space Ace of the Future*, partly a parody of the 1930s *Buck Rogers* and *Flash Gordon* movie serials, for the SF magazine *Ad Astra*. It was collected by the Preston SF Group in 1991 (right).

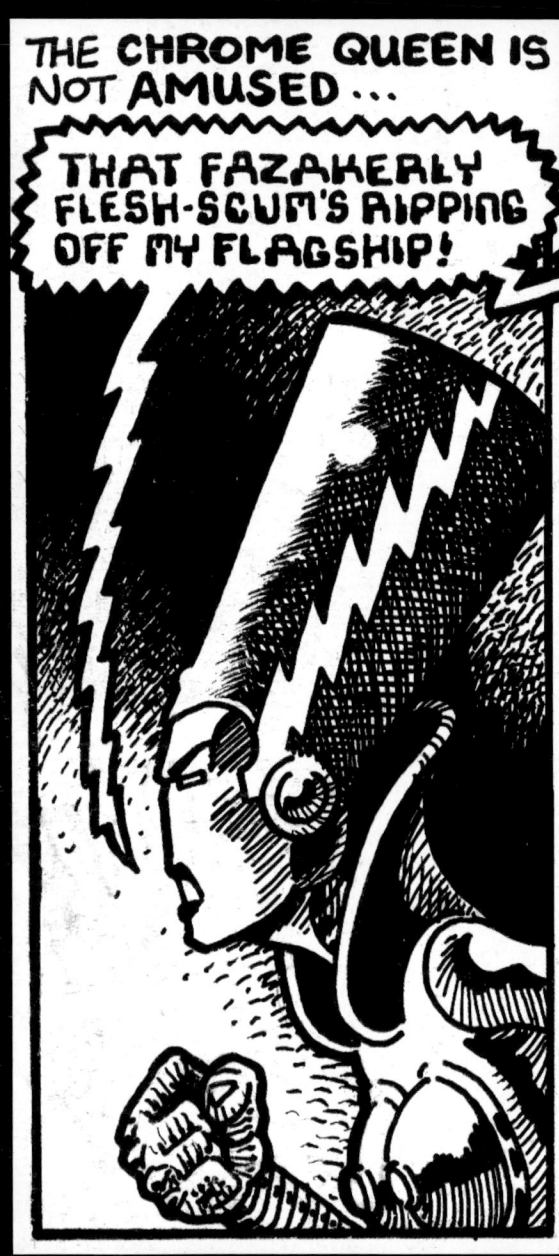

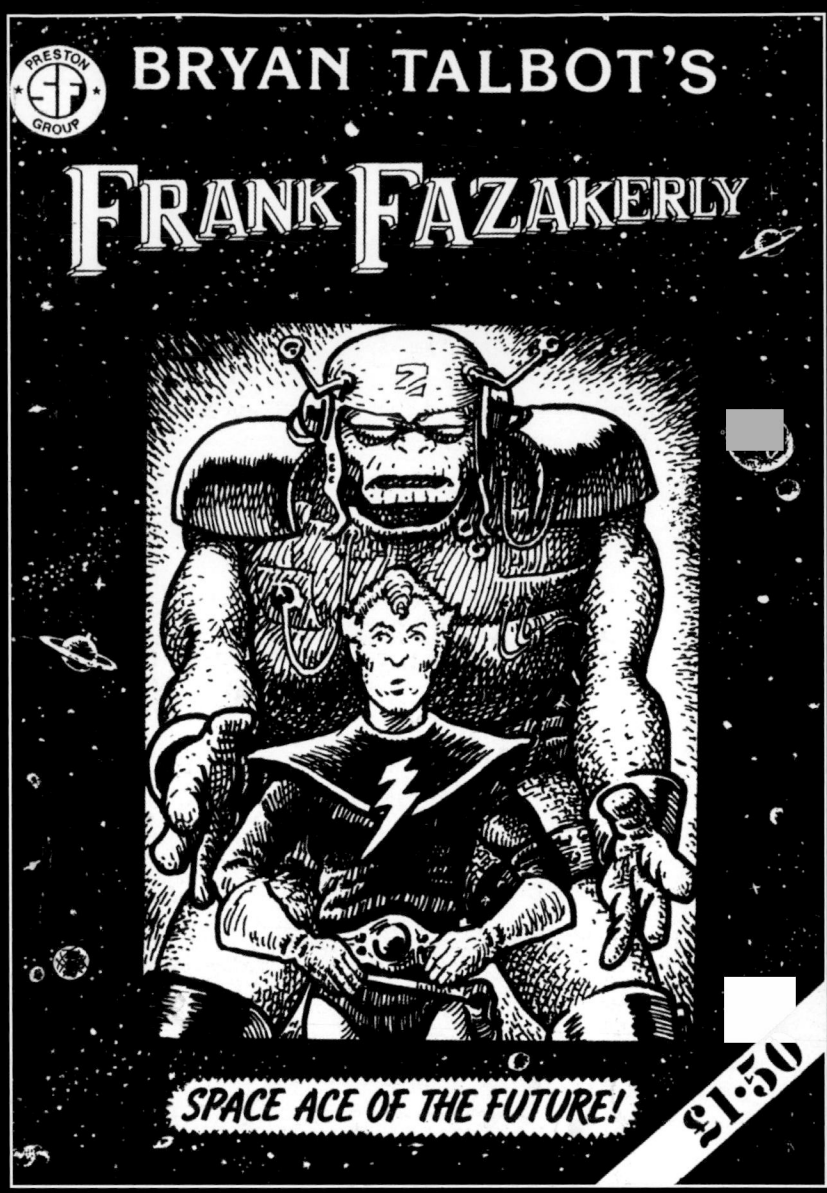

Food For Thought was a benefit comic for the *Band-Aid* Ethiopia relief fund. Alan Moore scripted *Cold Snap* (right) for it. 1985.

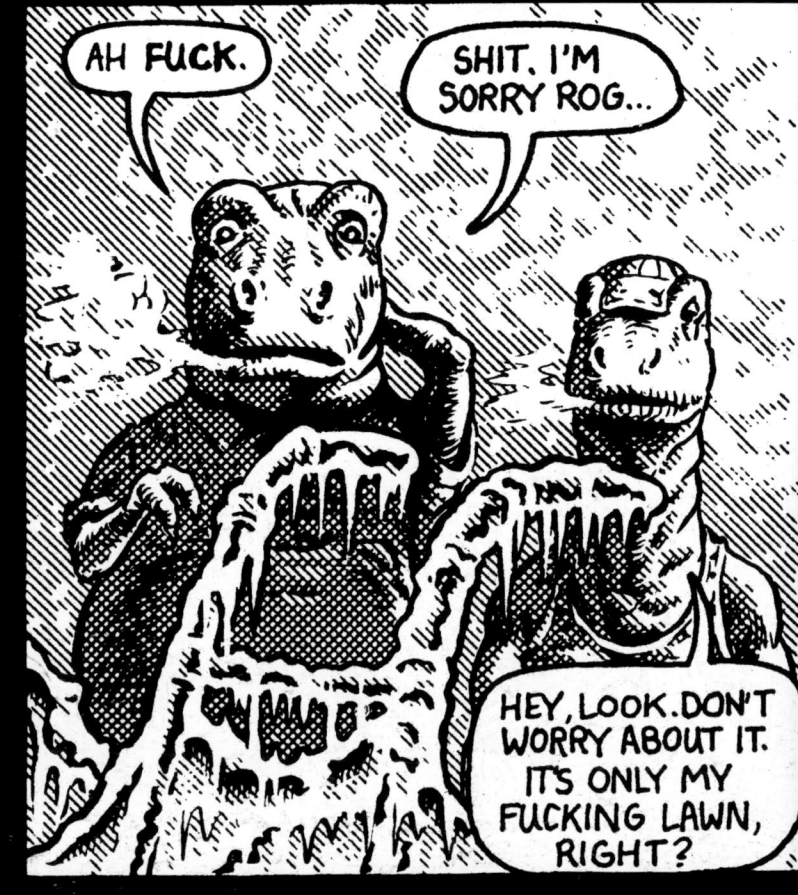

Sloth (right), a seven-page strip for Knockabout Comics' *Seven Deadly Sins*, scripted by Neil Gaiman. 1989.

I wrote and drew *Scumworld* (below) 1982-83 for the weekly UK rock newspaper *Sounds*.

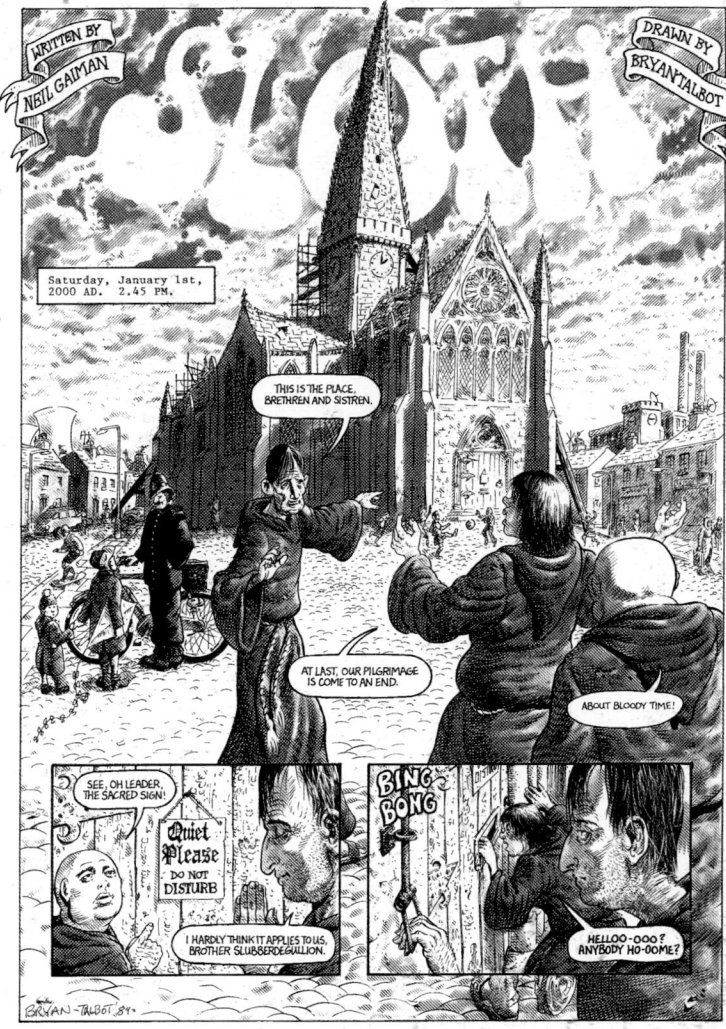

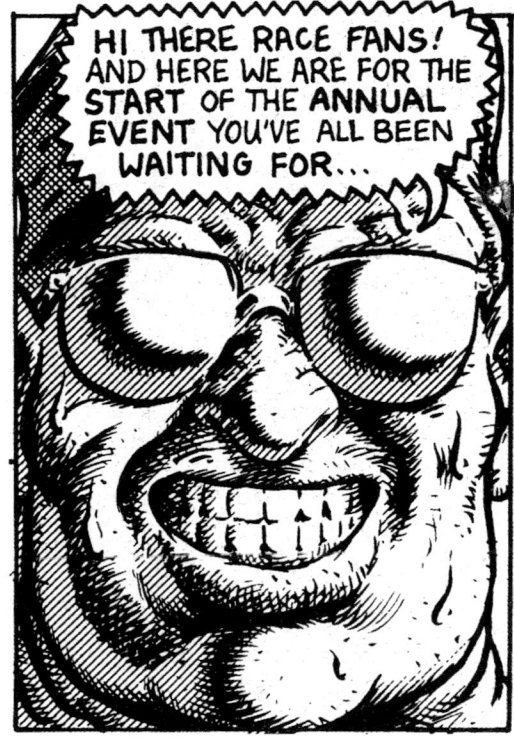

Below is a title logo done for Bruce Sweeney's long-running *Underground Station* UG news column in 2003.

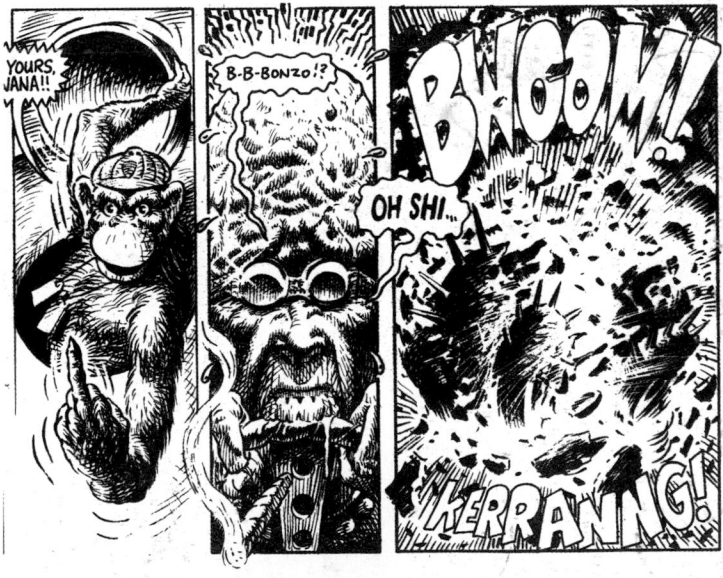

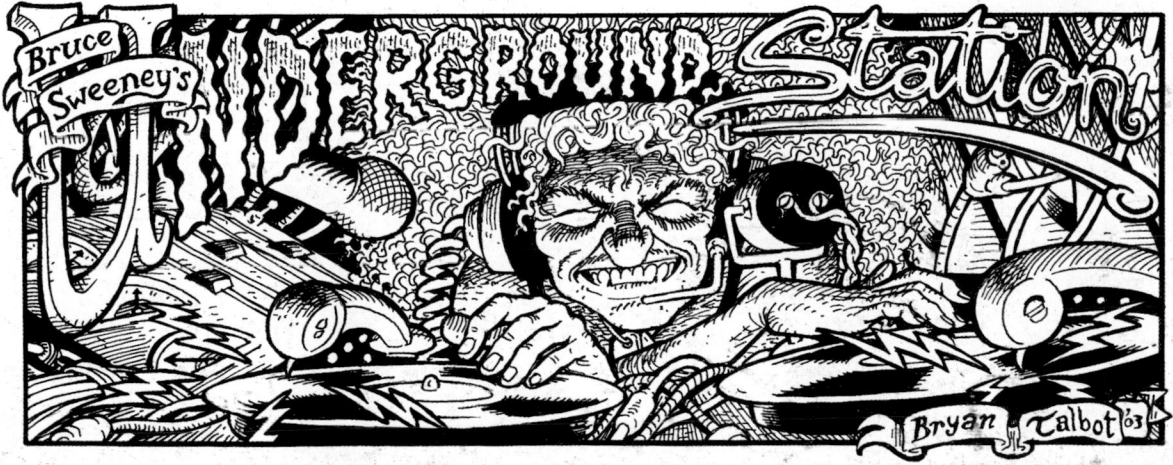

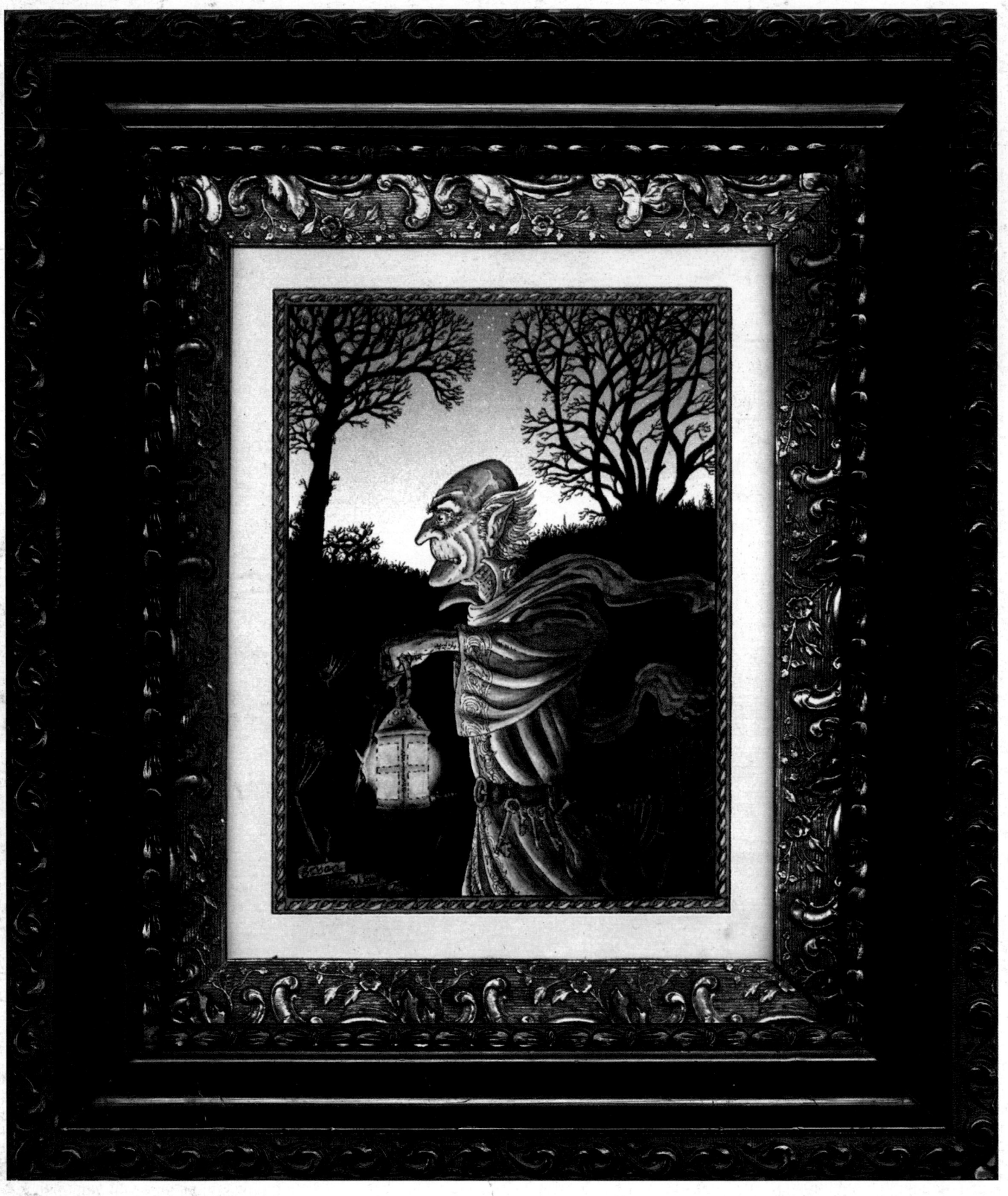

I drew *The Hermit* in 1975, the year of the first *Brainstorm Comix*, to fit the Victorian frame I'd found. Inks. Unpublished.

Facing is my favourite page from The *Adventures of Luther Arkwright*, my first graphic novel. It is said to be the first British GN, serialised in Rob King's *Near Myths* from 1978, then *Pssst!* The first volume was published in 1982 by Never Limited. This is the opening page of the second (1987). The theme of this volume was enlightenment, so here we have an essay in light and shade: the sunlight streams in through the window, the rest of the room is lit by its reflected light. The character is side lit by the match and, in the background, is Holman Hunt's *I am the Light of the World*, a reference to the messianic status that Arkwright achieves through his transfiguration.

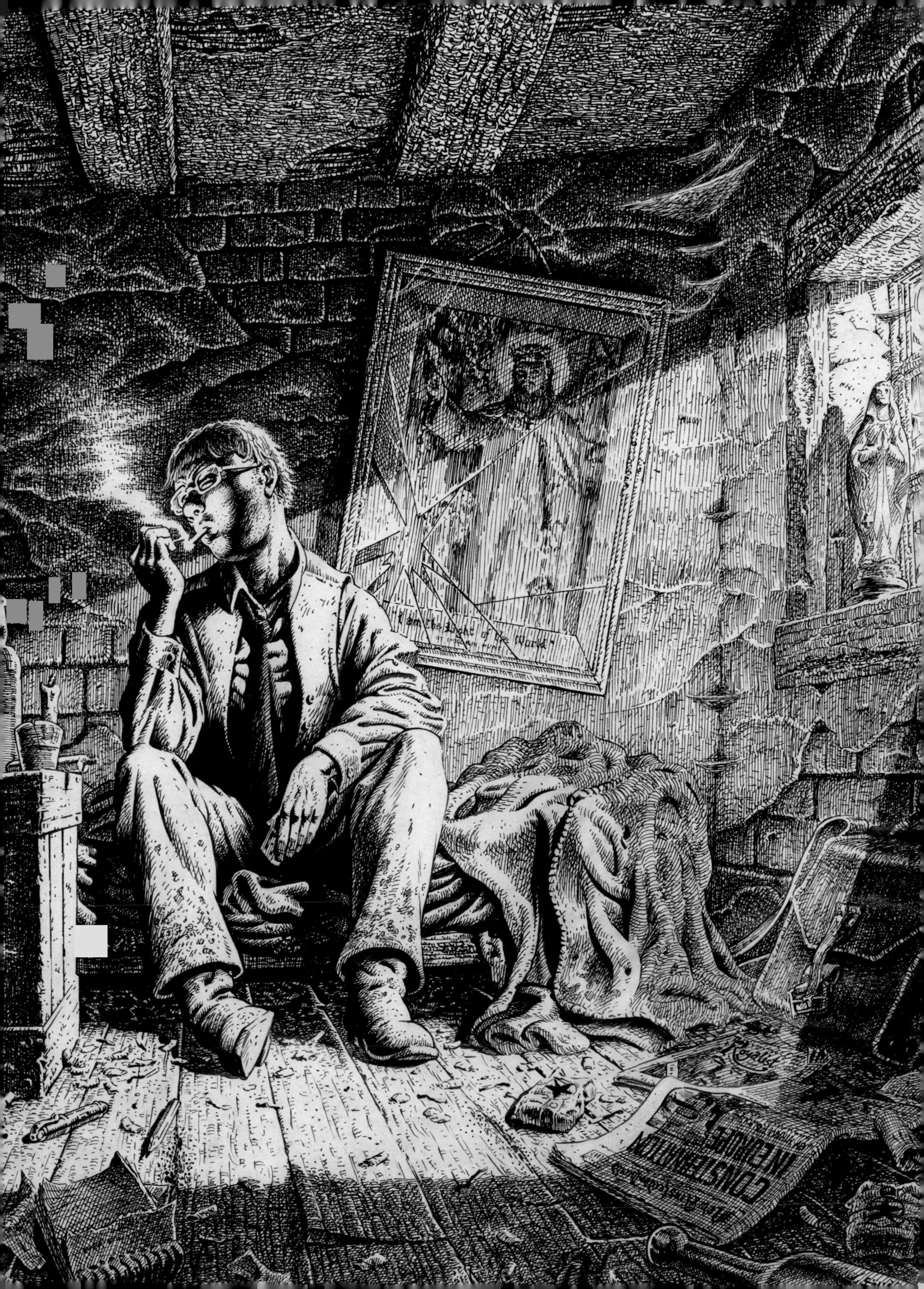

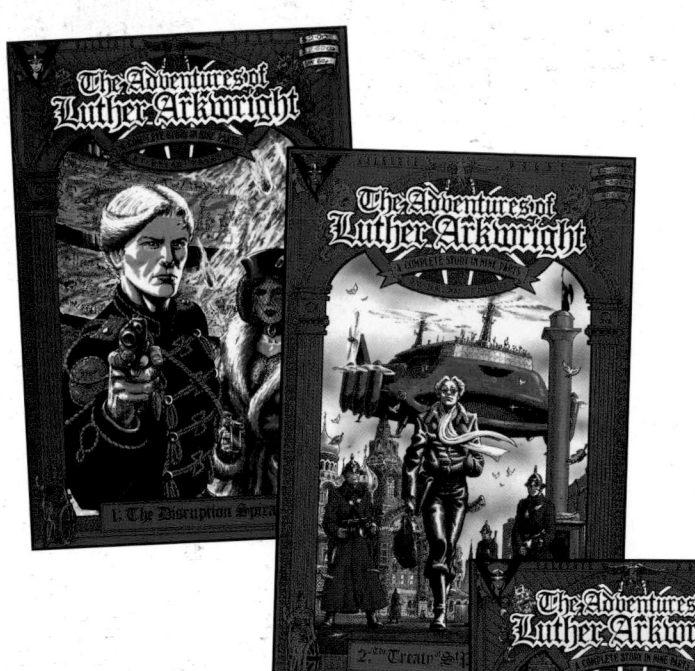

Arkwright was also serialised in the UK in comic book format by Valkyrie Press and the third and final volume, by Proutt, appeared in 1989. Never Limited and Proutt (the French comics sound effect for a fart) were the publishing imprints of French aristocrat Serge Boissevain, the publisher of the innovative UK monthly comics magazine *Pssst!*, and, like Lee Harris, he was an extremely important influence on my career. He was like a Victorian "artist's patron" in that he financed me to finish the story just so that he could read it himself. I'm eternally in his debt.

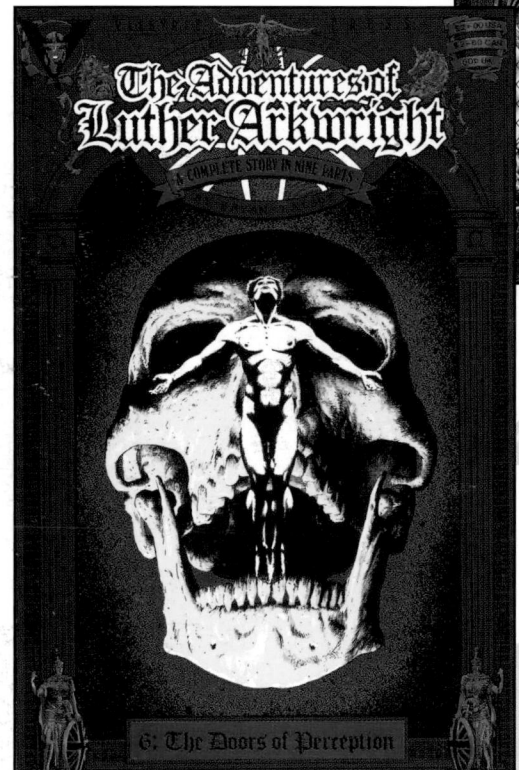

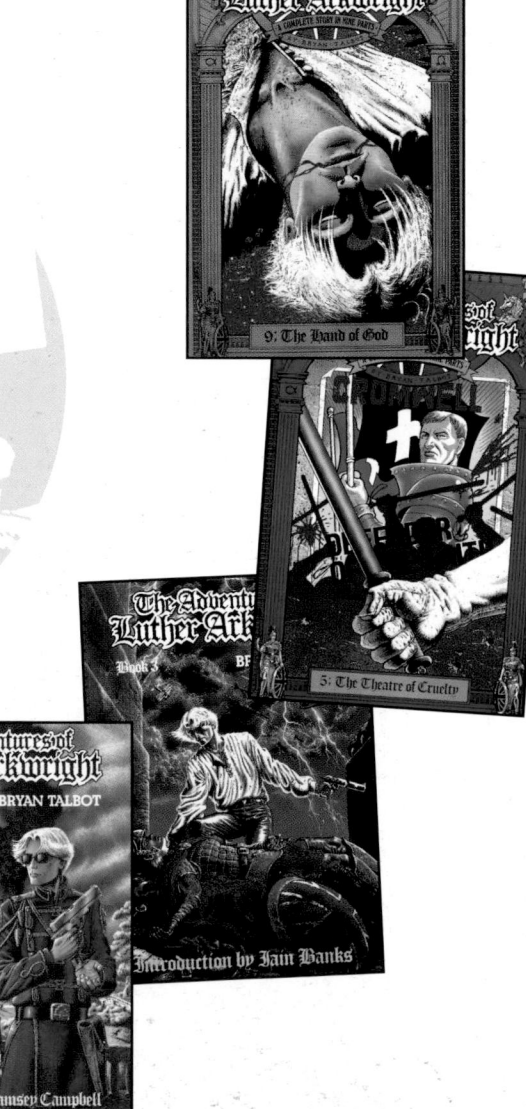

To the right is the cover for the original Arkwright RPG by James Brunton.

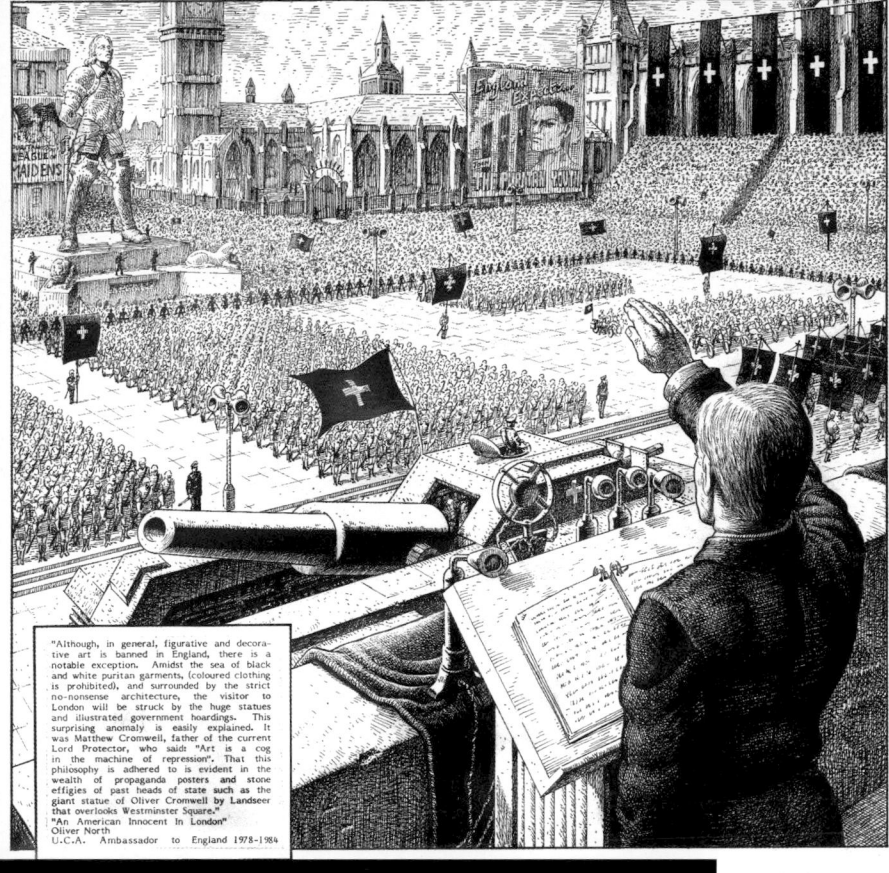

"Although, in general, figurative and decorative art is banned in England, there is a notable exception. Amidst the sea of black and white puritan garments, (coloured clothing is prohibited), and surrounded by the strict no-nonsense architecture, the visitor to London will be struck by the huge statues and illustrated government hoardings. This surprising anomaly is easily explained. It was Matthew Cromwell, father of the current Lord Protector, who said "Art is a cog in the machine of repression". That this philosophy is adhered to is evident in the wealth of propaganda posters and stone effigies of past heads of state such as the giant statue of Oliver Cromwell by Landseer that overlooks Westminster Square."
"An American Innocent In London"
Oliver North
U.C.A. Ambassador to England 1978-1984

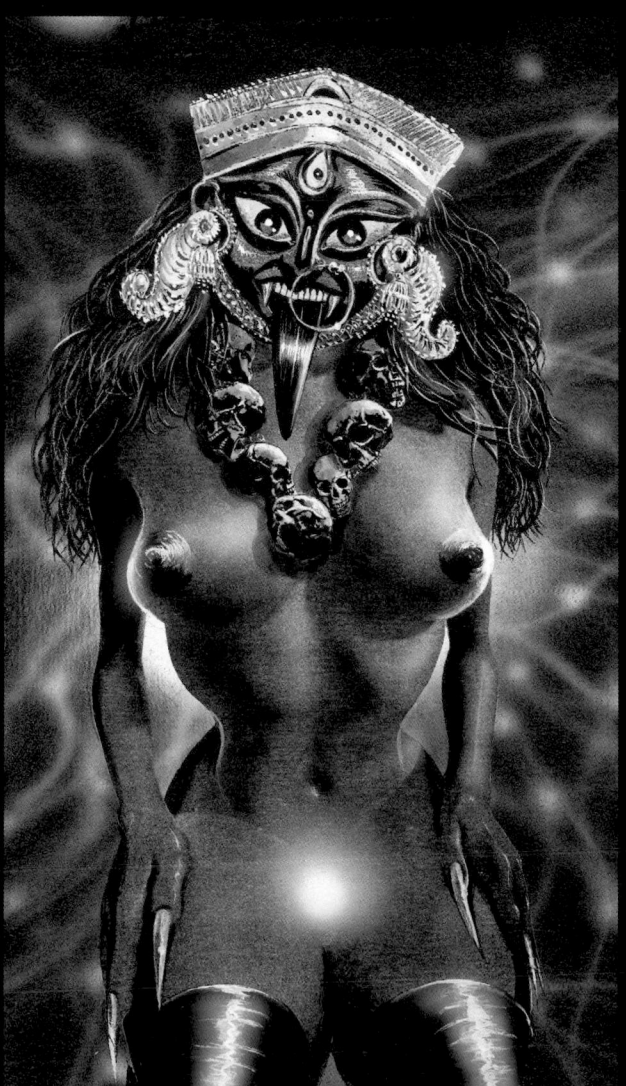

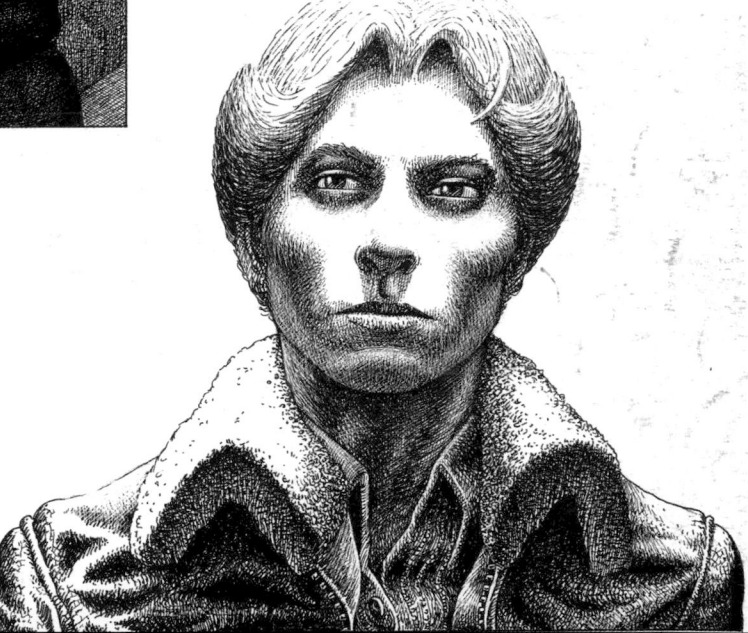

The story itself was intentionally experimental. One eleven-page sequence consisted of collaged images, such as the image of Kali, left, with large blocks of stream-of-consciousness prose. In another sequence I spread six seconds over seventy-two panels. The book was created during the rise in the UK of the extreme right-wing and this is reflected in its anti-fascist theme.

Dark Horse Comics published the American comic series, with new covers and lettering, in the early 90s, before collecting it into one volume in 1997.

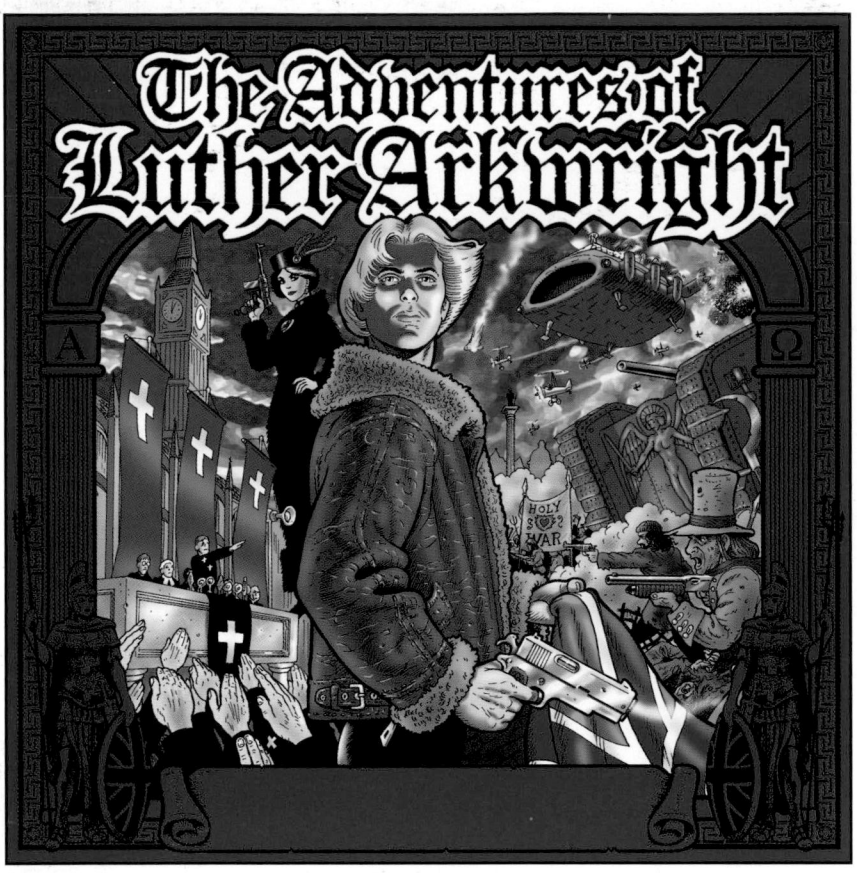

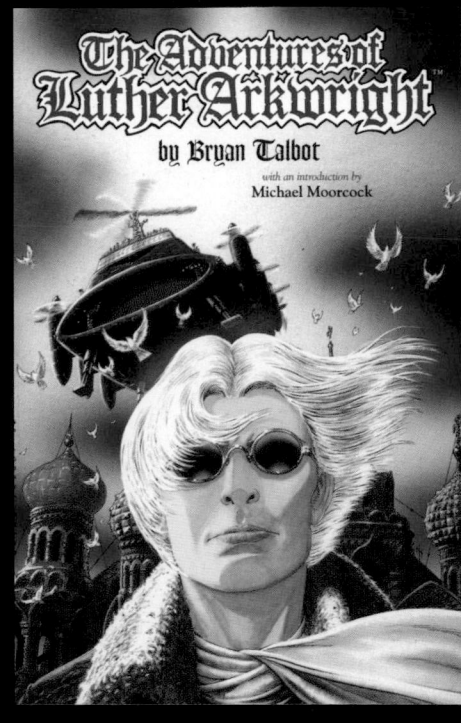

Above is the cover for the three-hour CD audio adaptation by Big Finish Productions, starring David Tennant as Arkwright. In the bar on the right, top: the one volume collection by Dark Horse, middle: the replica model of Arkwright's Vibro-beamer by Jason Wilbourn, bottom: the Czech edition which is the best ever: a fourteen inch tall hardback with digitally remastered artwork. The pewter figurine below was made by David Drage. Bottom right is the cover of the forthcoming RPG from Hogshead Games.

Facing page is the original for the cover of the second Proutt volume. Inks. 1987.

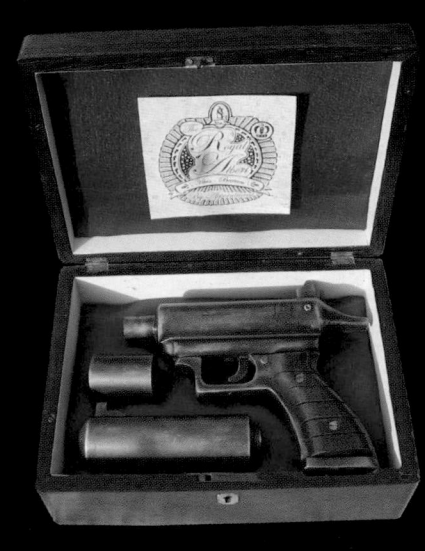

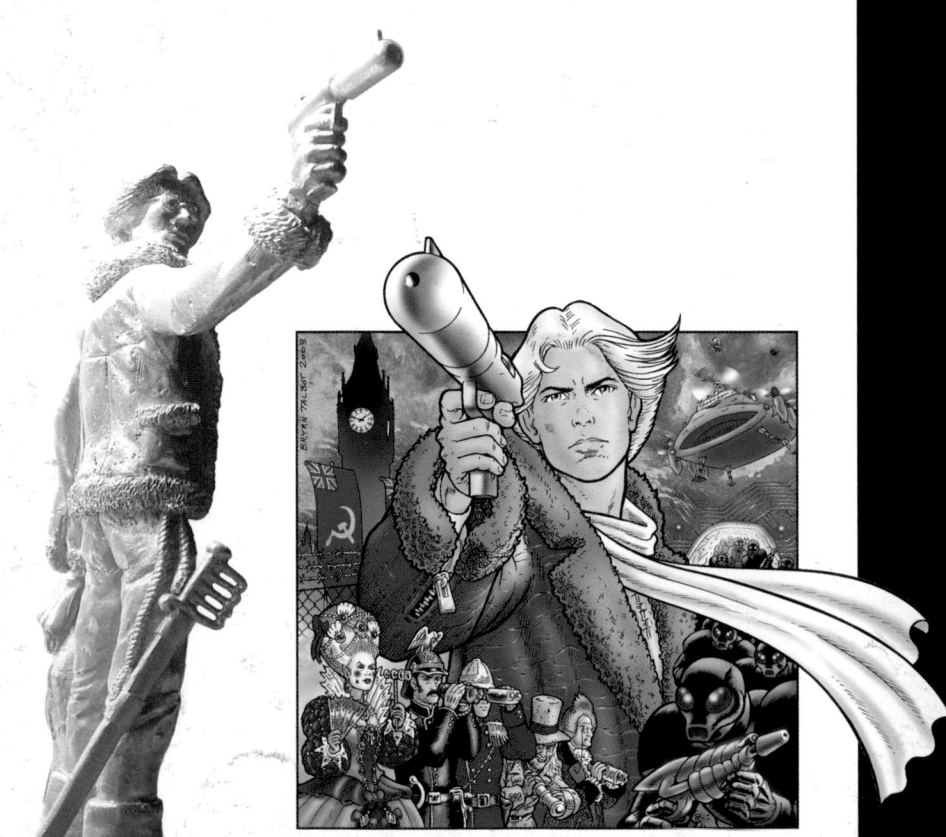

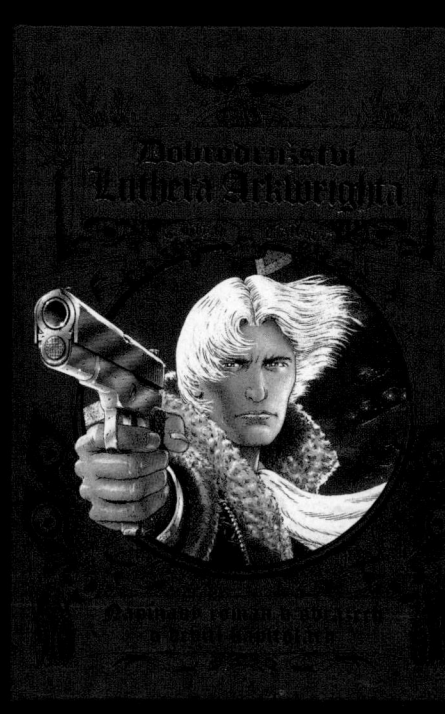

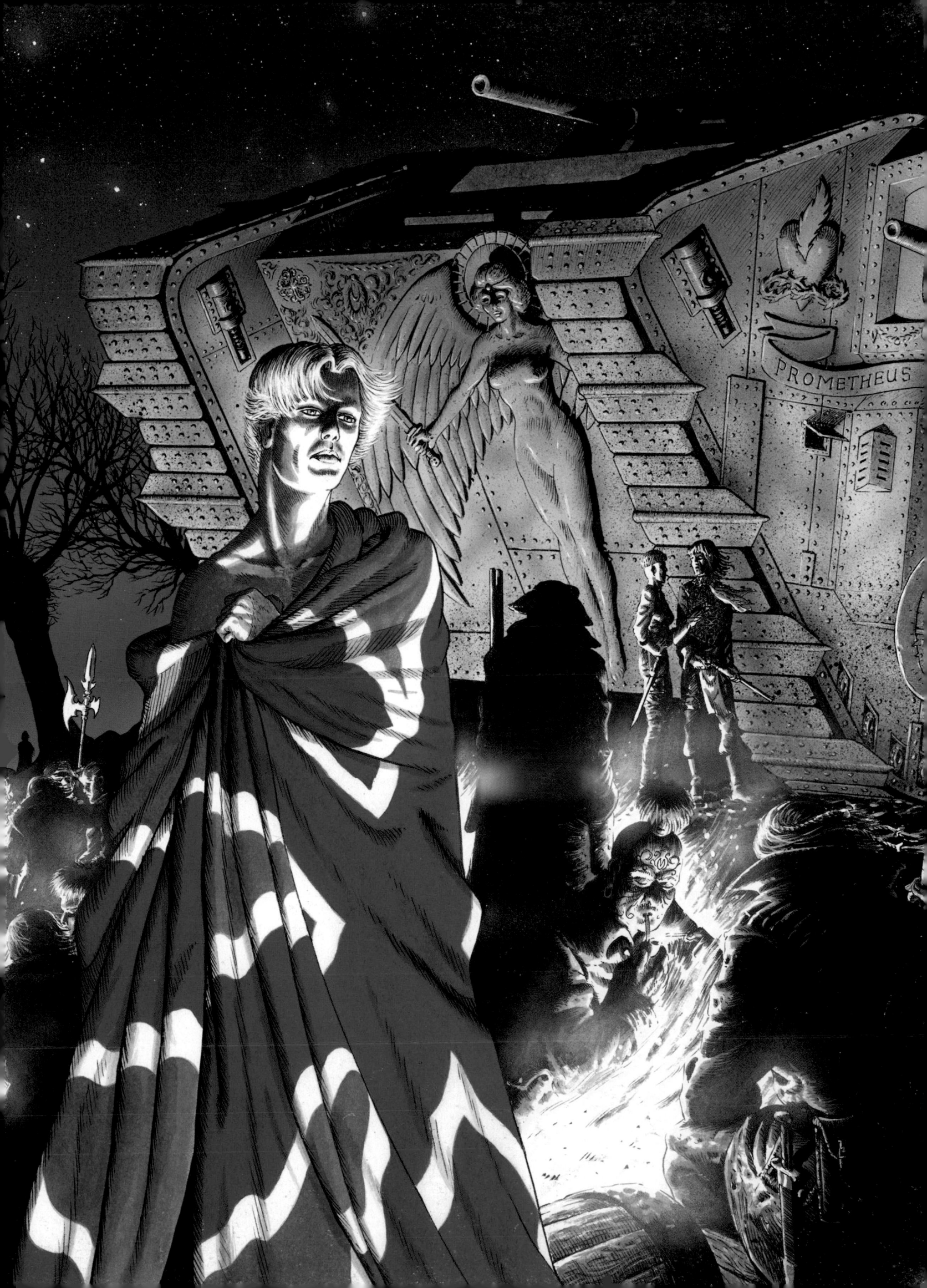

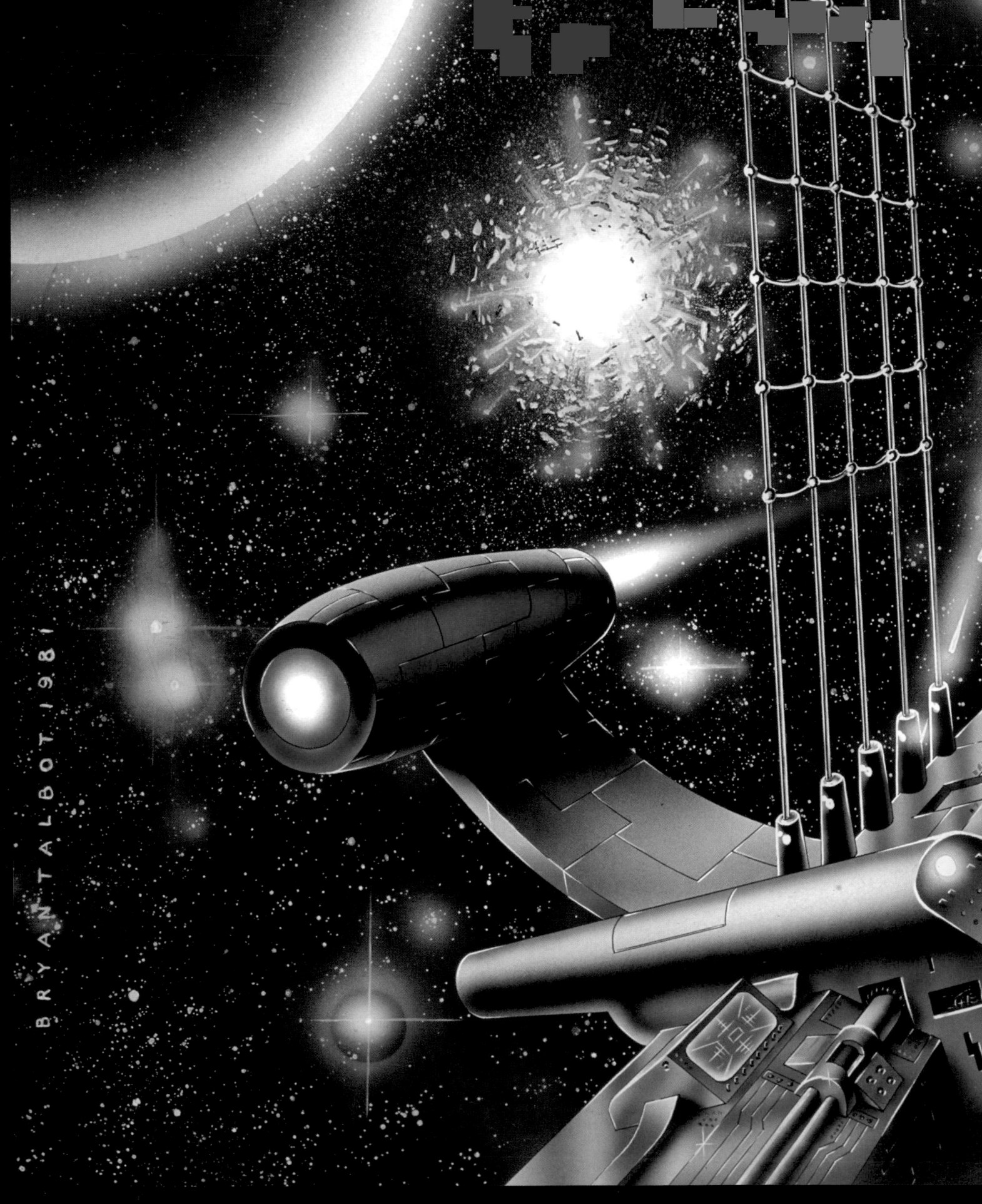

BRYANTALBOT1981

20

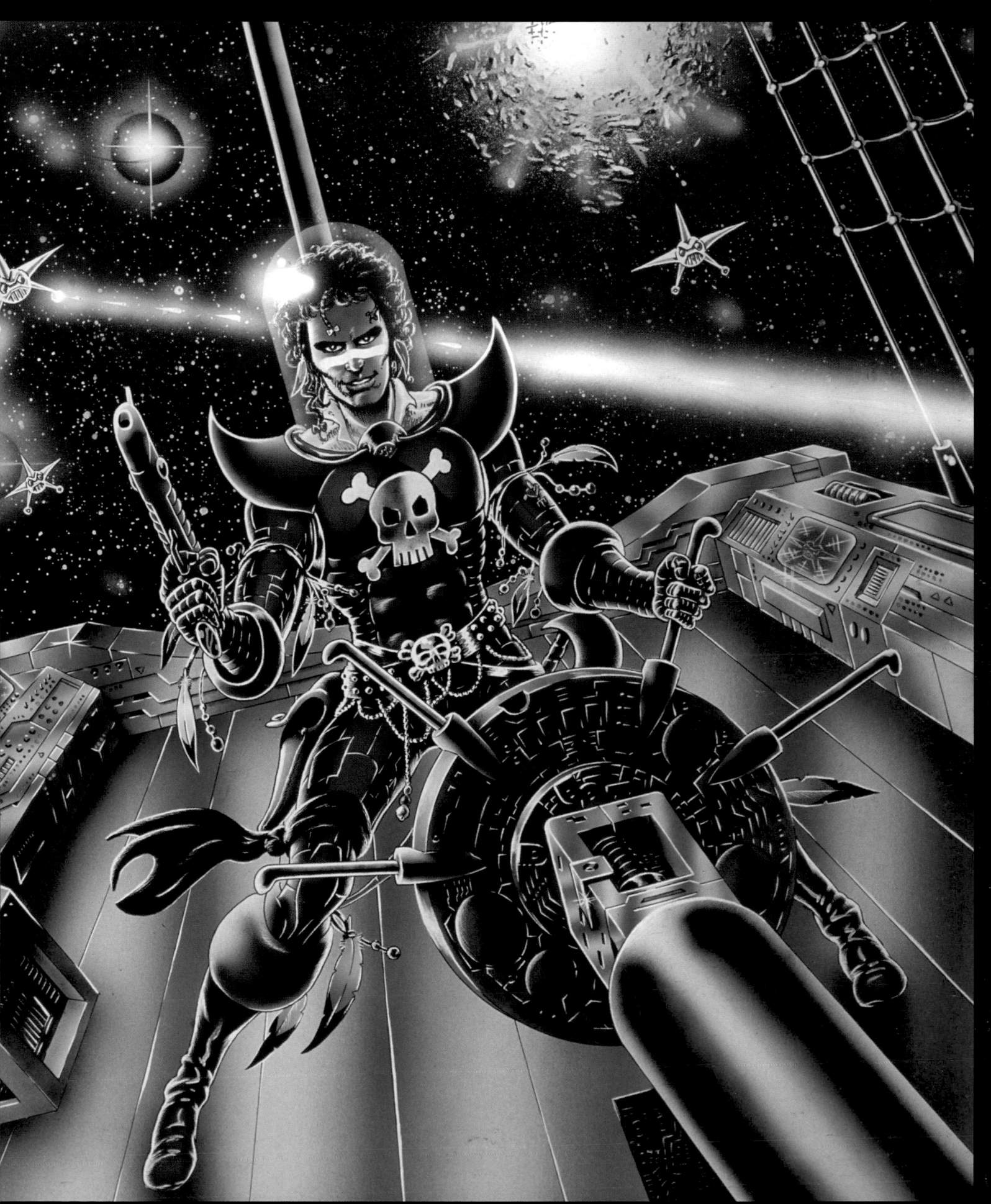

Adam Ant, Space Pirate from *Adam Ant Magazine*. Inks. 1981.

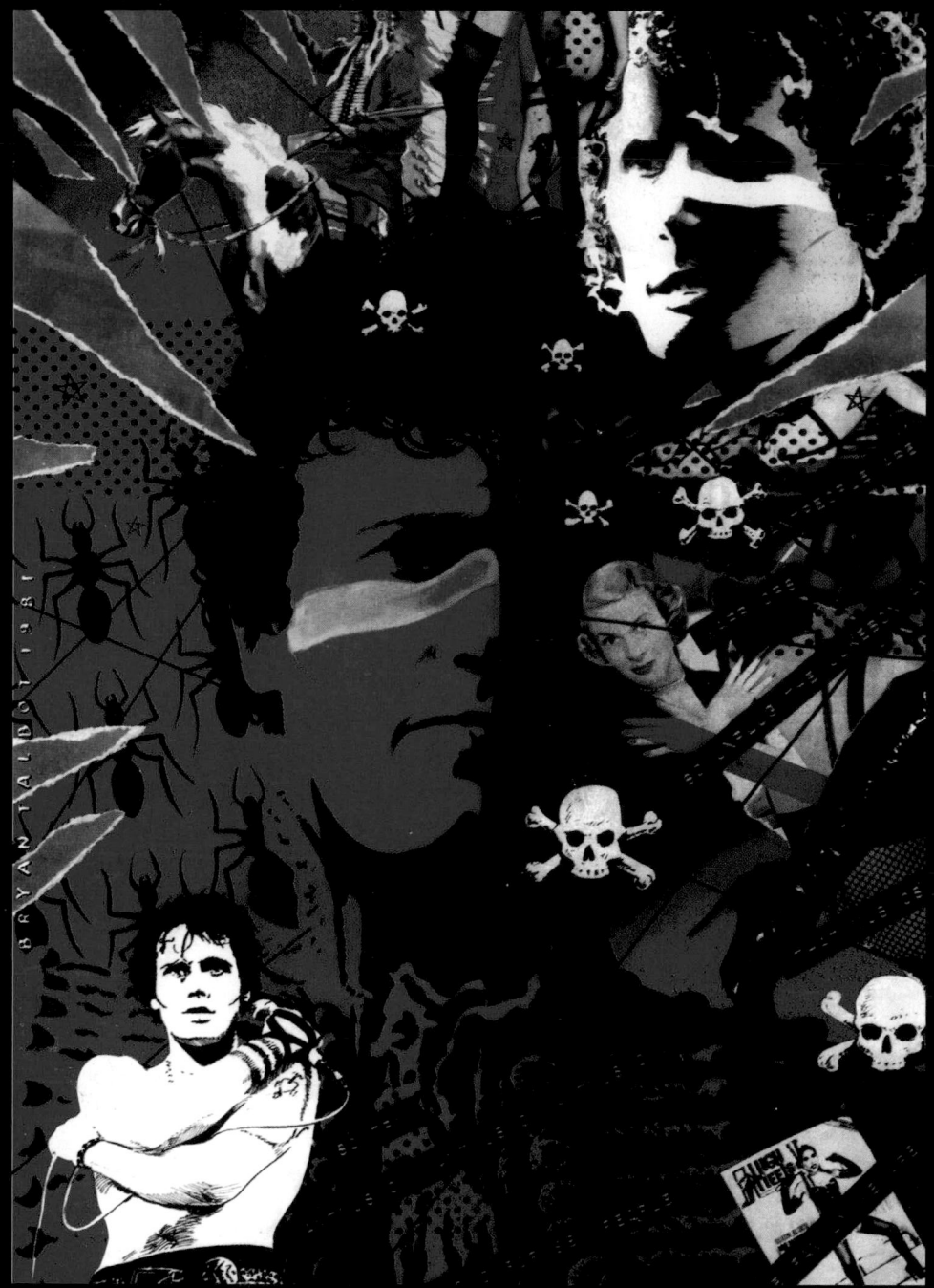

Having established myself in underground and alternative comics I started attracting paying work and in 1981 I went self-employed as a jobbing illustrator. One of my first commissions was for the UK magazine *Flexipop*, so named because of the free flexidisc each issue. They asked for Adam Ant, the frontman for then cult rock band *Adam and the Ants*. I had to borrow records and fanzines to research his themes. The result is above.

Suddenly, he became a phenomenon and the pop press was crying out for images. As I'd done his first published illo, I became branded as "the Adam Ant artist" and spent most of a year producing pics and logos for various Ant publications. The illo facing was produced for a giant-sized postermag. And, yes, he does actually have "Pure Sex" tattooed on his left deltoid. I eventually met him at a UK comic con. Inks and collage. 1981.

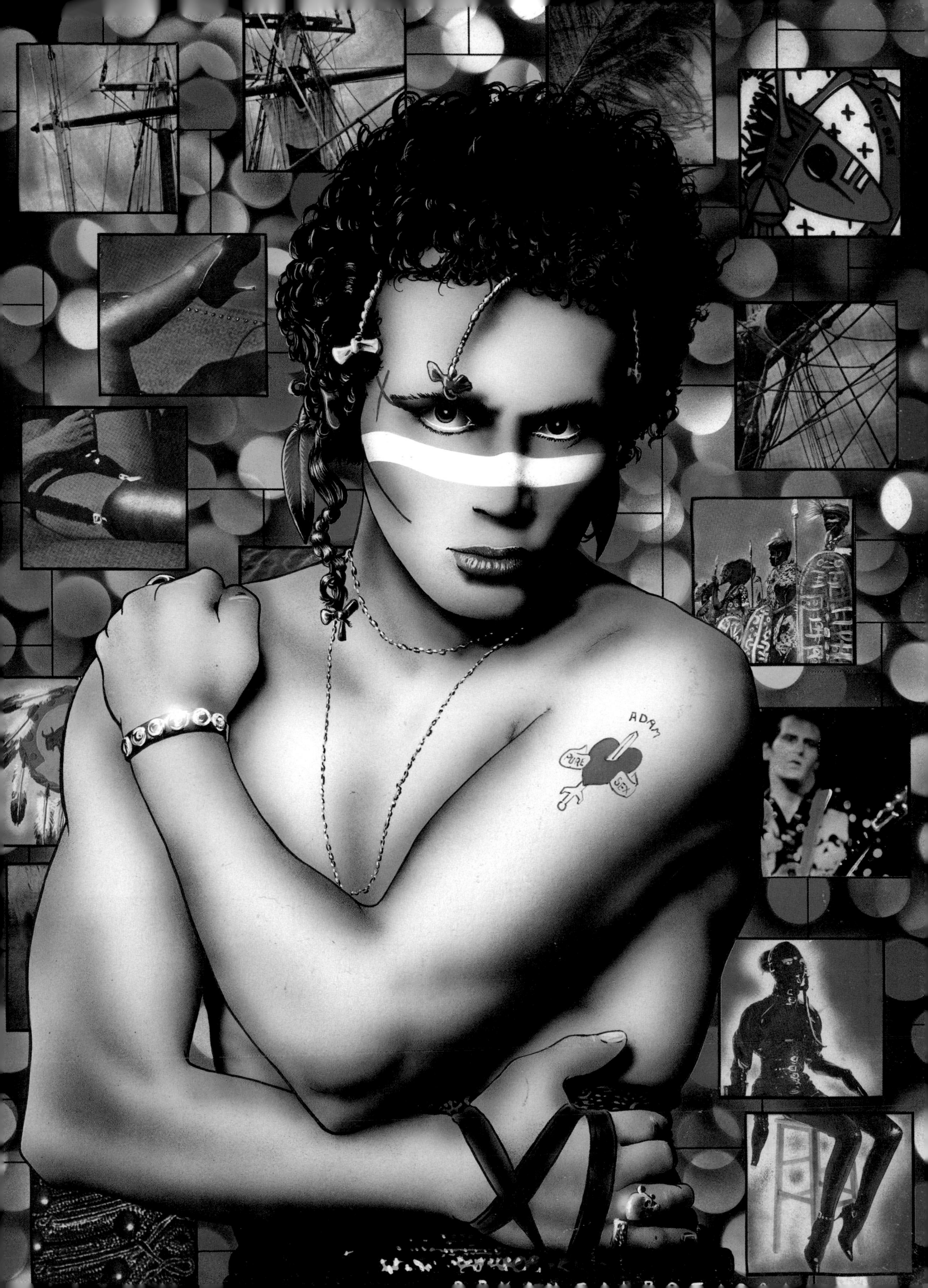

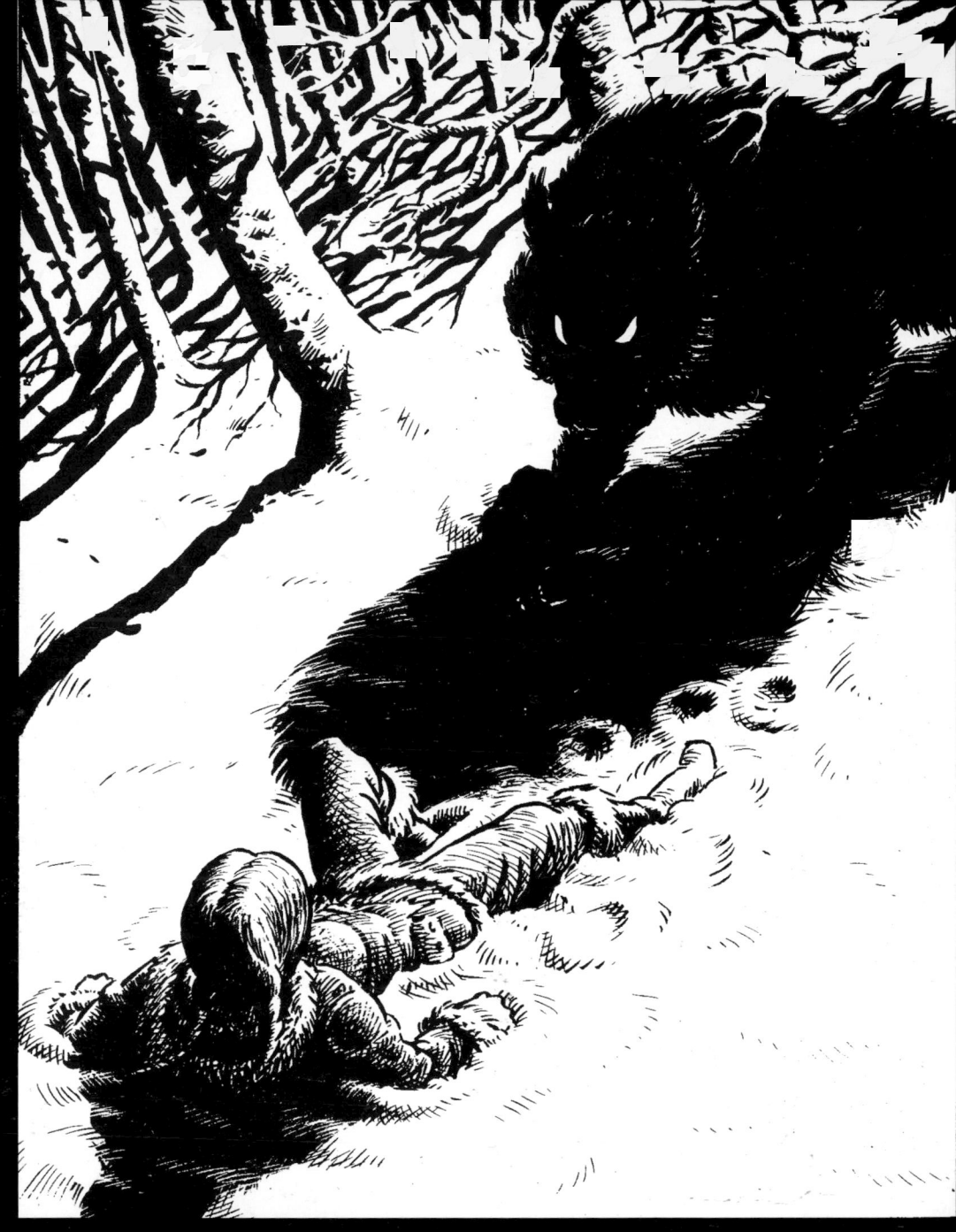

Above is a pen and ink promotional image for my friend Stephen Gallagher's novel *Follower*. It was used as the cover for the movie proposal. 1983.

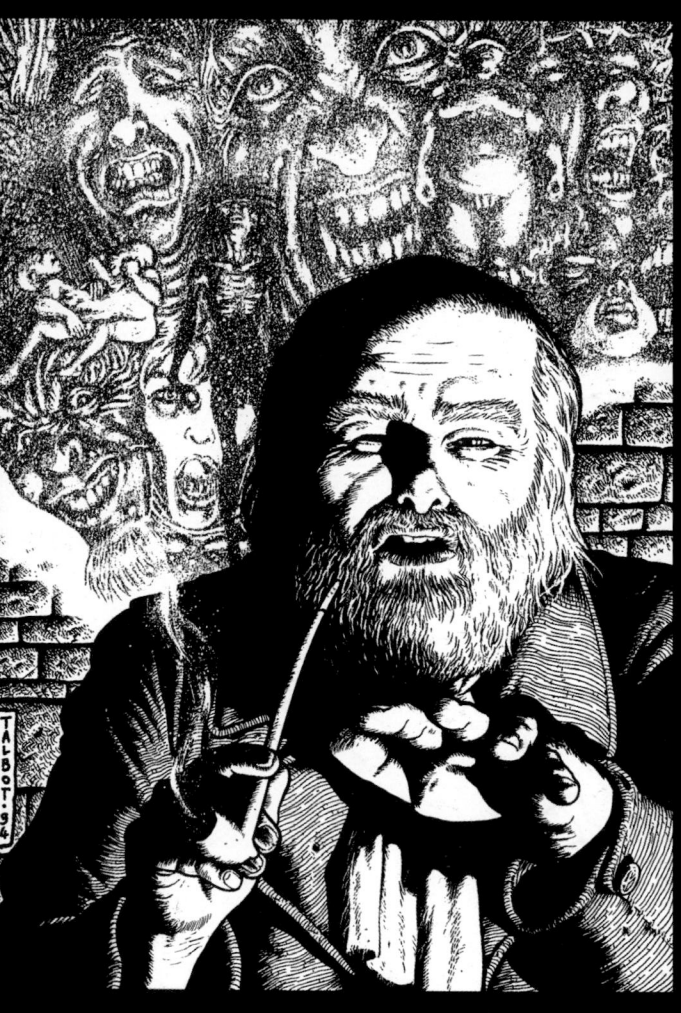

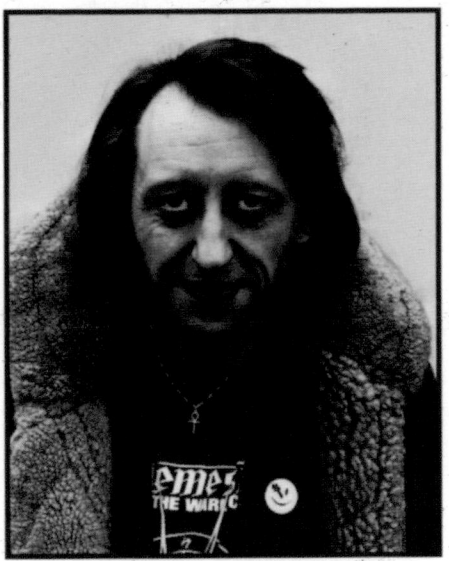

BRYAN TALBOT
Writer, Artist, Painter, Editor

This trading card above was from the *Famous Comic Book Creators* series (Eclipse 1992).

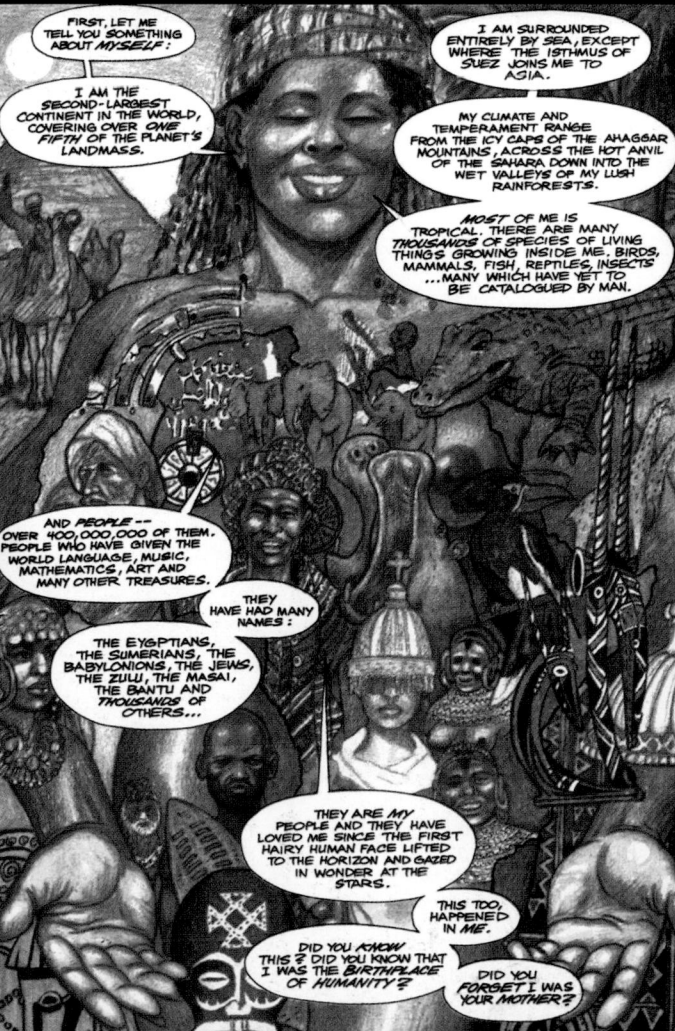

The Storyteller, above left, was the frontispiece of *Northern Chills*, an anthology of horror stories by Kimota Publishing, 1994. Keith Marsland posed for the picture. He also posed for the character Sam in *The Tale of One Bad Rat*.

On the bottom left is one of the three pages of *Africa*, done for *The Comic Relief Comic* benefit book, 1991. The script was by Igor Goldkind. It was colored in pencils by Al Davison.

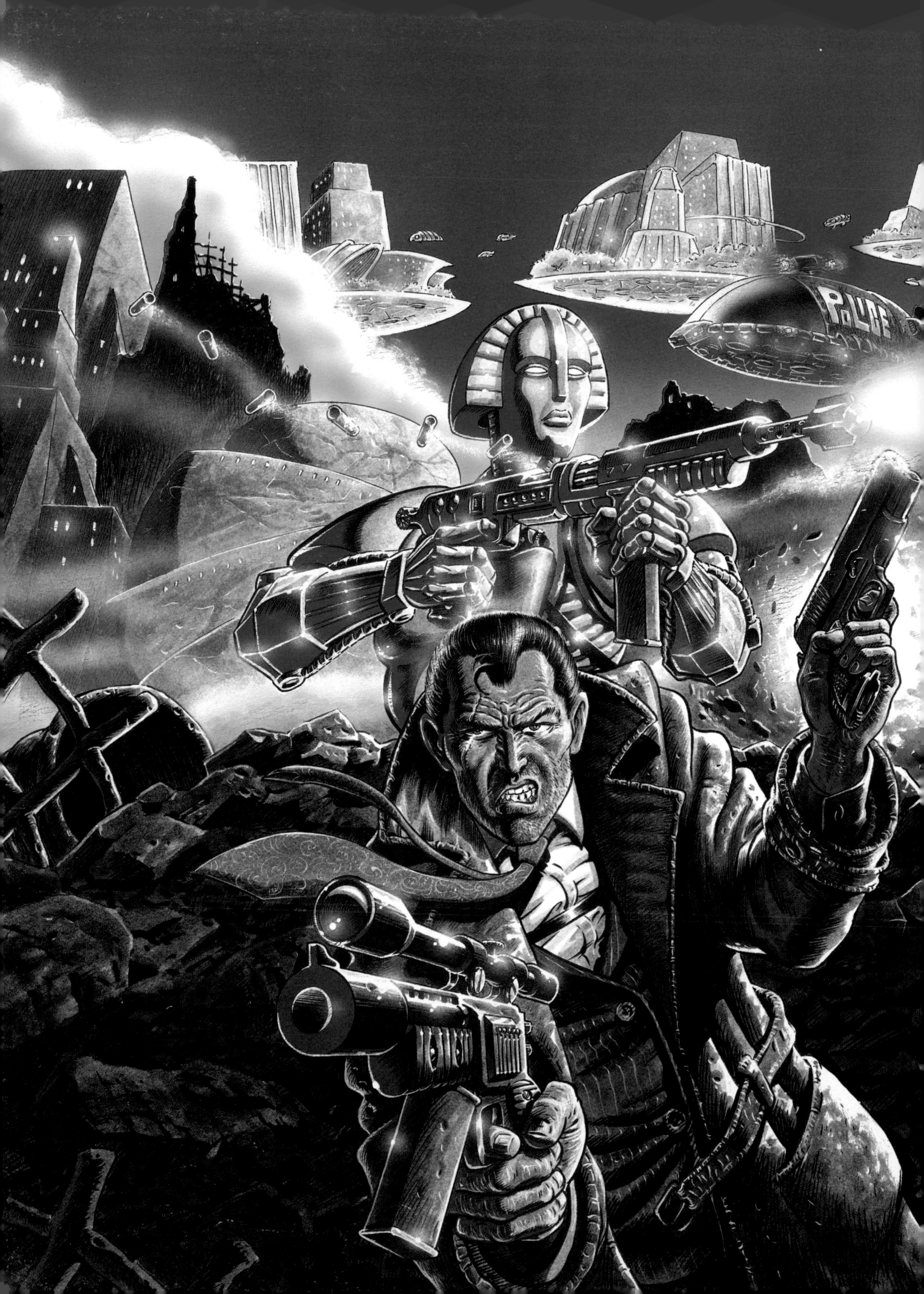

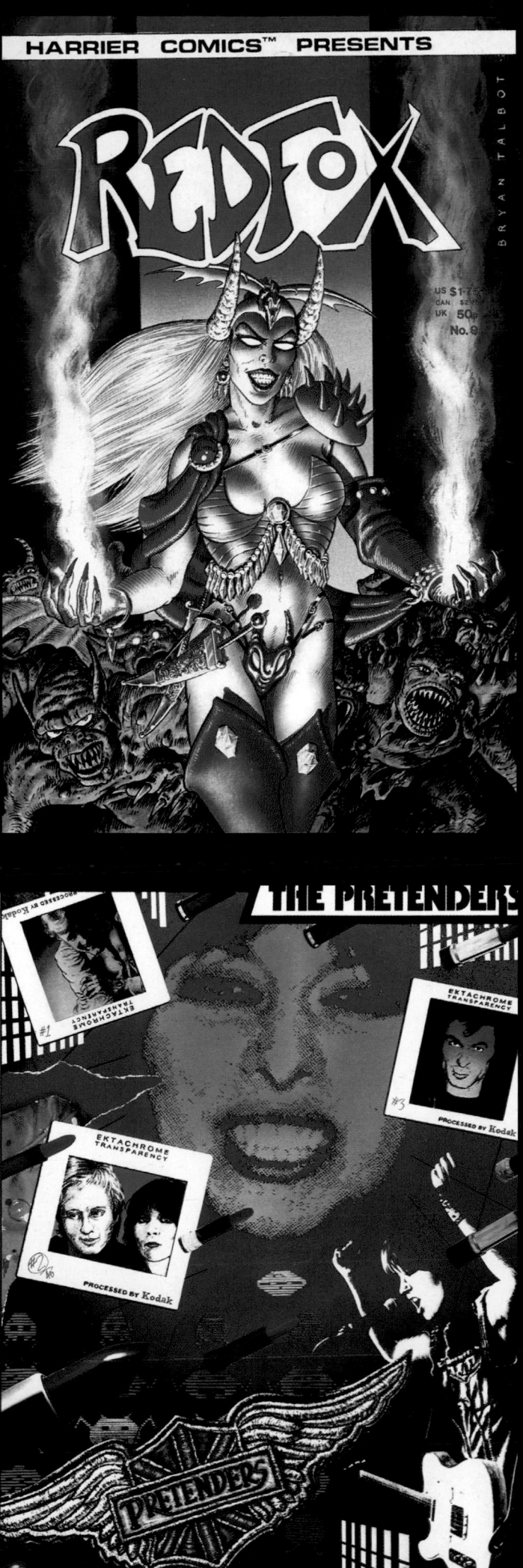

I drew *G-Man*, a six-page strip written by Pat Mills for Egmont's proposed glossy comic magazine *Heroes*, intended as a rival to IPC's phenomenally successful SF comic *2000AD*. Opposite is the cover illo for the dummy issue. It was never published. Inks. 1986.

Left above: cover for Valkyrie Press. *Redfox*, by Chris Bell and Fox, was the only other comic series they published apart from Arkwright. Inks. 1987.

I produced a series of paintings for Rock Art Prints Ltd in the late 70s, including this one of The *Pretenders*, published in the book *Visions of Rock*. Acrylics, inks and collage. 1980.

For the same book I did punk poet John Cooper Clarke (overleaf) but it wasn't used because the editor thought that it wouldn't go down well in Middle America. All the images in this piece were direct references to lines or themes in his poems. I still know several of his poems off by heart and often spontaneously trot them out when I'm drunk. Unpublished. Inks and collage. 1979.

Facing Clarke is Frank Zappa, produced as a Rock Art Print. Again, it's full of references to his songs. I never liked the background so have reworked it on computer especially for this book. Acrylics and computer. 1979 & 2007.

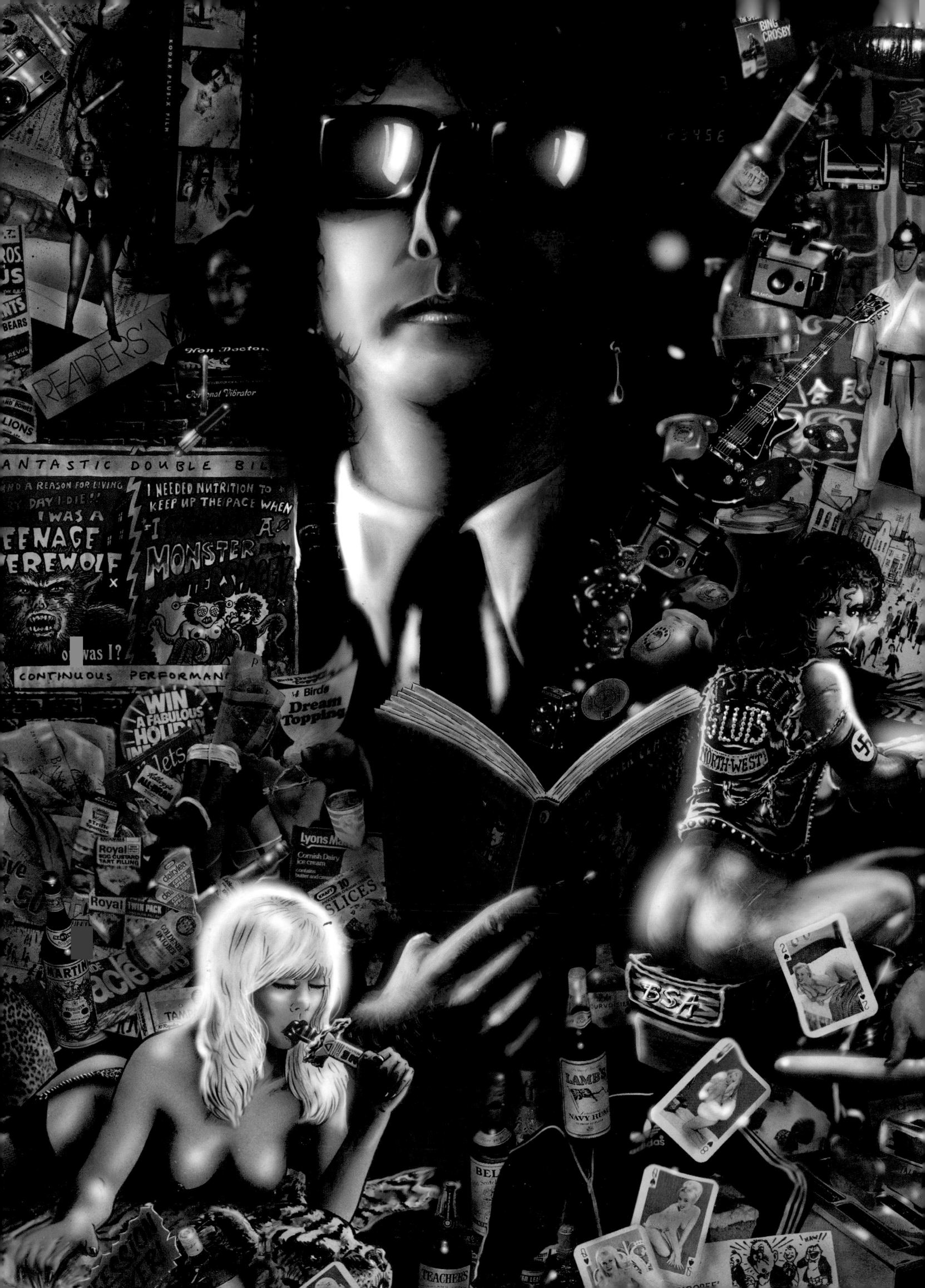

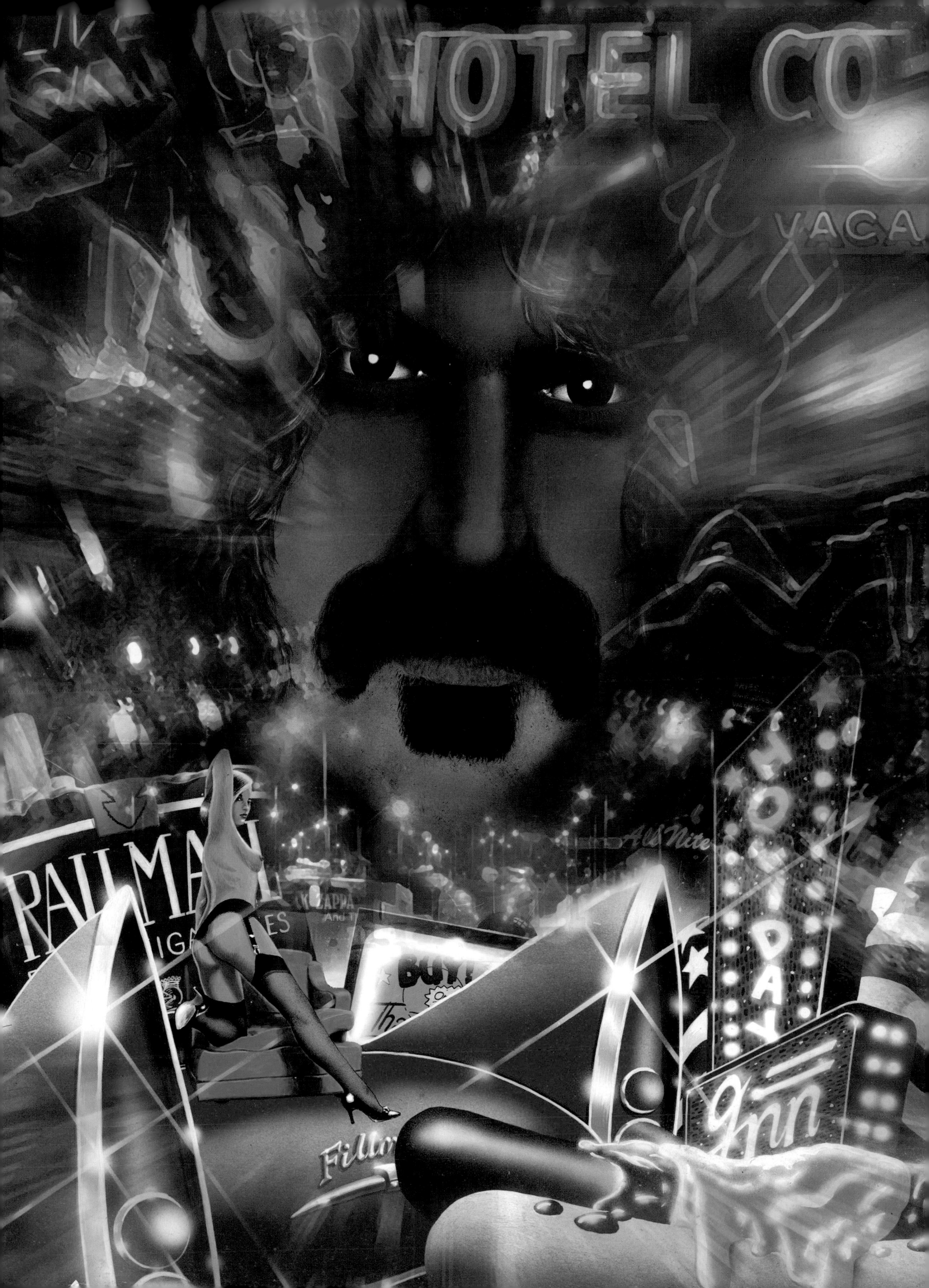

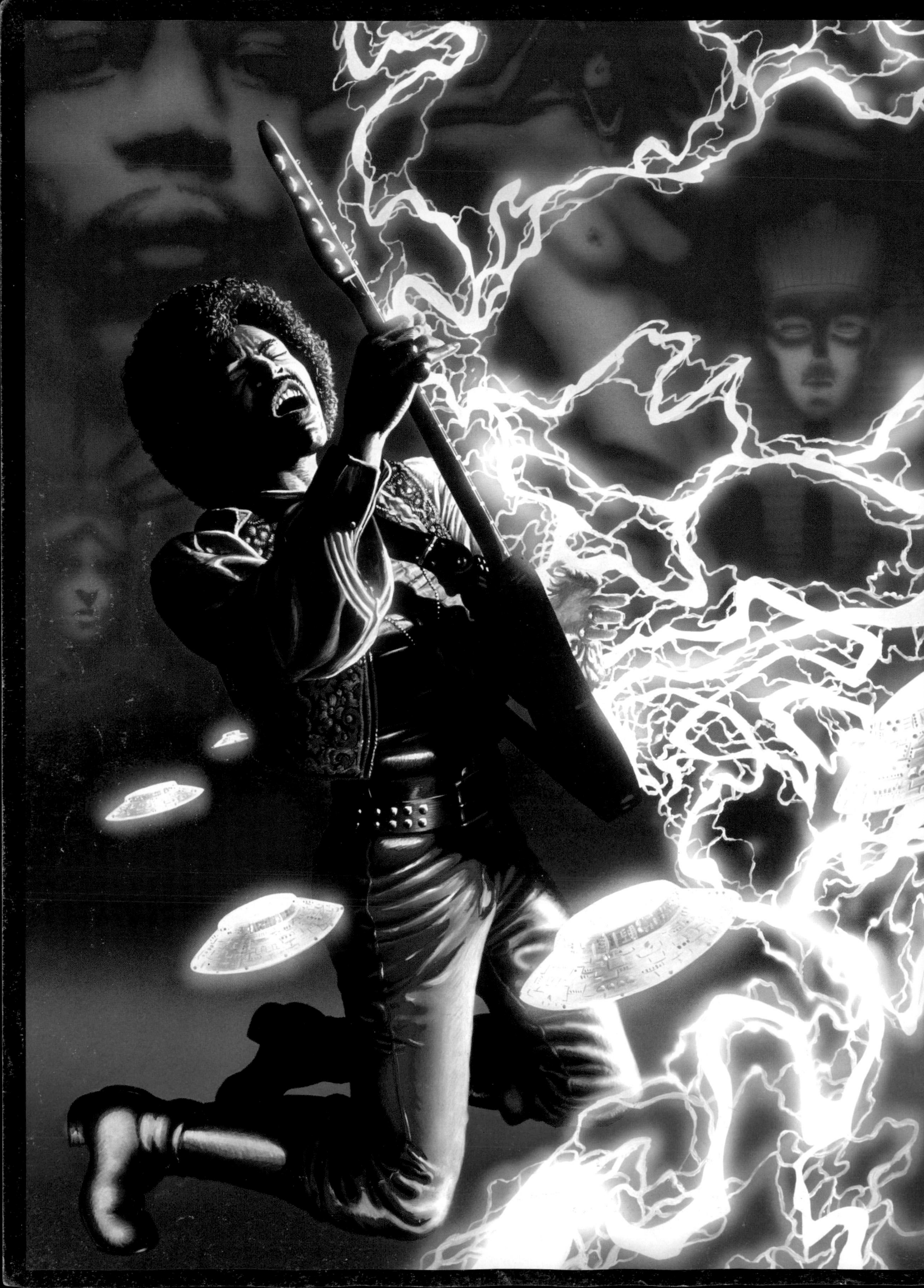

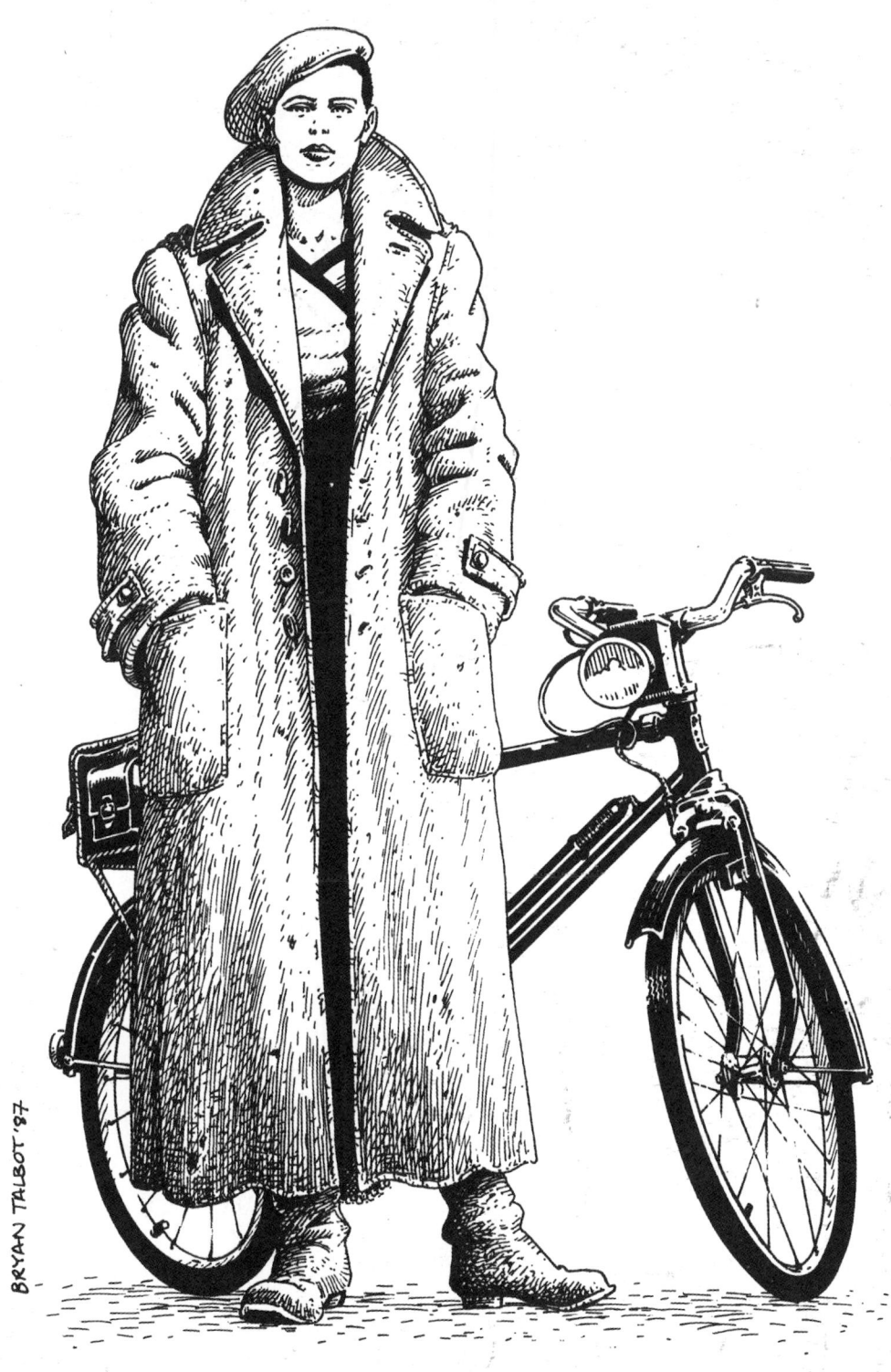

Jimi Hendix, opposite, another of my faves, was also done for Rock Art Prints (RAP). It appeared on a greetings card and as a giant poster. A few years later, it was ripped off by Warner Brothers and used without my permission and without payment as a cover to a Hendrix video. Acrylics and inks. 1979.

Above is, going by my admittedly senile memory, my first commissioned book illustration – for *The Murderer's Song* by Michael Moorcock in the first publication by Titan Books, *Tales from the Forbidden Planet*. 1987.

RAP also produced a line of SF Pin-ups. Overleaf is one of the two I did for them. Acrylics and inks. 1979.

Facing it is *Zaffra and the Dragon*. I self-published this as a limited edition print and later colored it for a cover for *Gamemaster* RPG magazine. Inks. 1985.

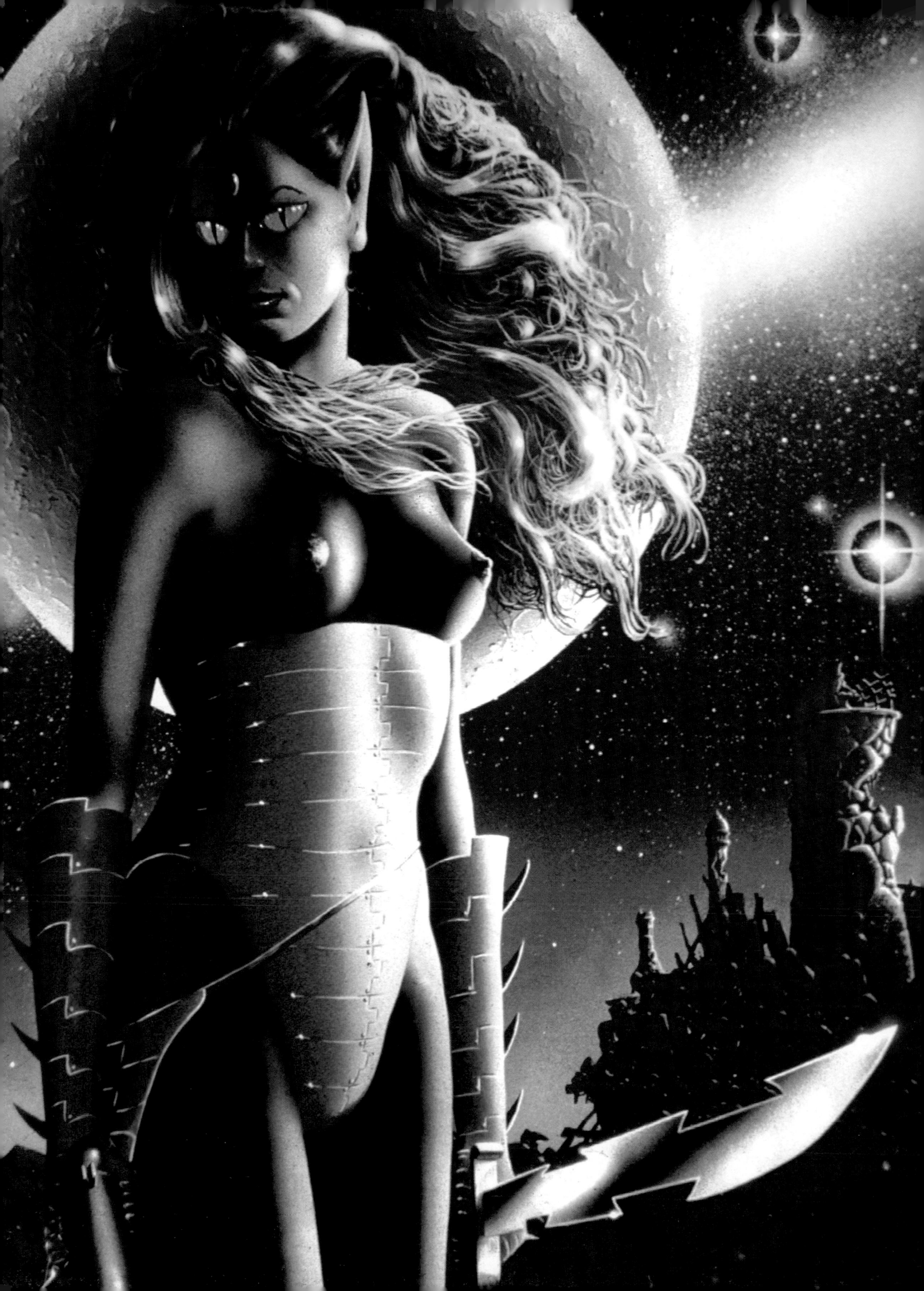

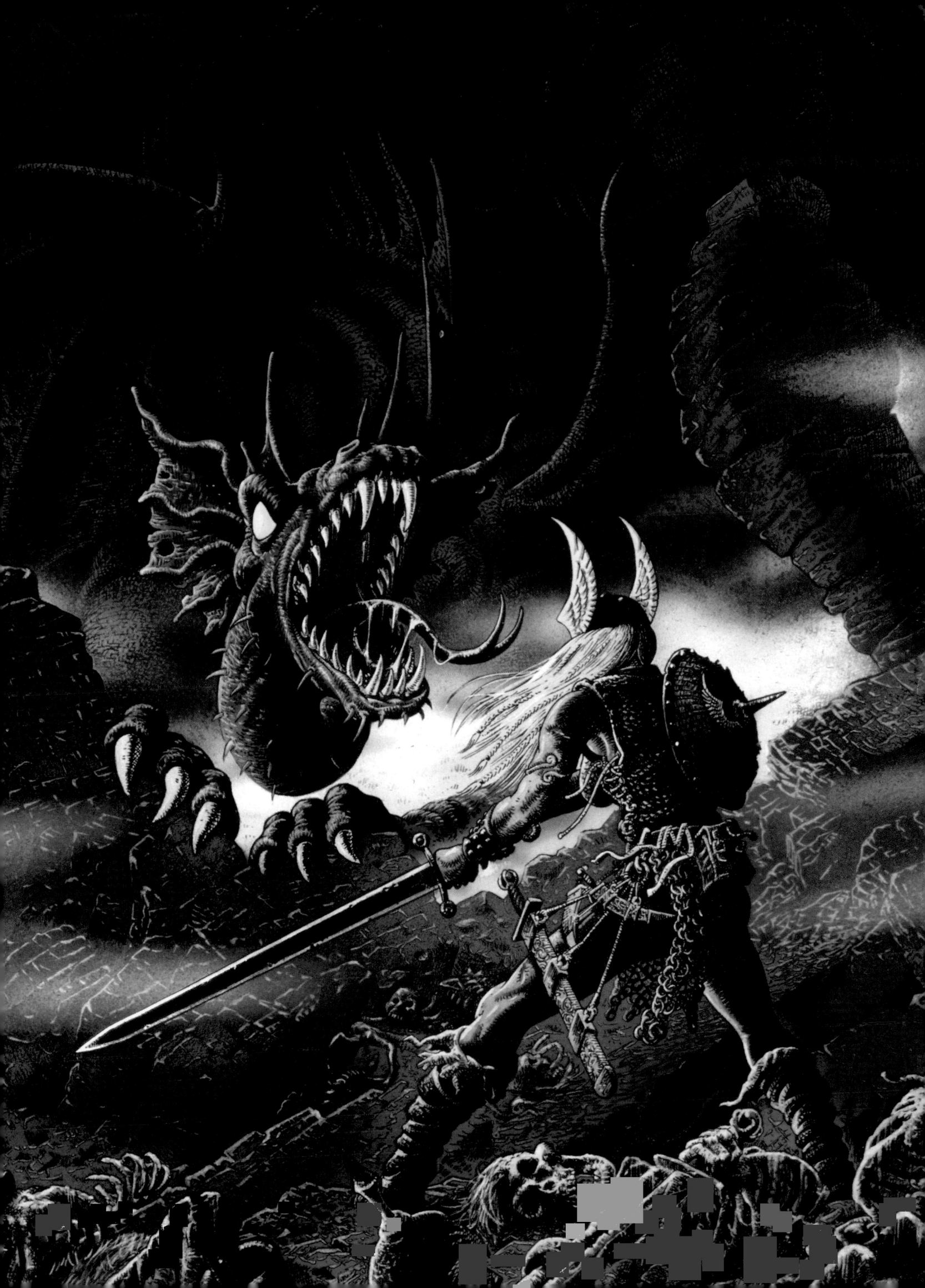

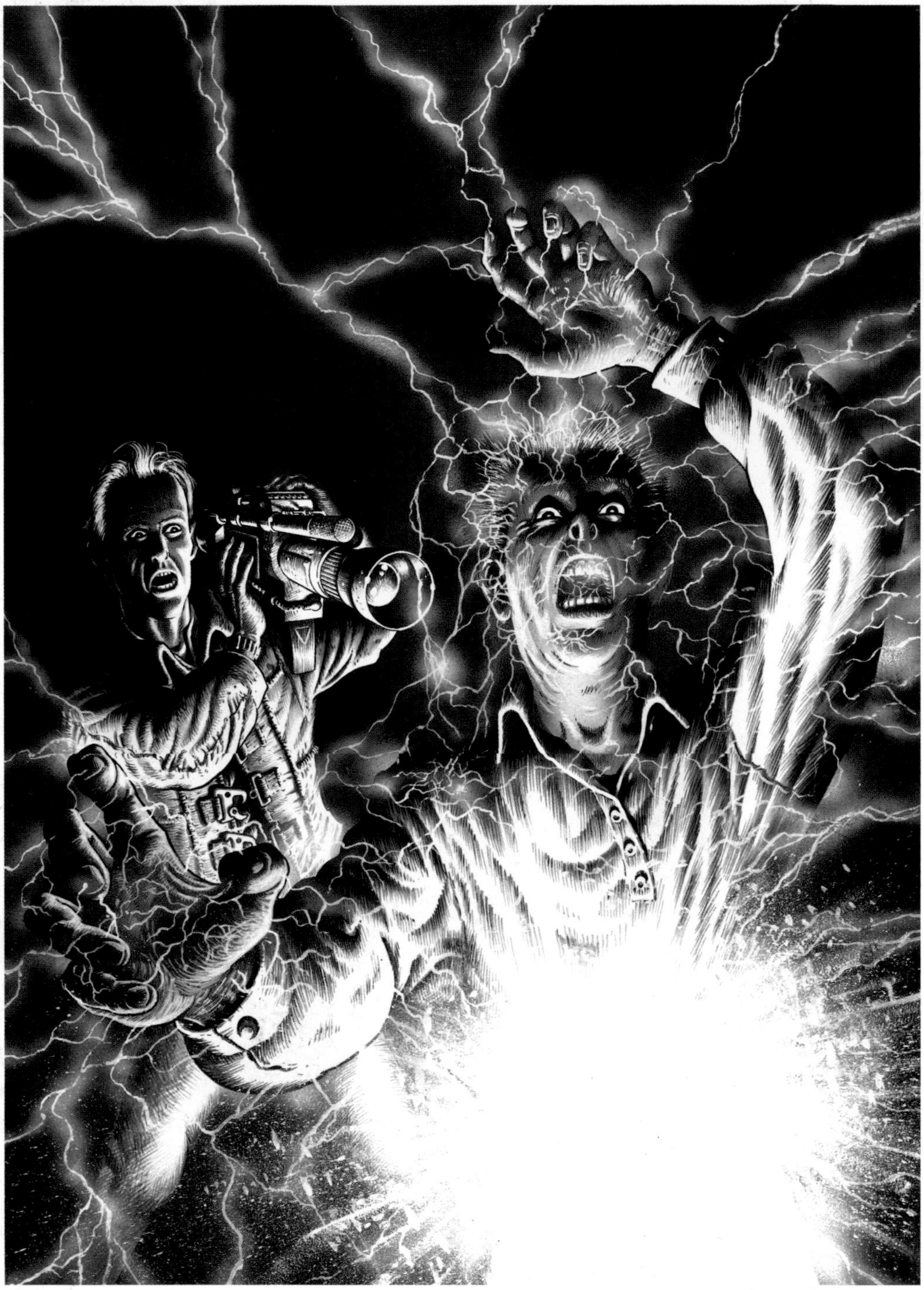

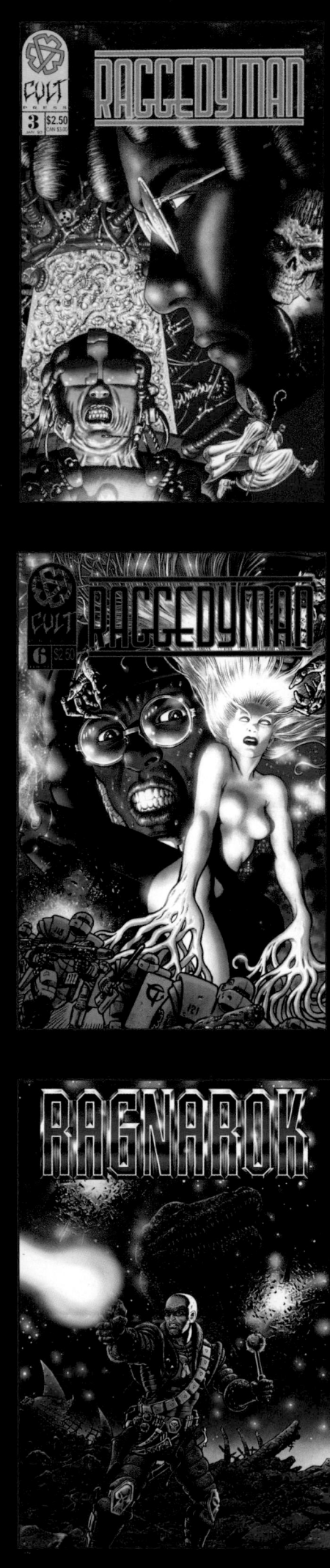

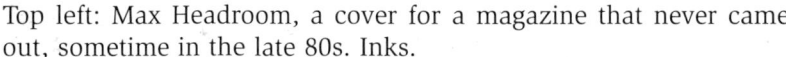

Top left: Max Headroom, a cover for a magazine that never came out, sometime in the late 80s. Inks.

Top right: I did six covers for the Cult Press cyberpunk series Raggedyman, written by Tasha Lowe and drawn by Tony Hicks. Inks. 1992.

Below right: Ragnarok, the poster and cover to the animated video written by Alan Moore. I designed the character and logo but didn't work on the video. Inks. 1982.

Facing: Dan Dare, the classic British comic hero from The Eagle weekly comic of the 1950s. This illustration was produced for the cover of Computer and Video Games when the game was released. Inks. 1985.

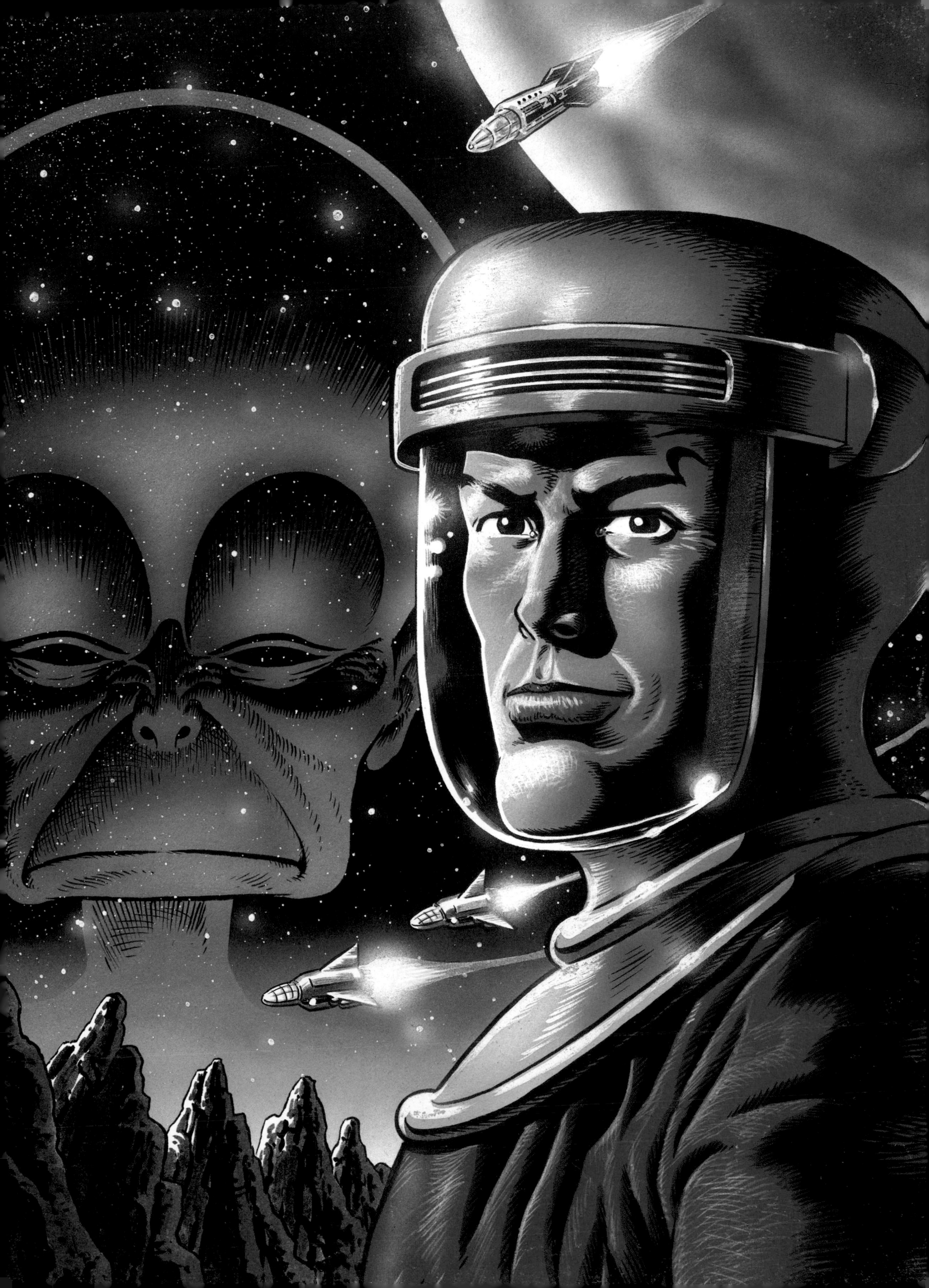

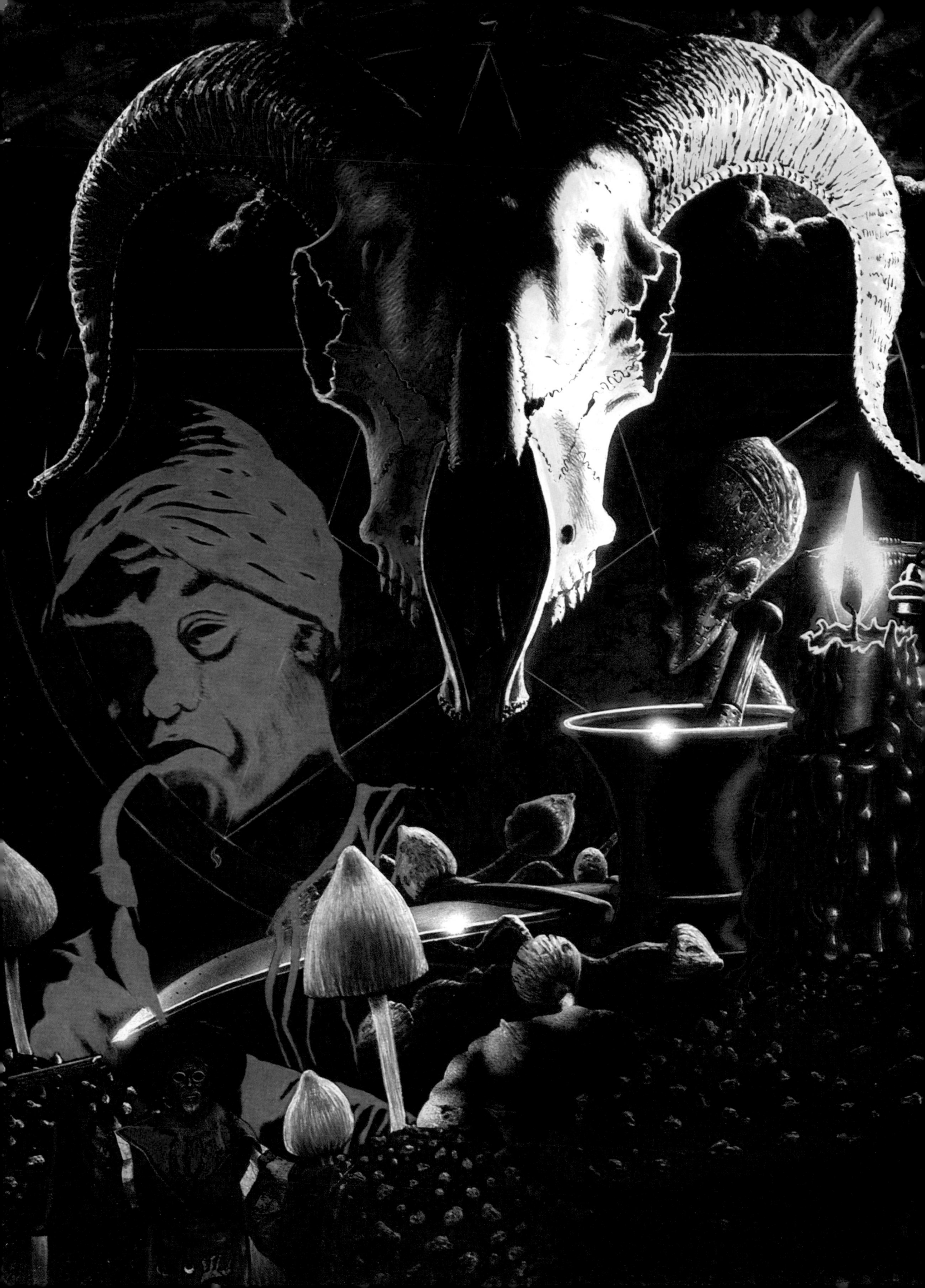

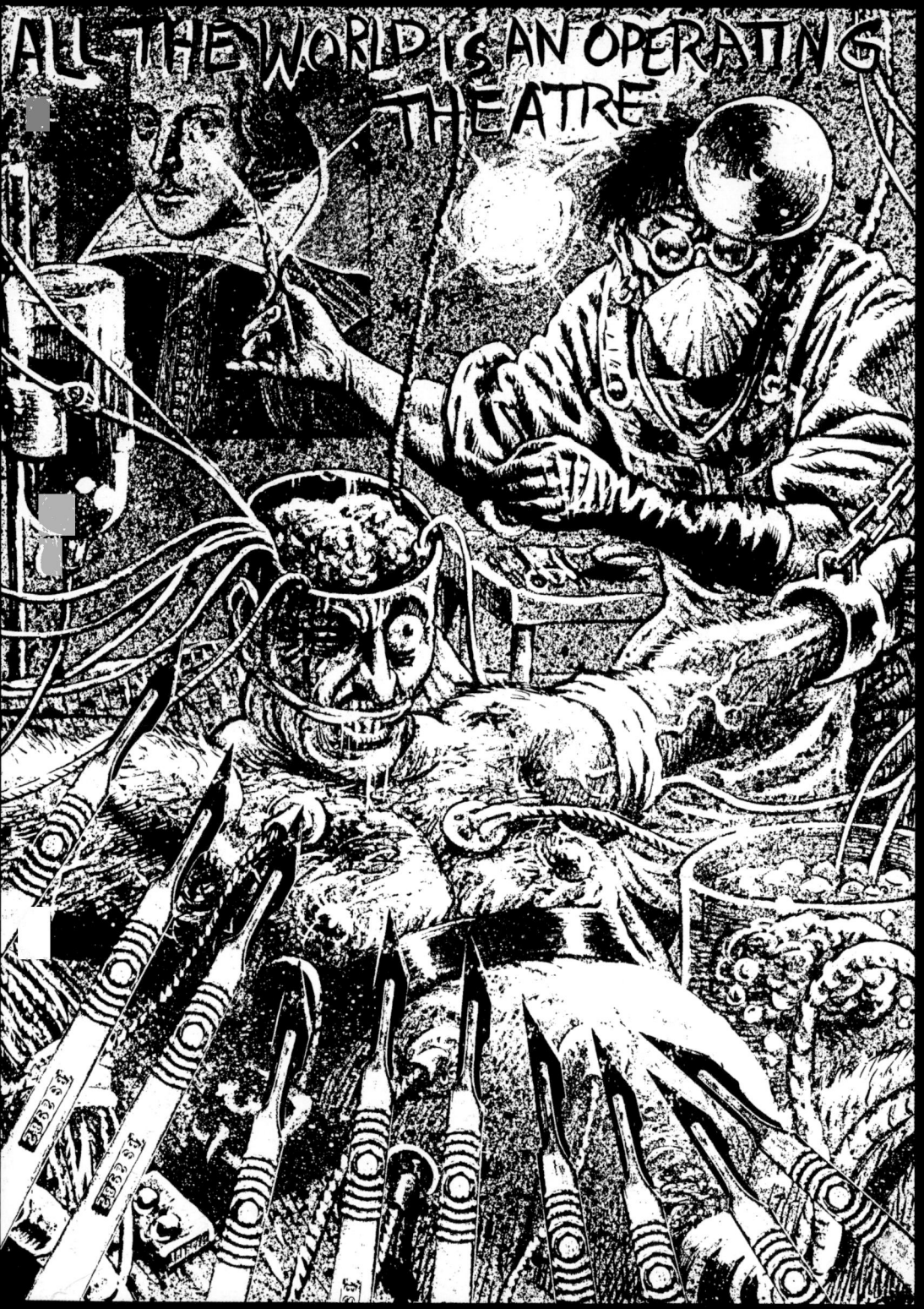

Opposite: a cover for Lee Harris' *Home Grown* magazine, the theme of the issue being drugs and magic. Acrylics, inks and collage. 1981.

Above: *Doc Chaos*, written by Dave Thorpe was a UK alternative comic character. This illo was done for the Doc Chaos prose novella *The Chernobyl Effect*, Hooligan Press, 1988.

I pencilled and inked DC's four-part prestige format mini-series *The Nazz*, written by Tom Veitch. I still think that Tom's script was one of the best post-*Watchmen* super-hero stories. Not set in the DC universe, its theme was *power corrupts*.
Overleaf: the originals for the covers of issues two and four. Inks. 1990 and 1991 respectively.

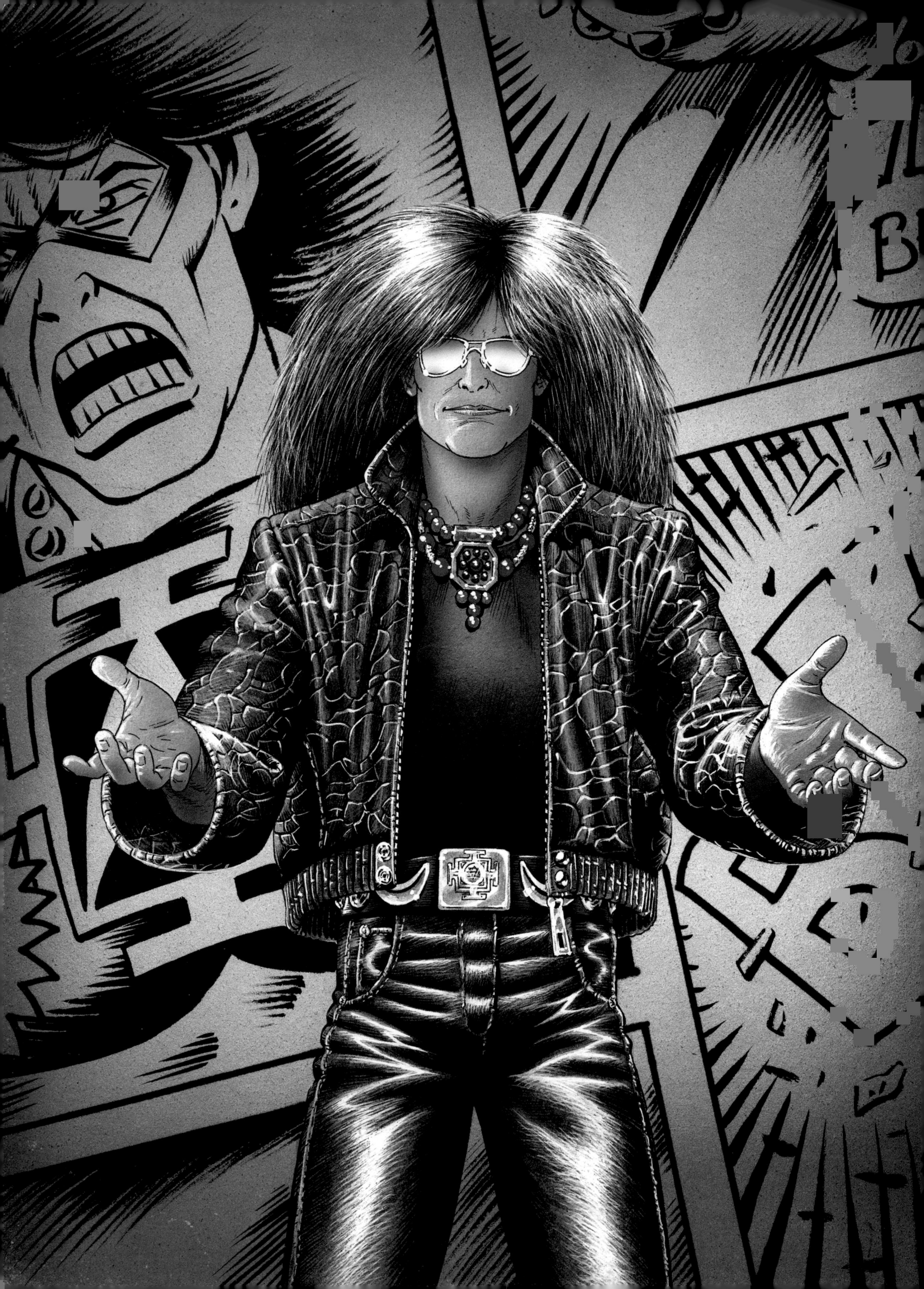

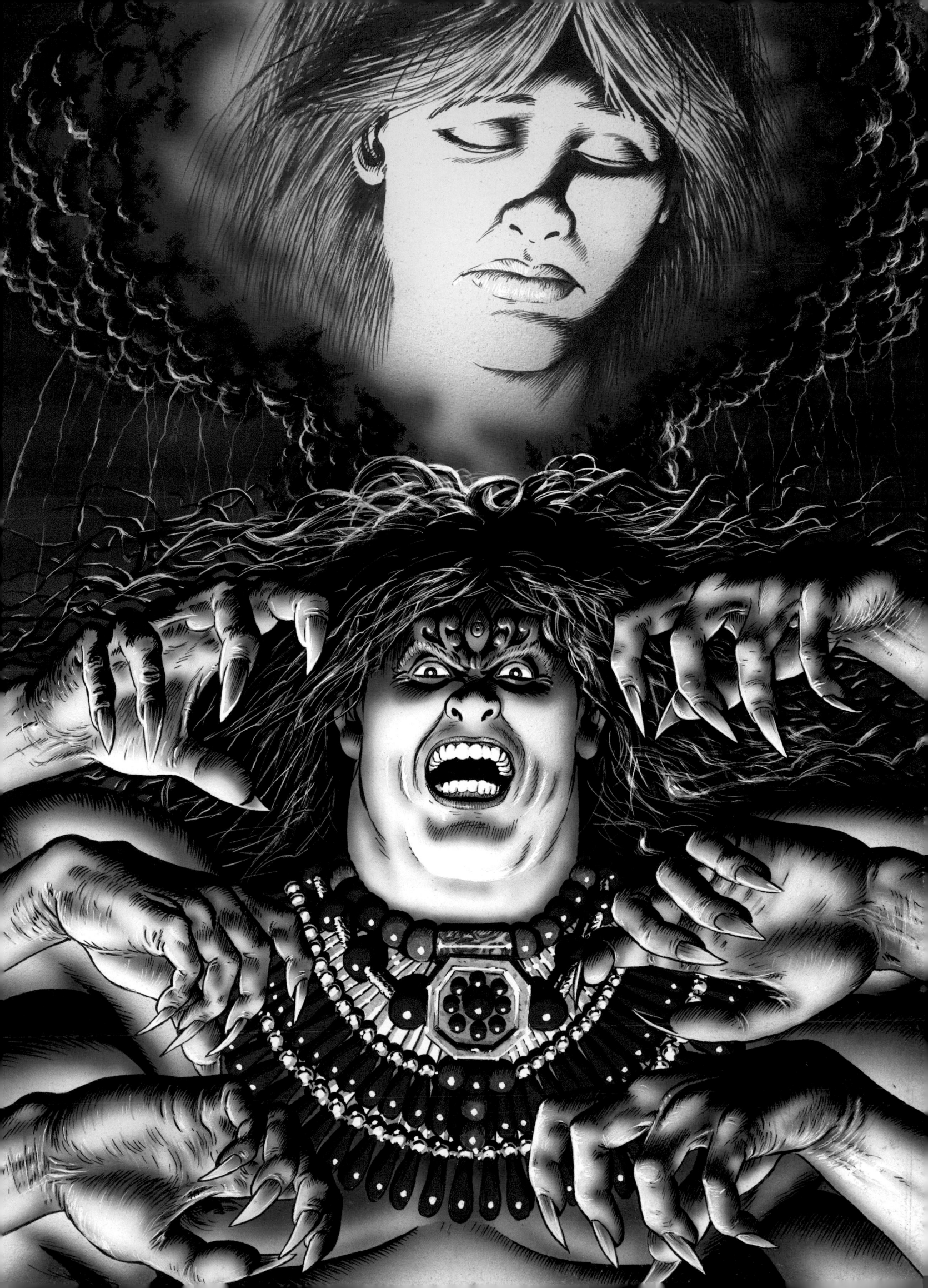

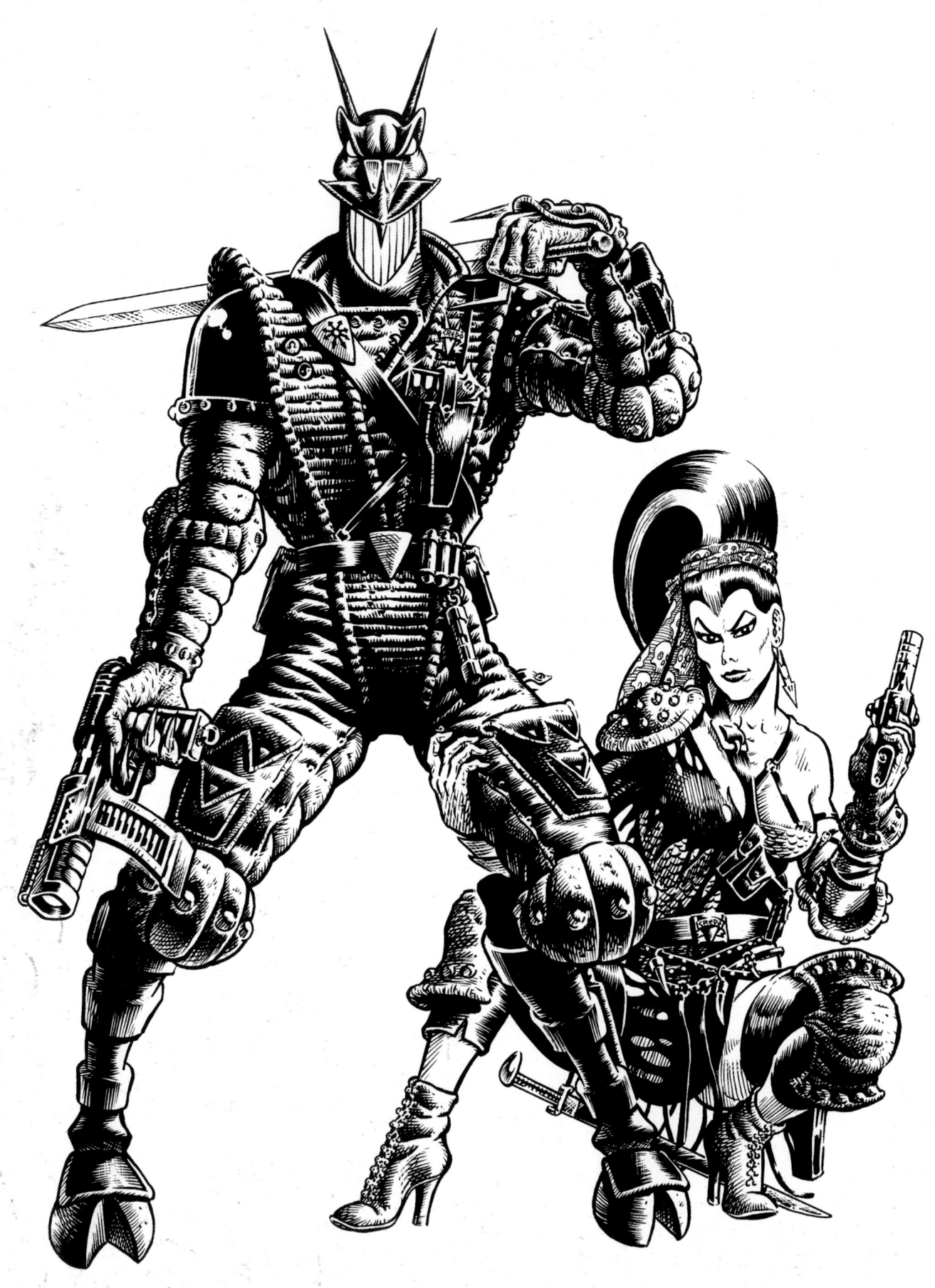

Nemesis and Purity Brown. Frontispiece to Titan Book's 1986 collection of *Nemesis the Warlock Book Four*.

WARNING: NEM AT WORK!

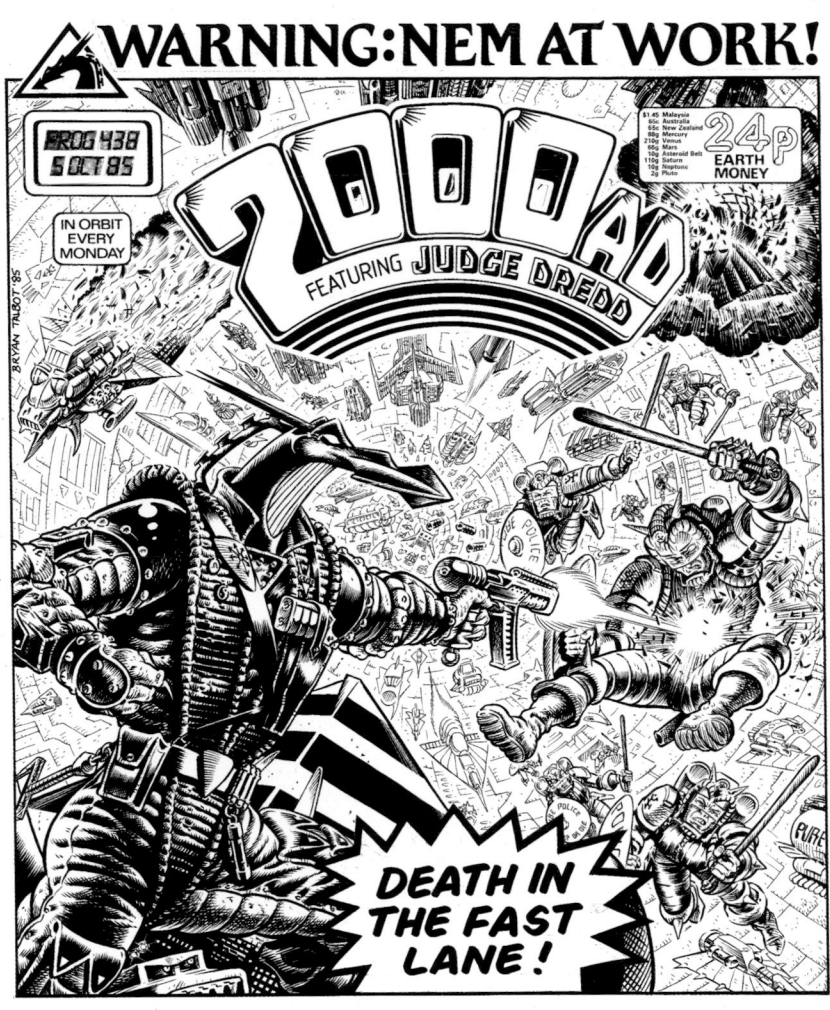

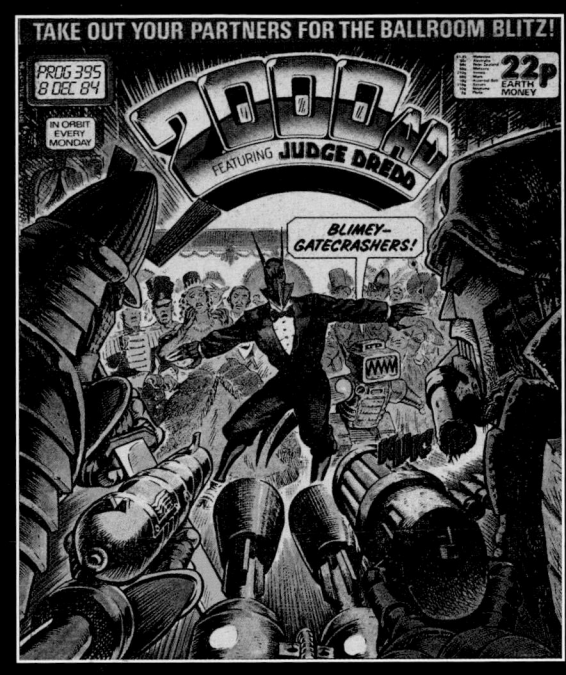

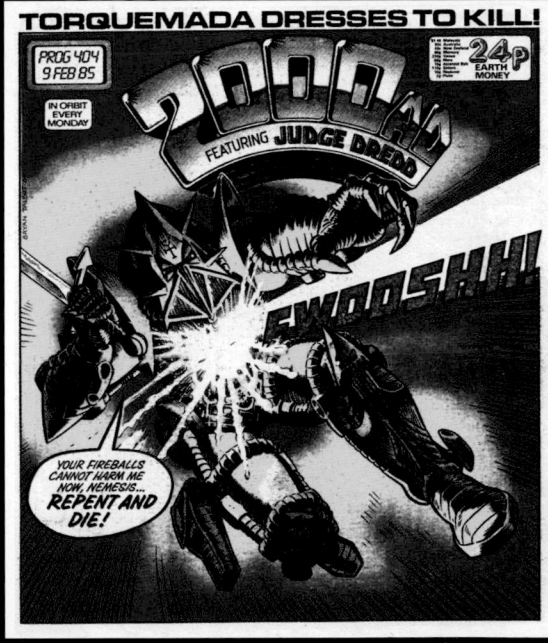

Nemesis the Warlock was the brainchild of writer Pat Mills and artist Kevin O'Neill and his adventures were serialised in IPC's 2000AD. When Kevin left the strip to work for DC Comics Pat, who liked my work on Luther Arkwright, asked if I'd take over. Of course I would! 2000AD was the cutting edge of UK comics and sold a rock-solid 120,000 copies a week. I put Arkwright on hold and worked for them for about four years, 1983–87.

Pat's scripts were a joy to work with. Nemesis was the leader of the alien resistance movement against *Tomas de Torquemada*, the fascist dictator of a future Earth. Torquemada regularly won the *Eagle Award* for "Favourite Villain". A favourite character of mine was the South African *Arch-Bigot of Necropolis* (below), written during the height of apartheid.

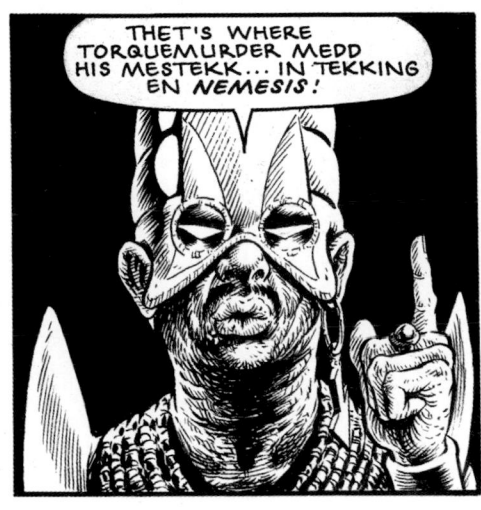

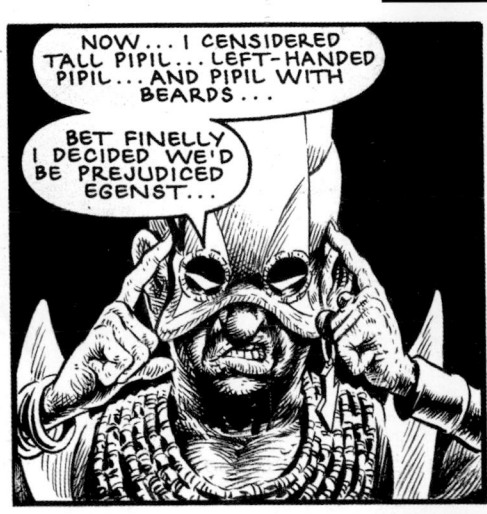

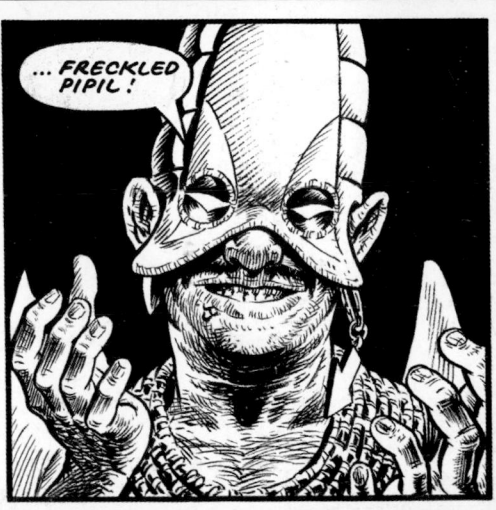

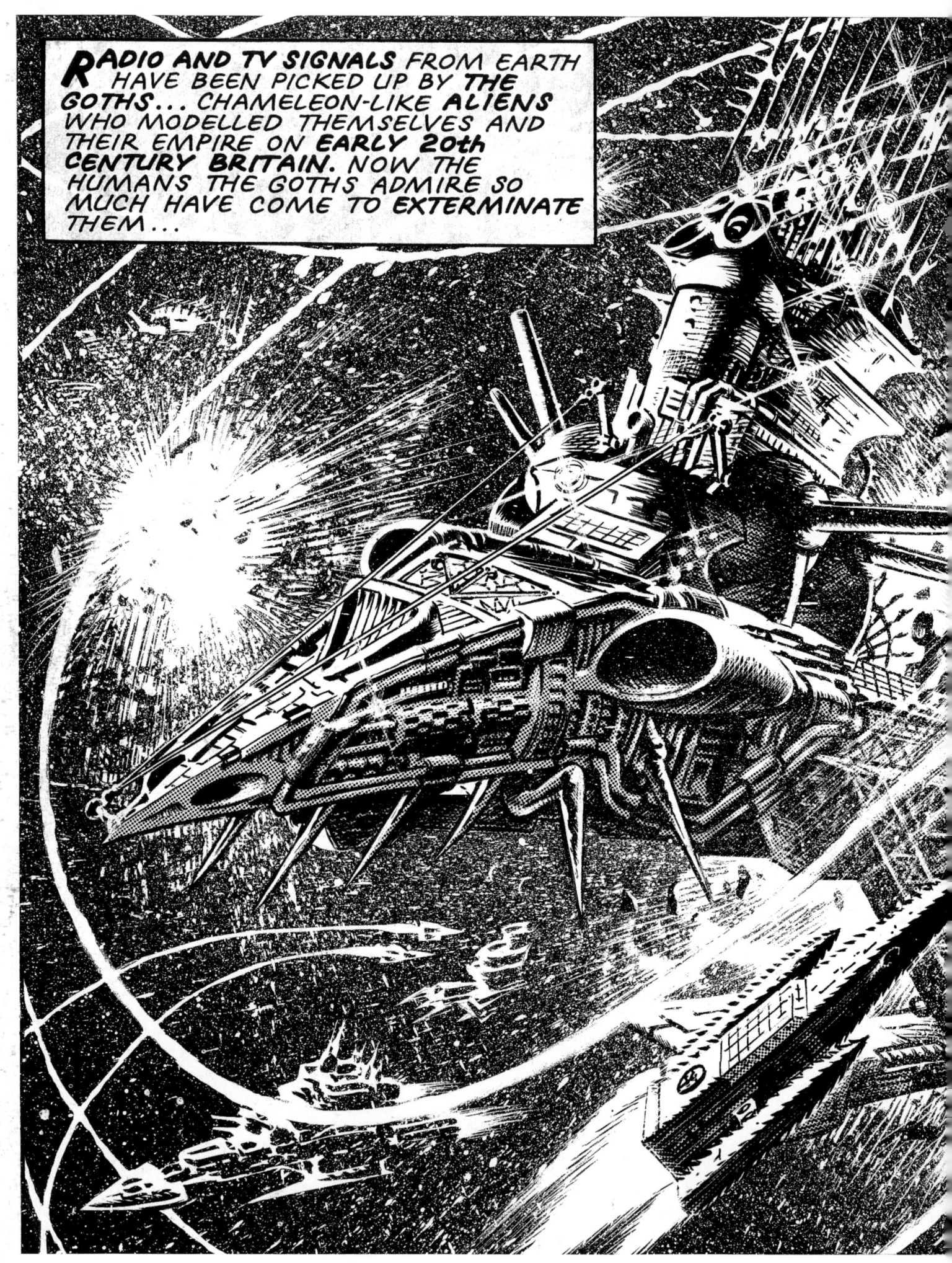

RADIO AND TV SIGNALS FROM EARTH HAVE BEEN PICKED UP BY THE GOTHS... CHAMELEON-LIKE ALIENS WHO MODELLED THEMSELVES AND THEIR EMPIRE ON EARLY 20th CENTURY BRITAIN. NOW THE HUMANS THE GOTHS ADMIRE SO MUCH HAVE COME TO EXTERMINATE THEM...

A panel from the first Nemesis series I worked on, *The Gothic Empire*. This is still many aging 2000AD fans' favourite Nemesis story. It was reprinted in 2006 by Rebellion, the new publisher of 2000AD, in *The Complete Nemesis the Warlock: Book One*.

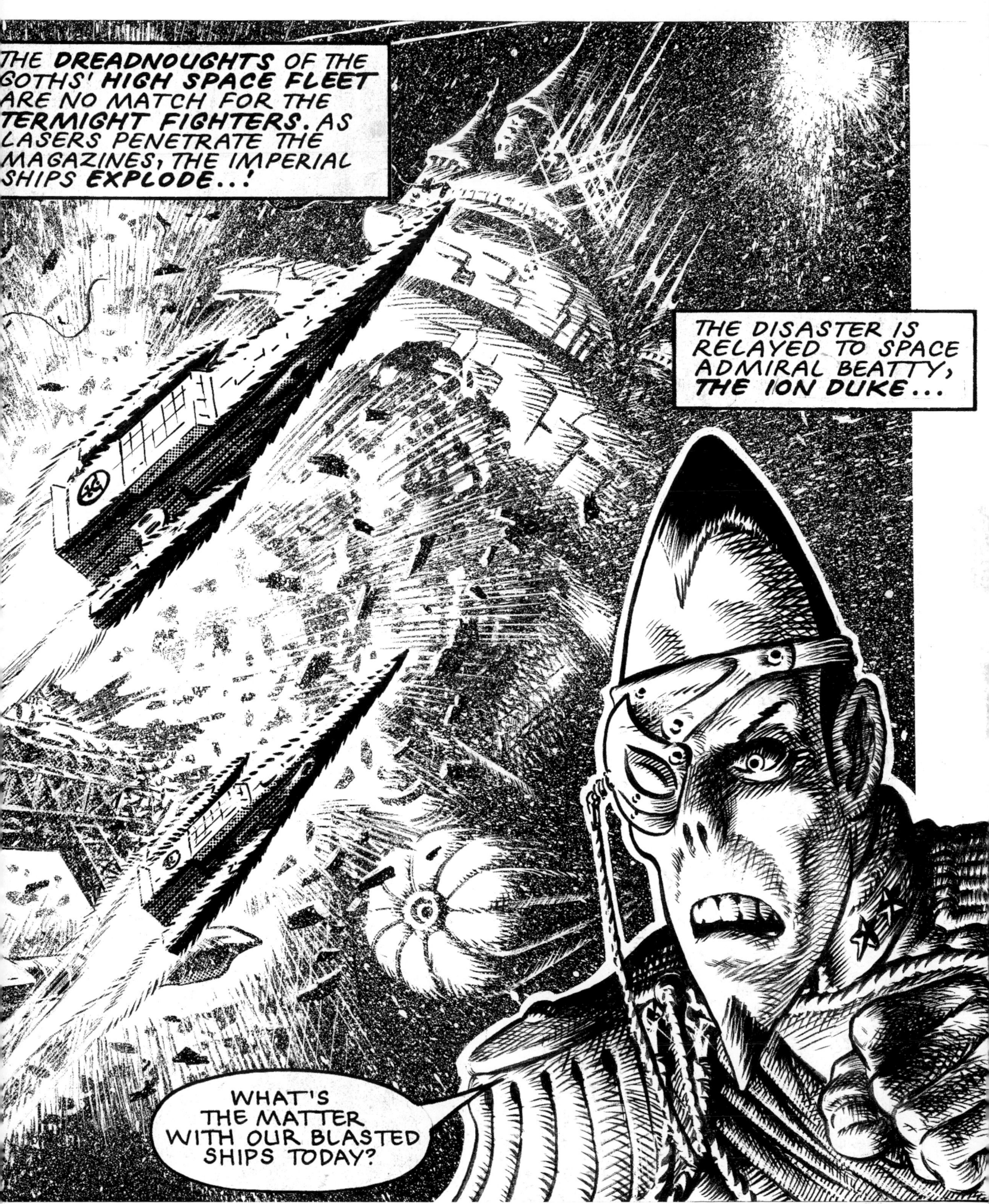

43

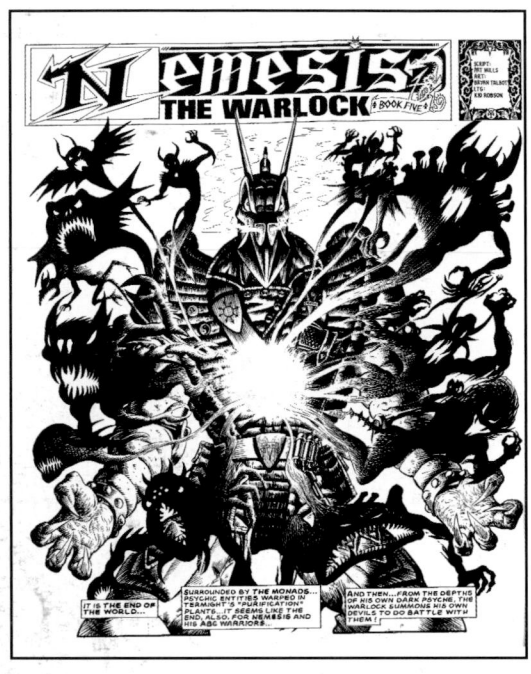

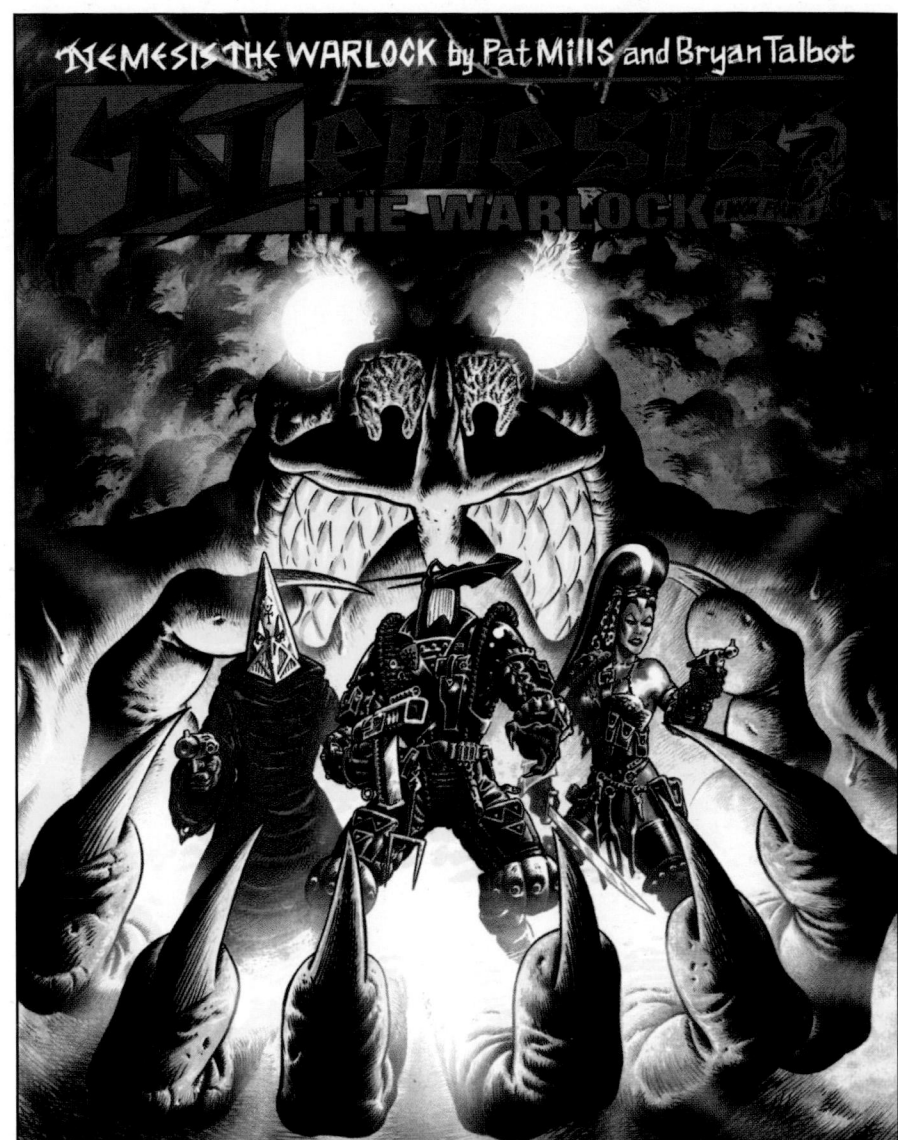

The Nemesis stories were originally collected into trade paperbacks by Titan Books and I did the majority of the covers. In 1987 Software Communications Ltd produced the computer game.

Facing is the original of the cover to the Titan edition of Book Six. Inks. 1987.

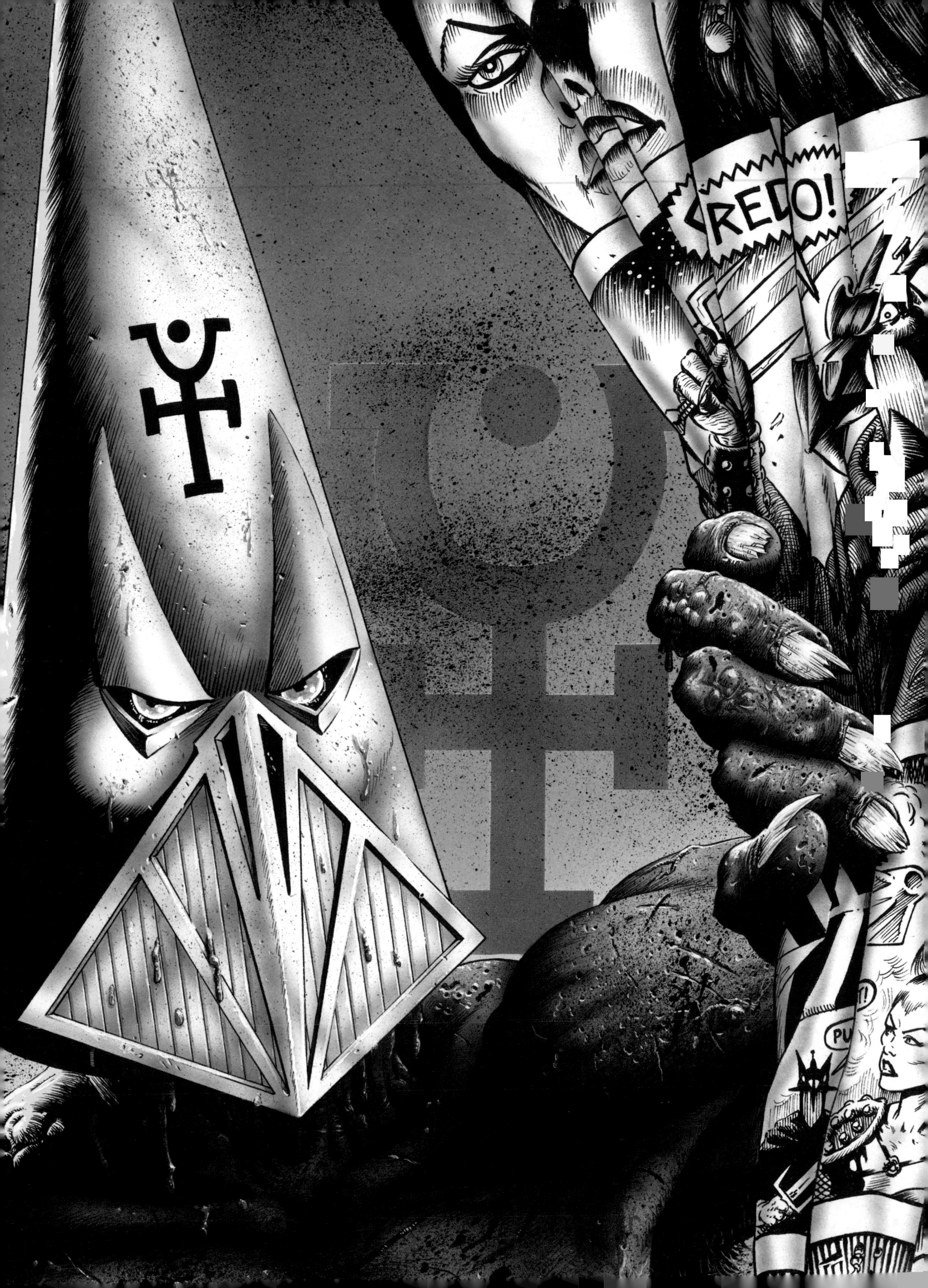

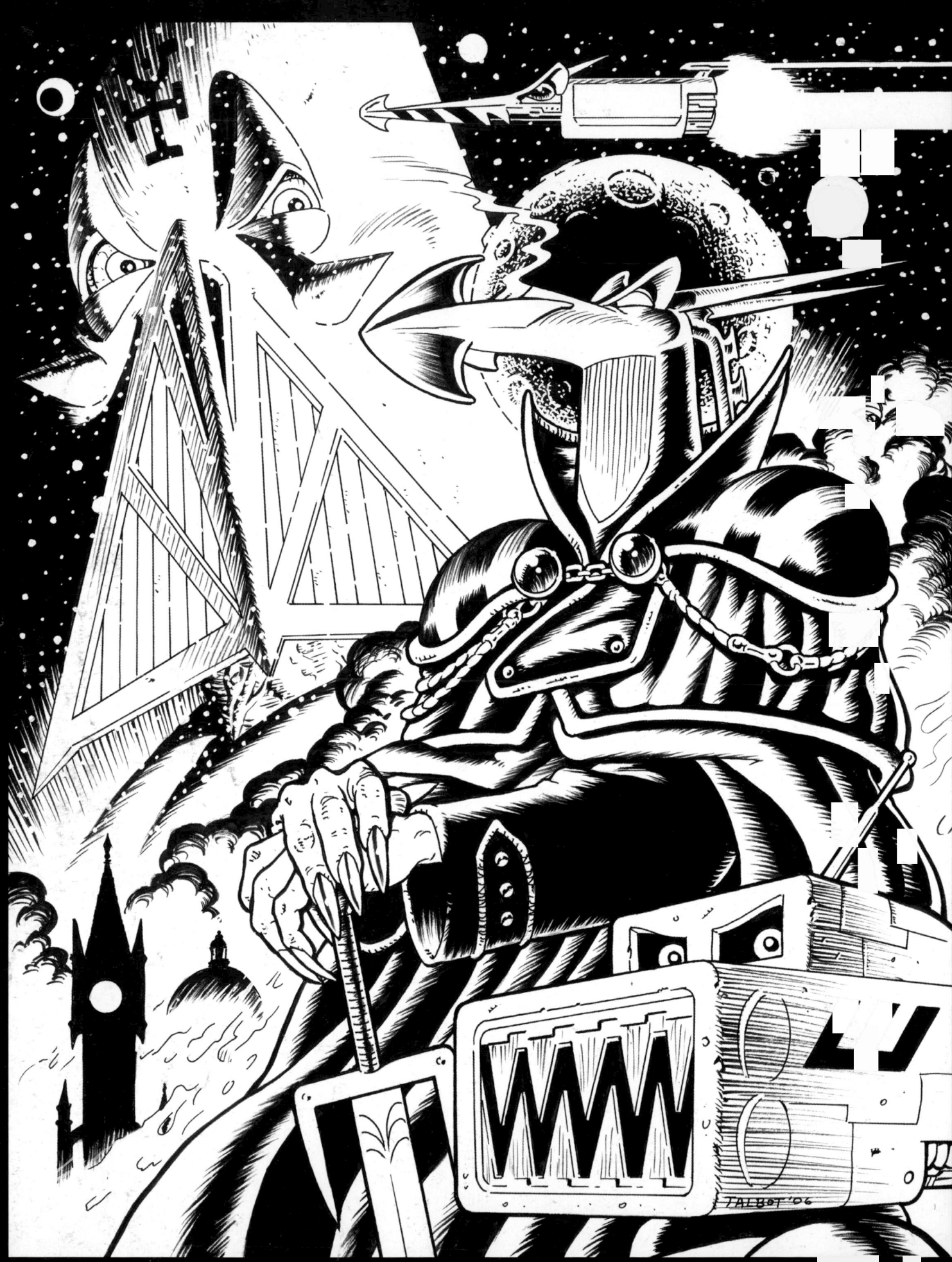

I still occasionally work for 2000AD, the last strip being *Memento*, a twelve page fully painted "silent" SF story, in 2004. This year, 2007, is 2000AD's thirtieth anniversary and, to mark the event, they're running a series of pin-ups of classic stories, such as the above: *The Gothic Empire*. December 2006.

Facing: the original of the cover of the Titan edition of Nemesis Book Nine.

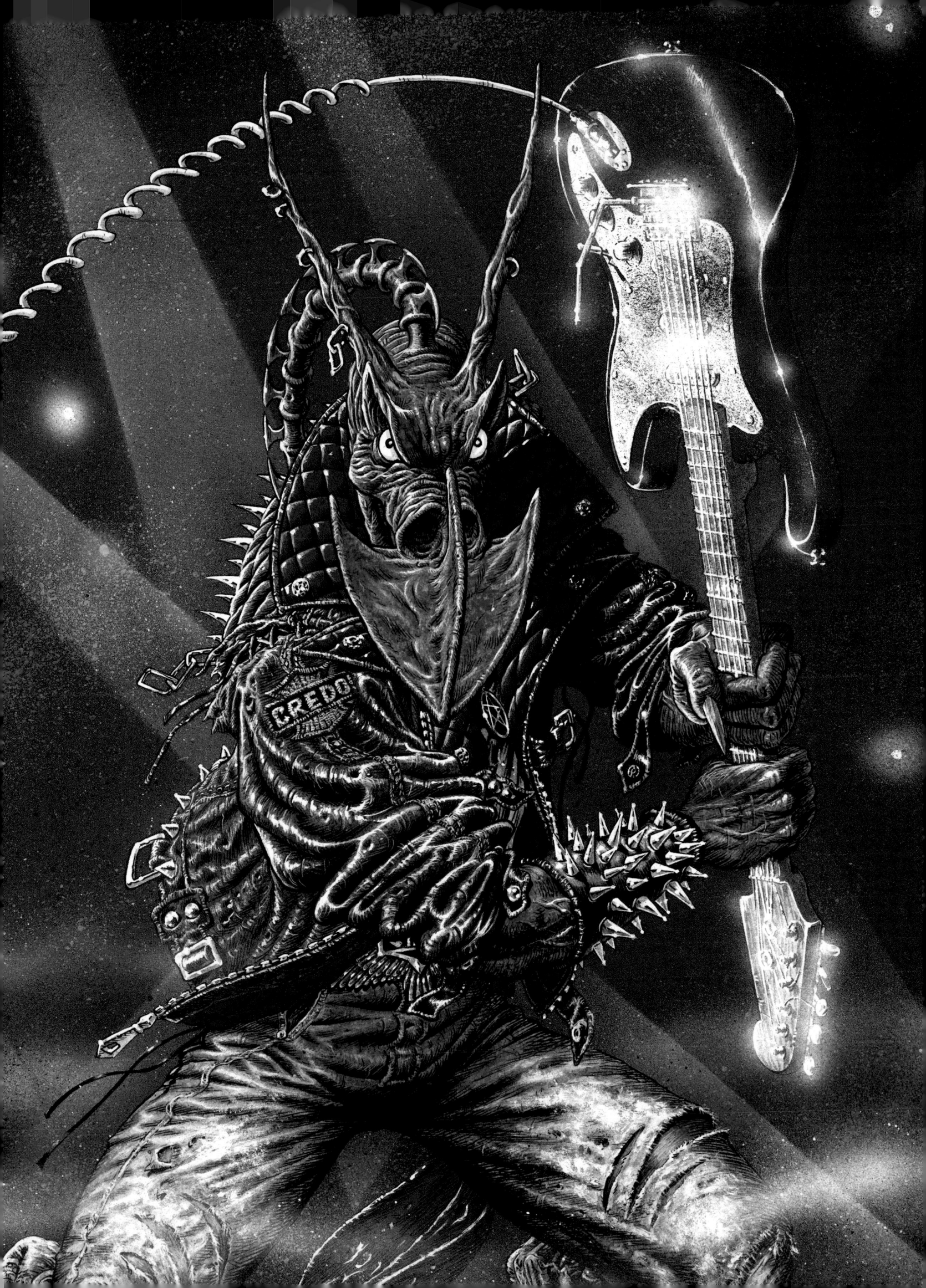

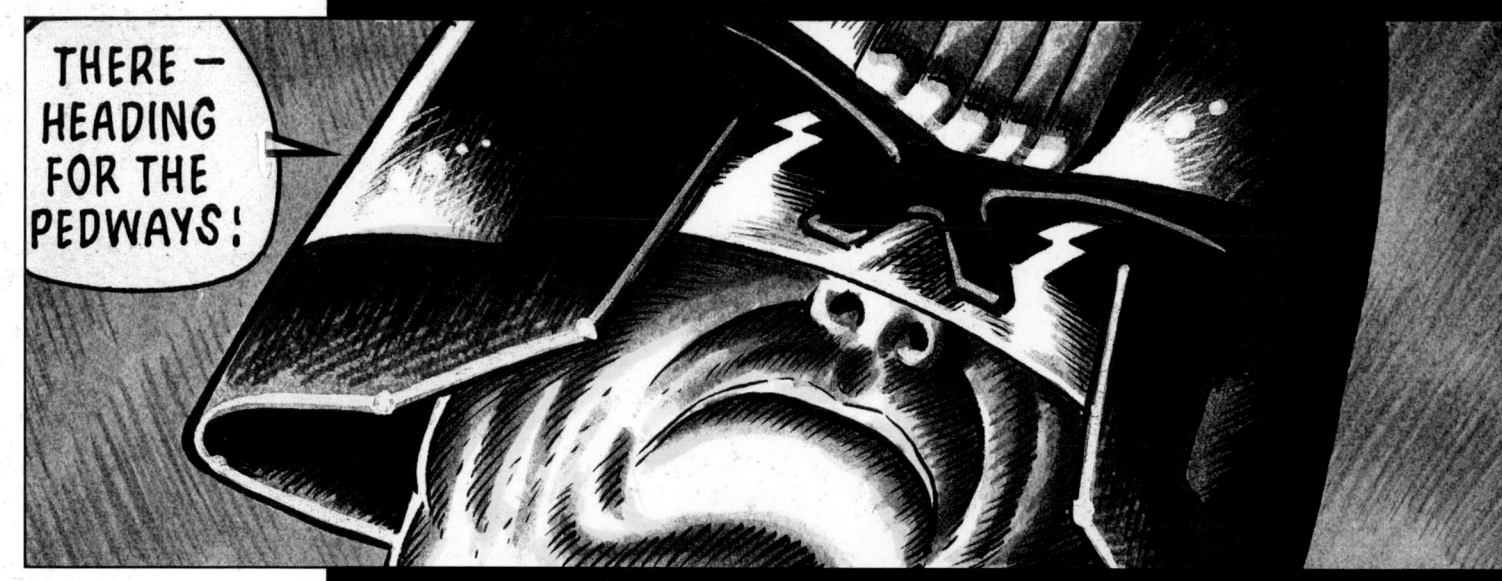

THERE – HEADING FOR THE PEDWAYS!

For 2008AD I also did some work on *Judge Dredd*, including *Ladies Night* (top – Inks. 1987) and the role-playing comic *House of Death* (below and opposite - 1986) for *Diceman* magazine, both written by Alan Grant (aka TB Grover) and John Wagner. The game was devised and rescripted by Pat Mills.

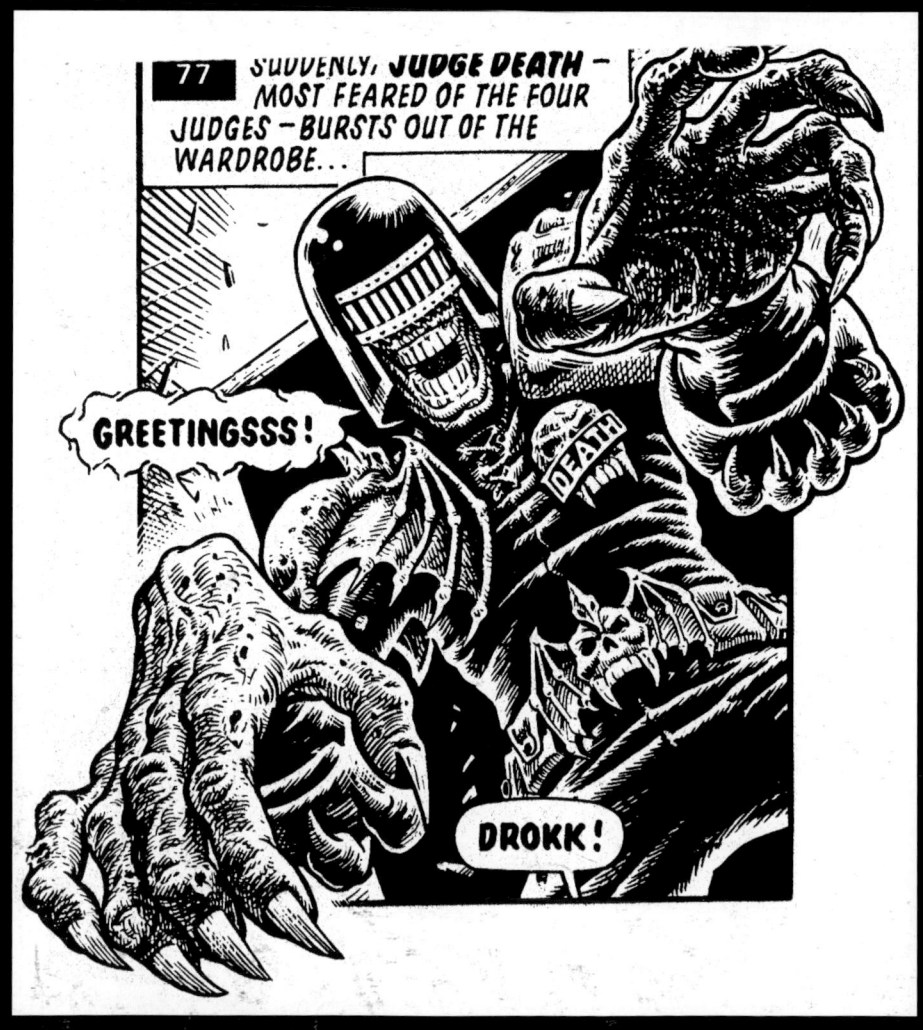

77 SUDDENLY, **JUDGE DEATH** – MOST FEARED OF THE FOUR JUDGES – BURSTS OUT OF THE WARDROBE...

GREETINGSSS!

DROKK!

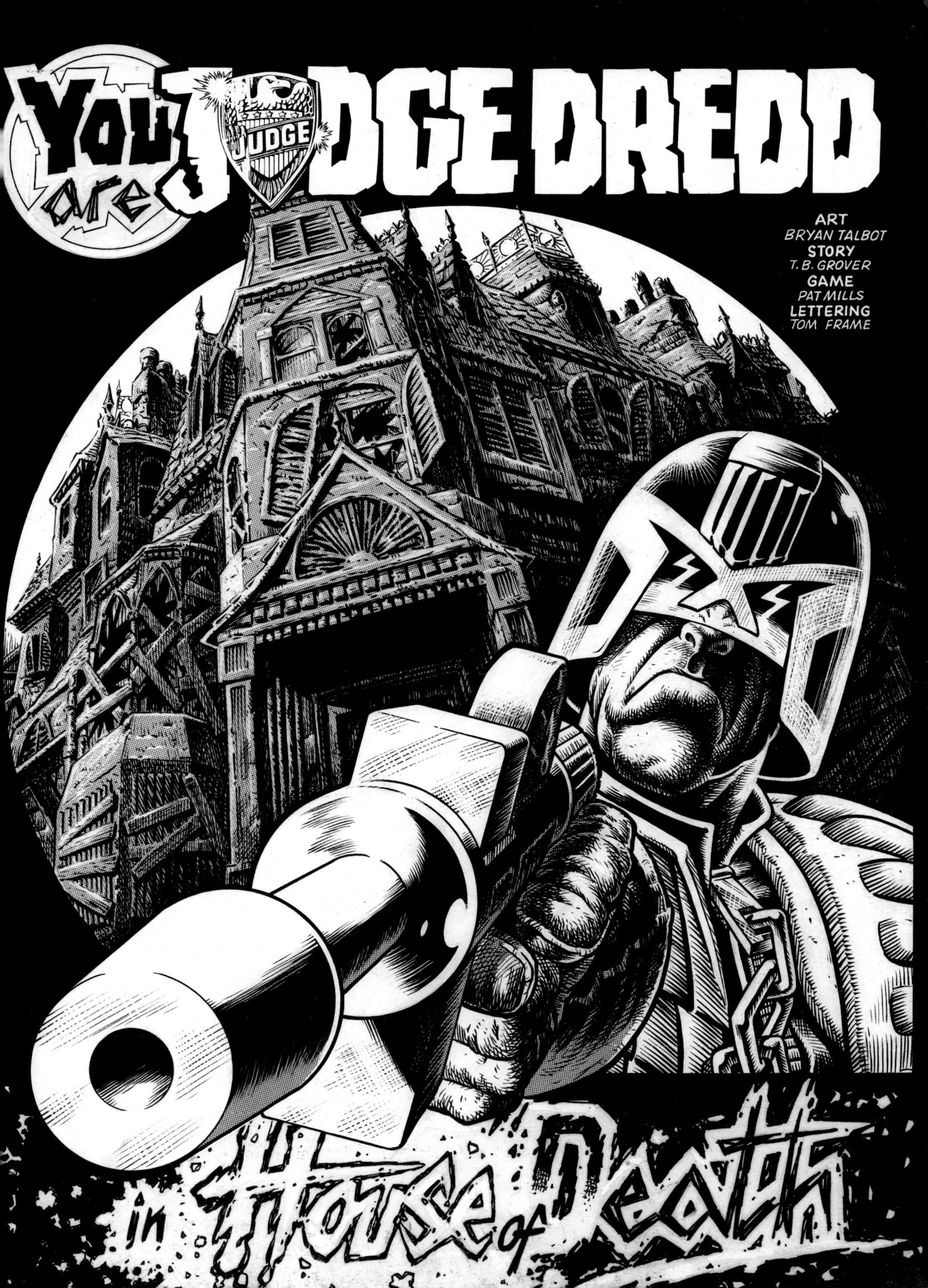

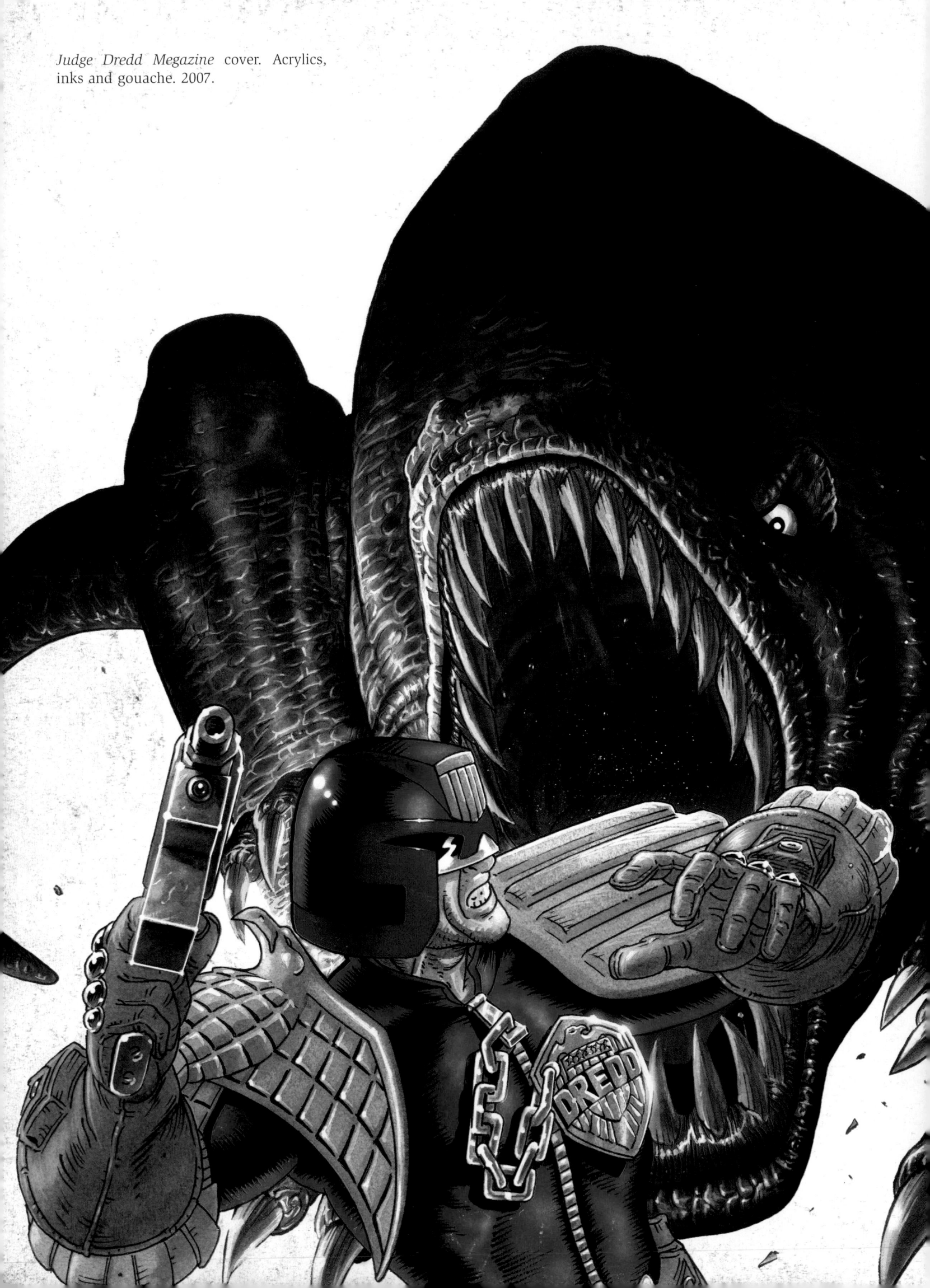

Judge Dredd Megazine cover. Acrylics, inks and gouache. 2007.

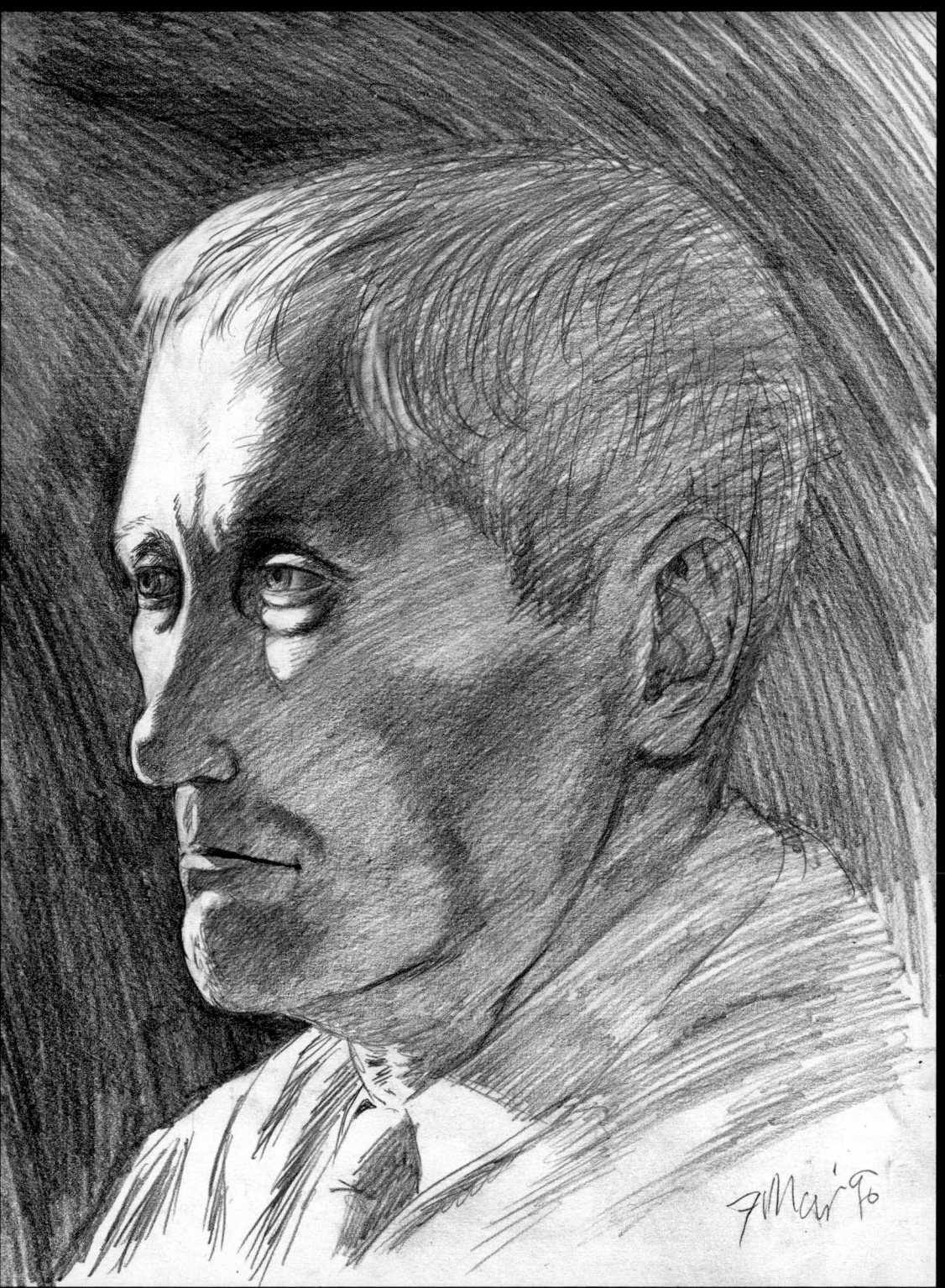

From 1988 to 1993 I attended life drawing evening classes at a local college. If I'd been given these lessons during my supposed art education I'd be a much better artist now. I really should find the time to do it again.

With the exception of the pen and ink drawing (top overleaf) they are all in pencil. Some took up to two hours to draw, though I found that often the quick sketches contained more energy.

All unpublished.

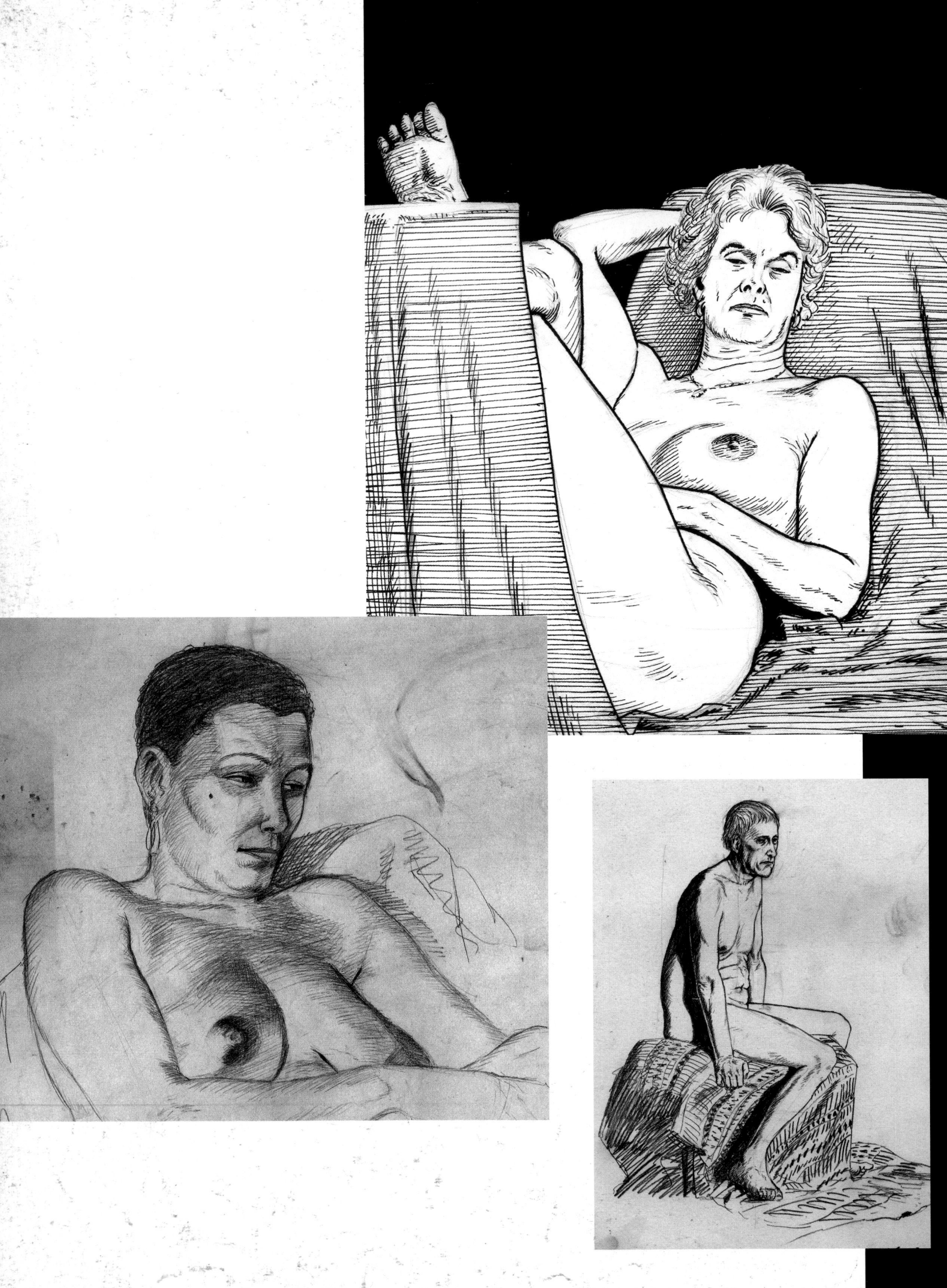

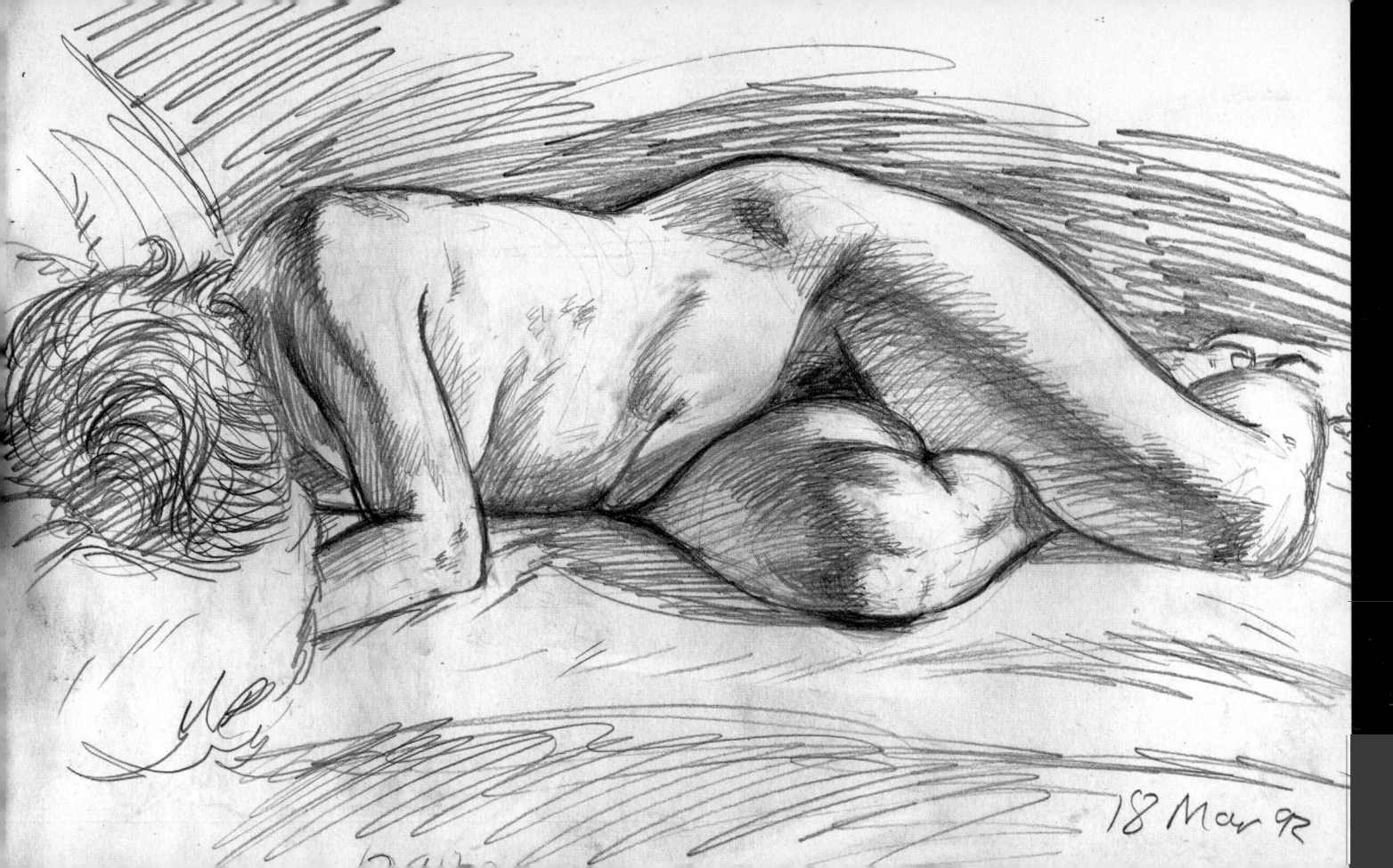

18 Mar 93

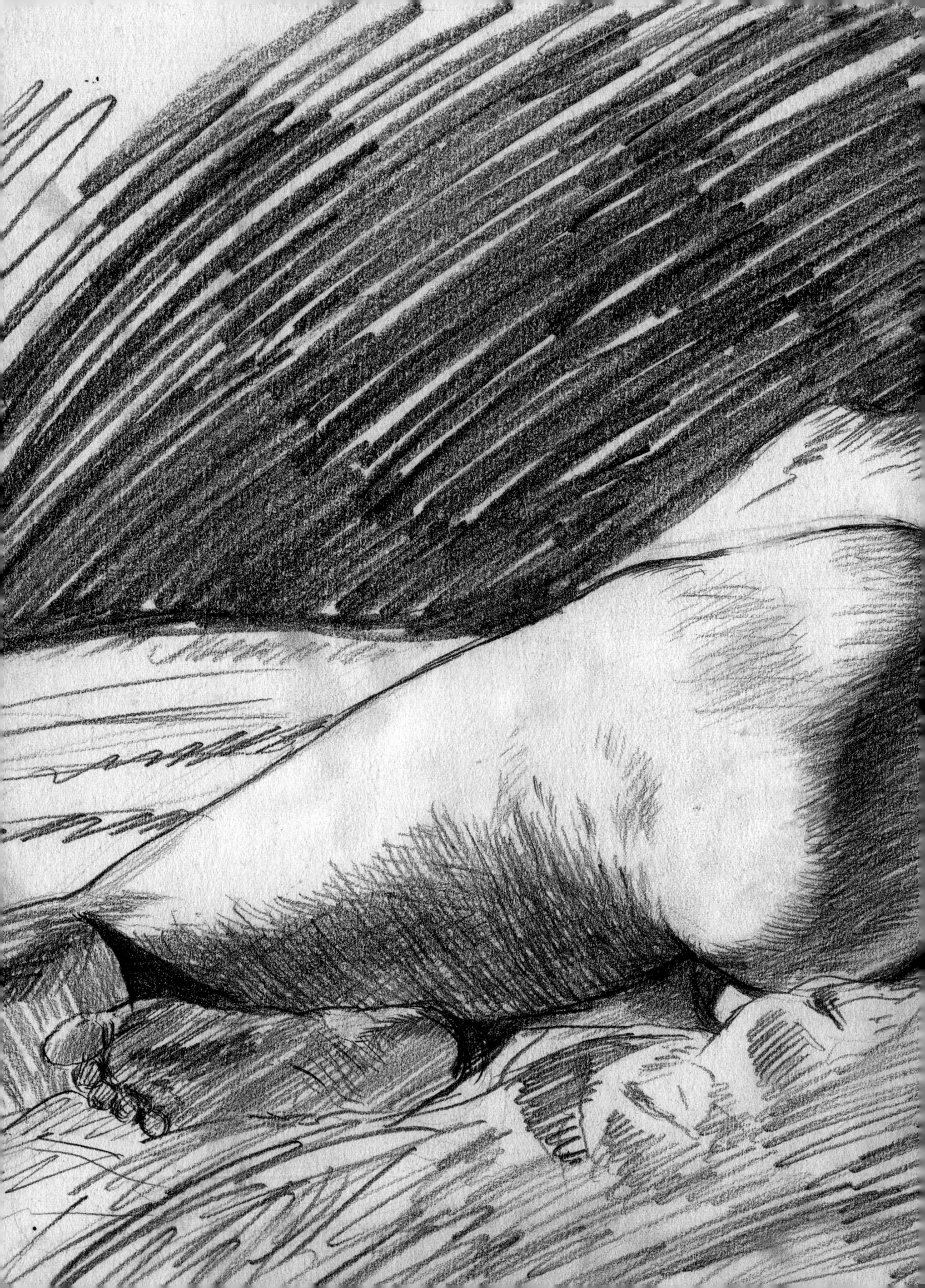

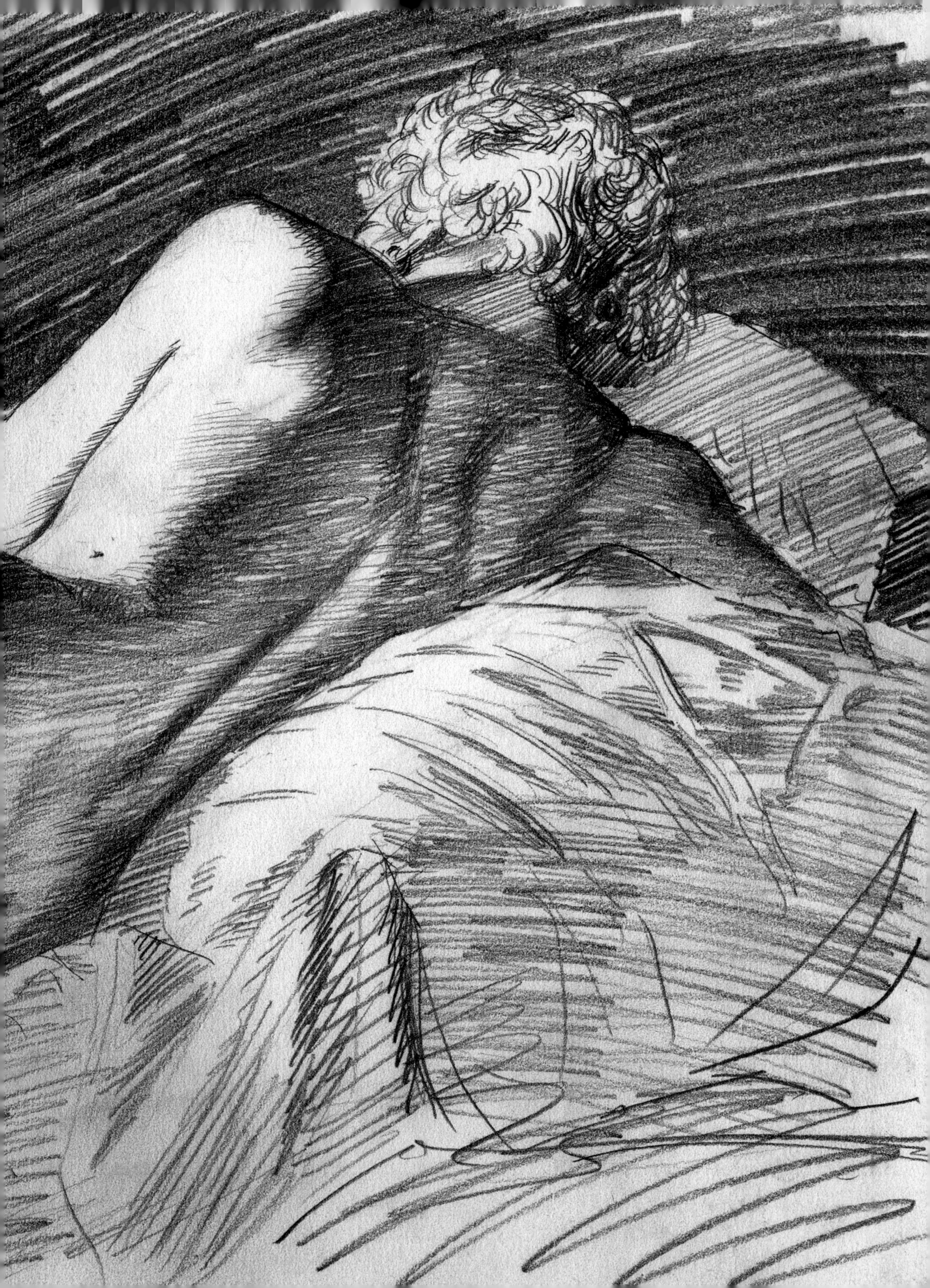

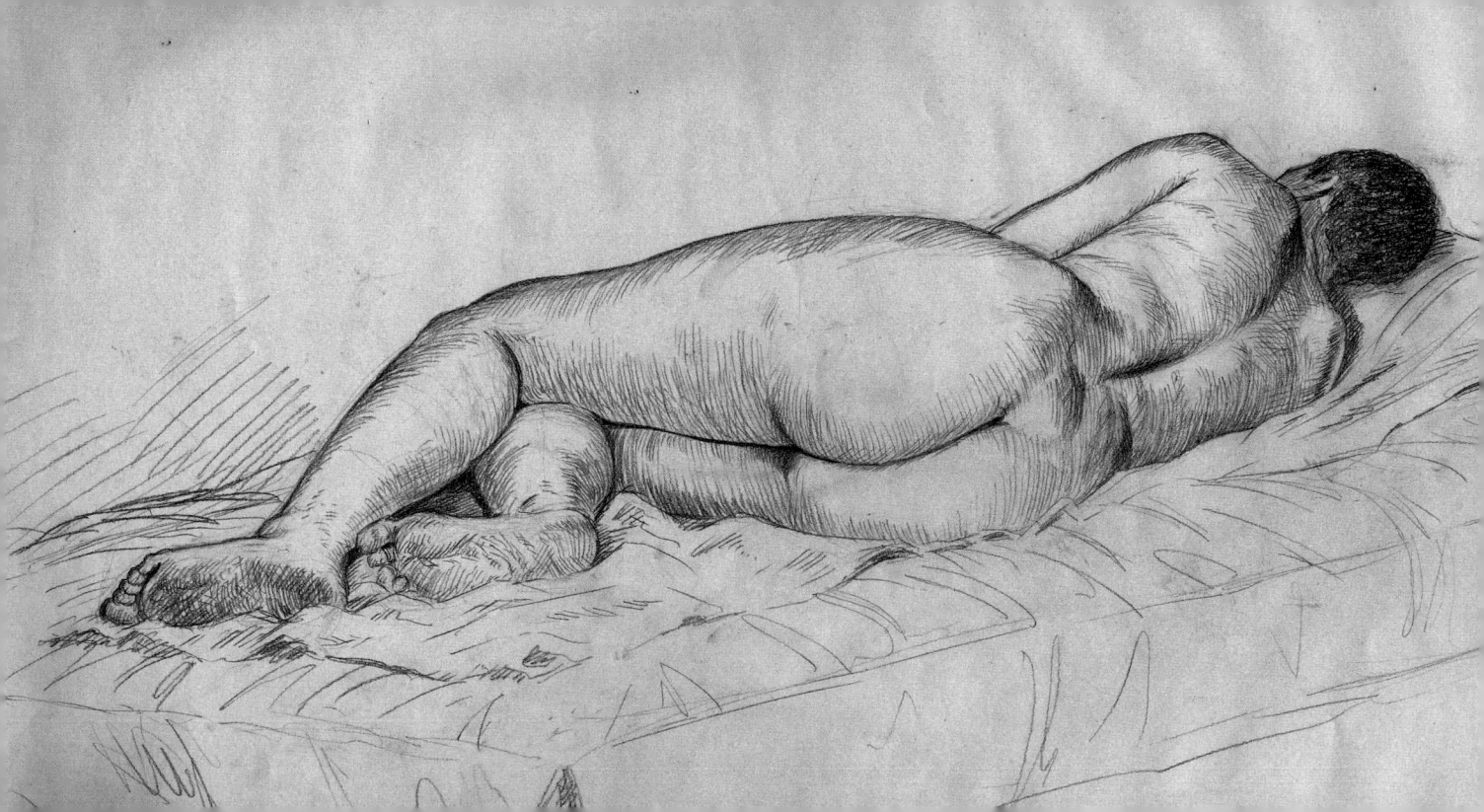

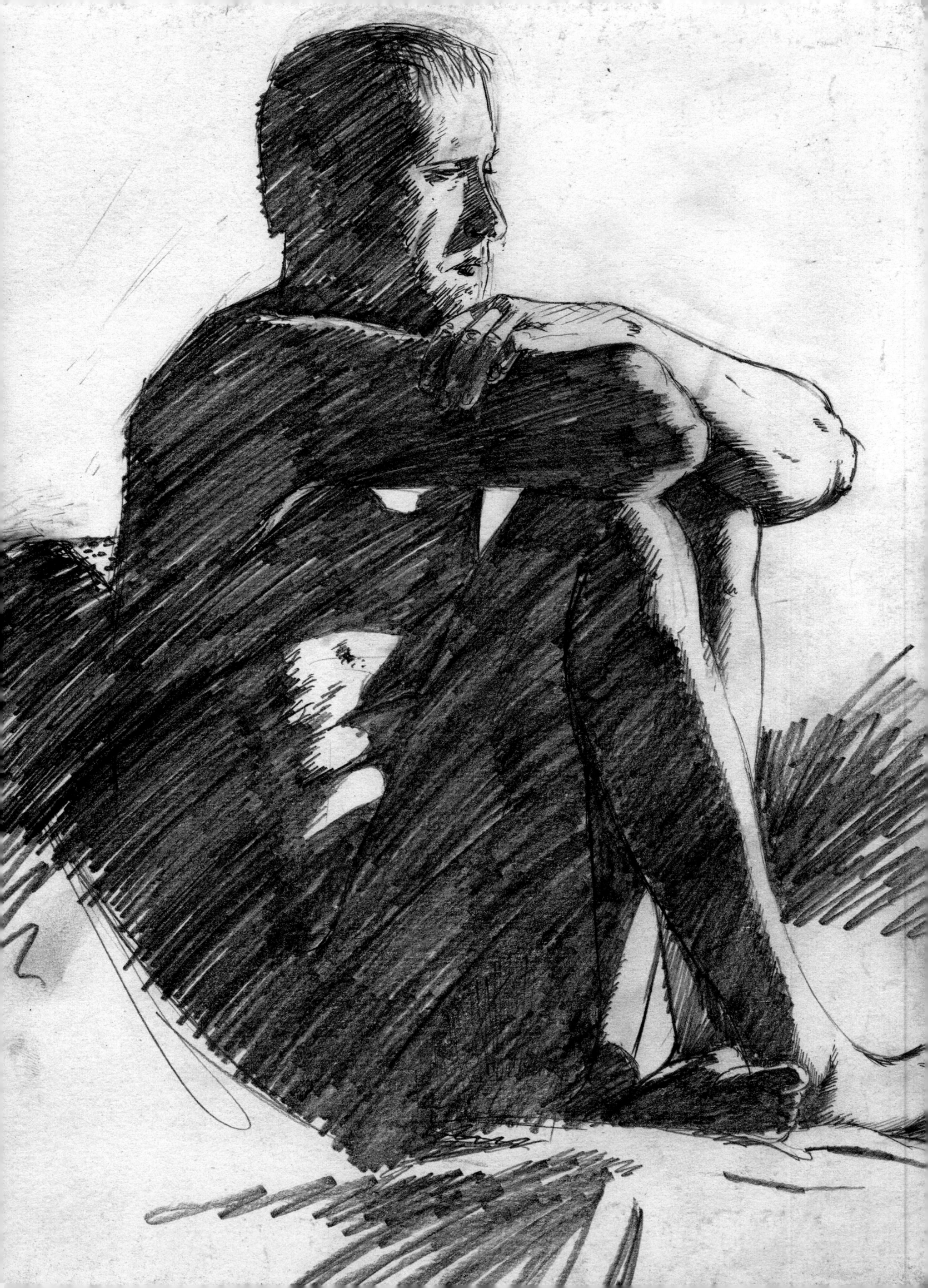

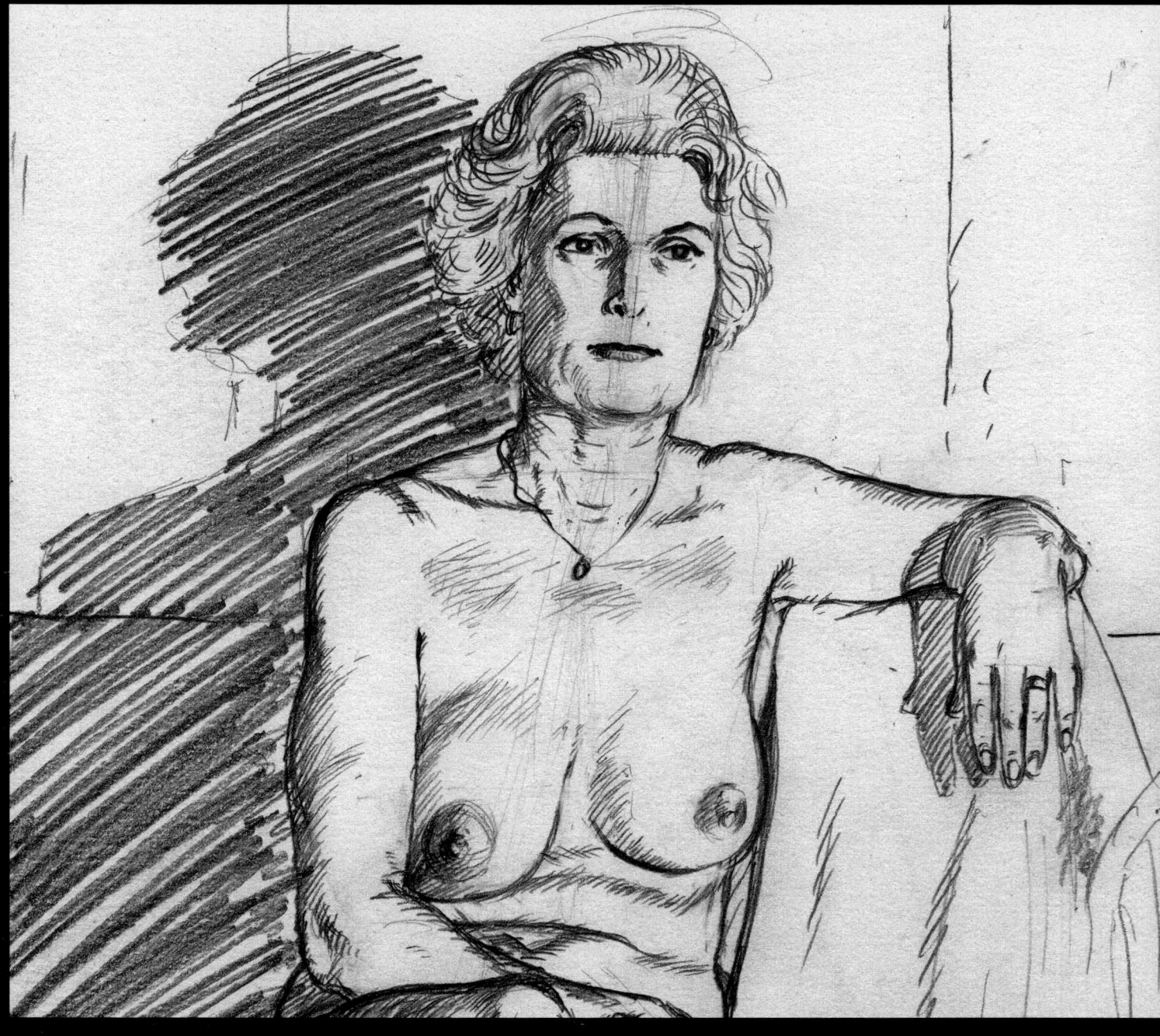

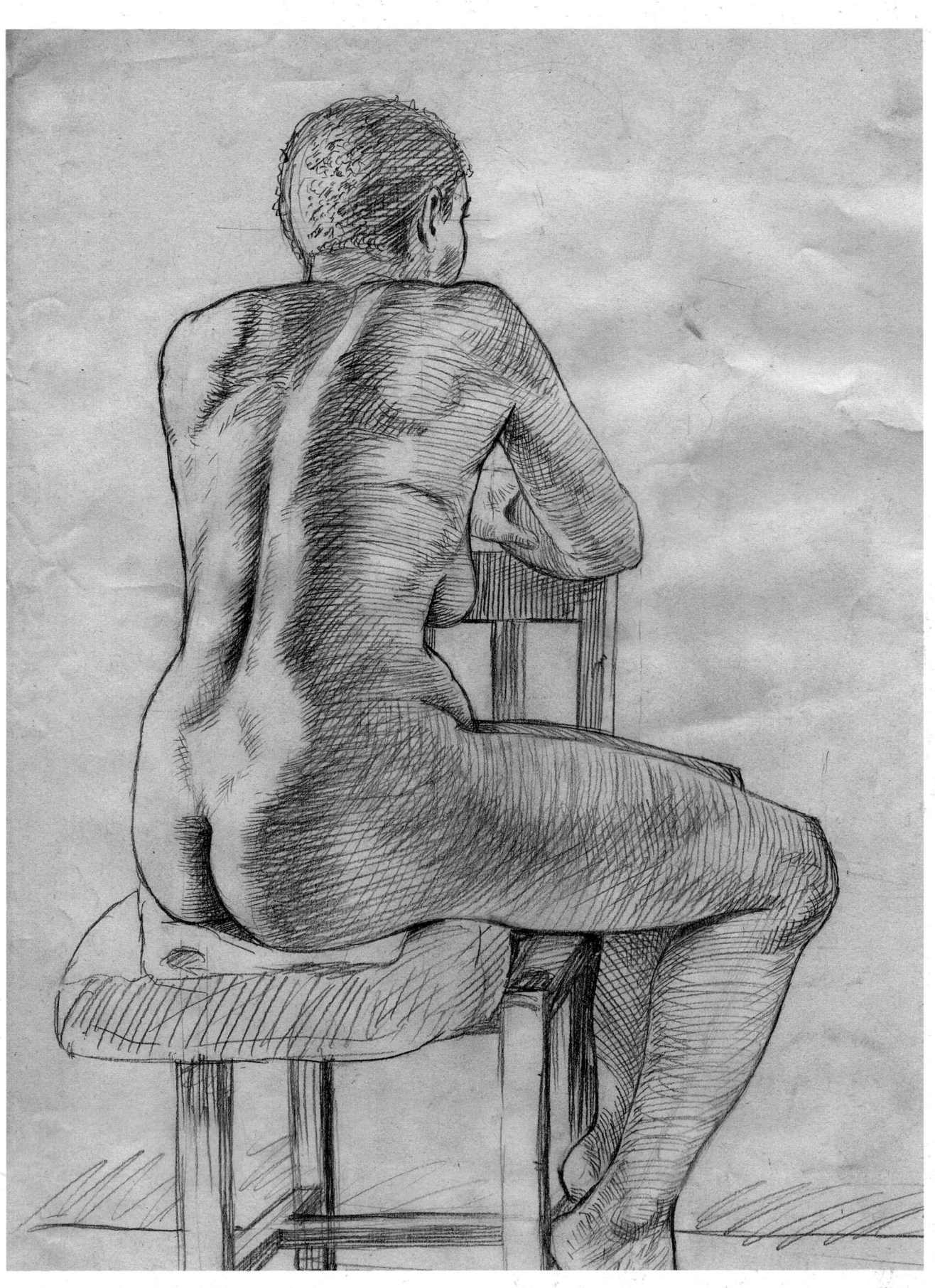

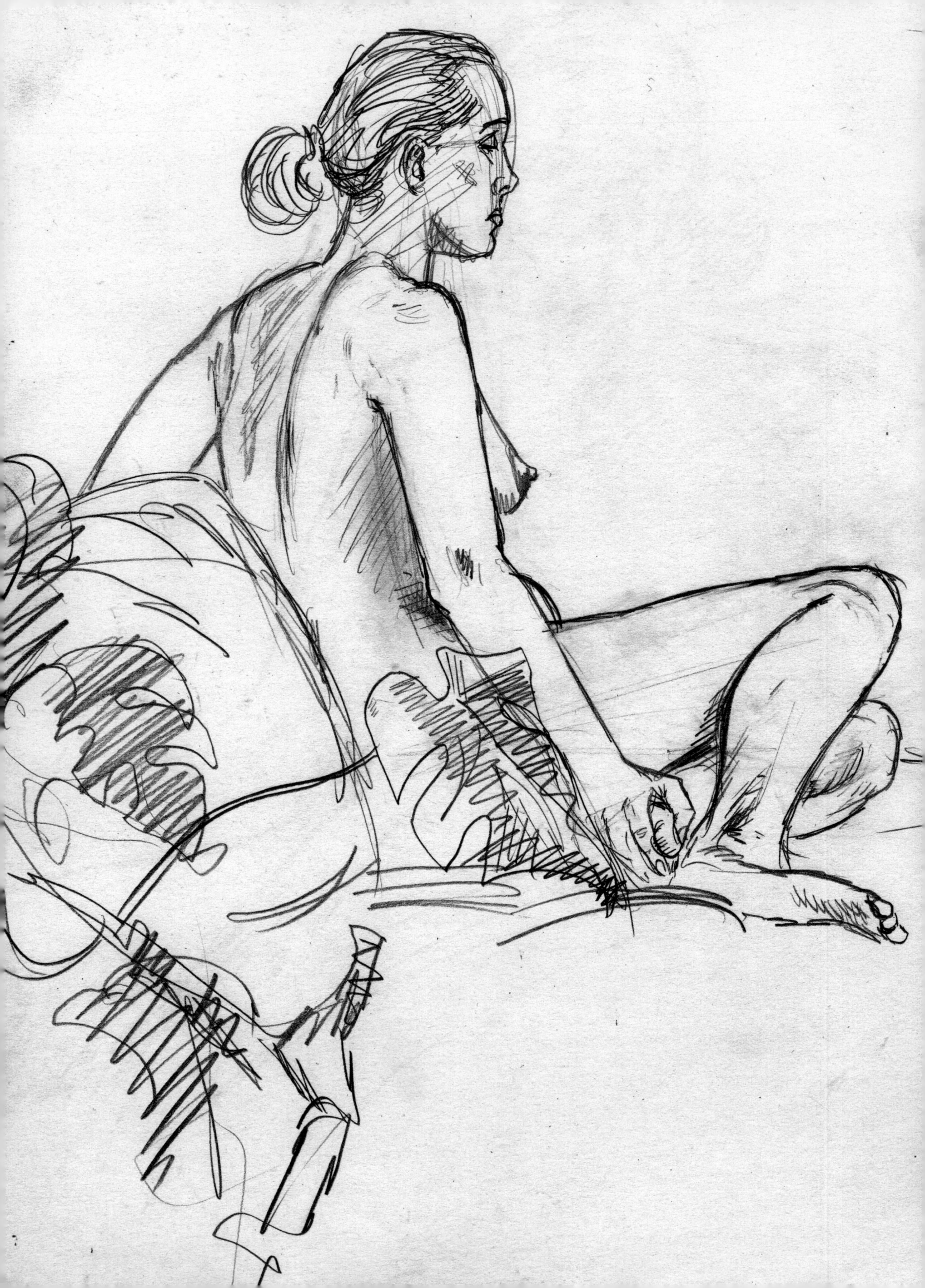

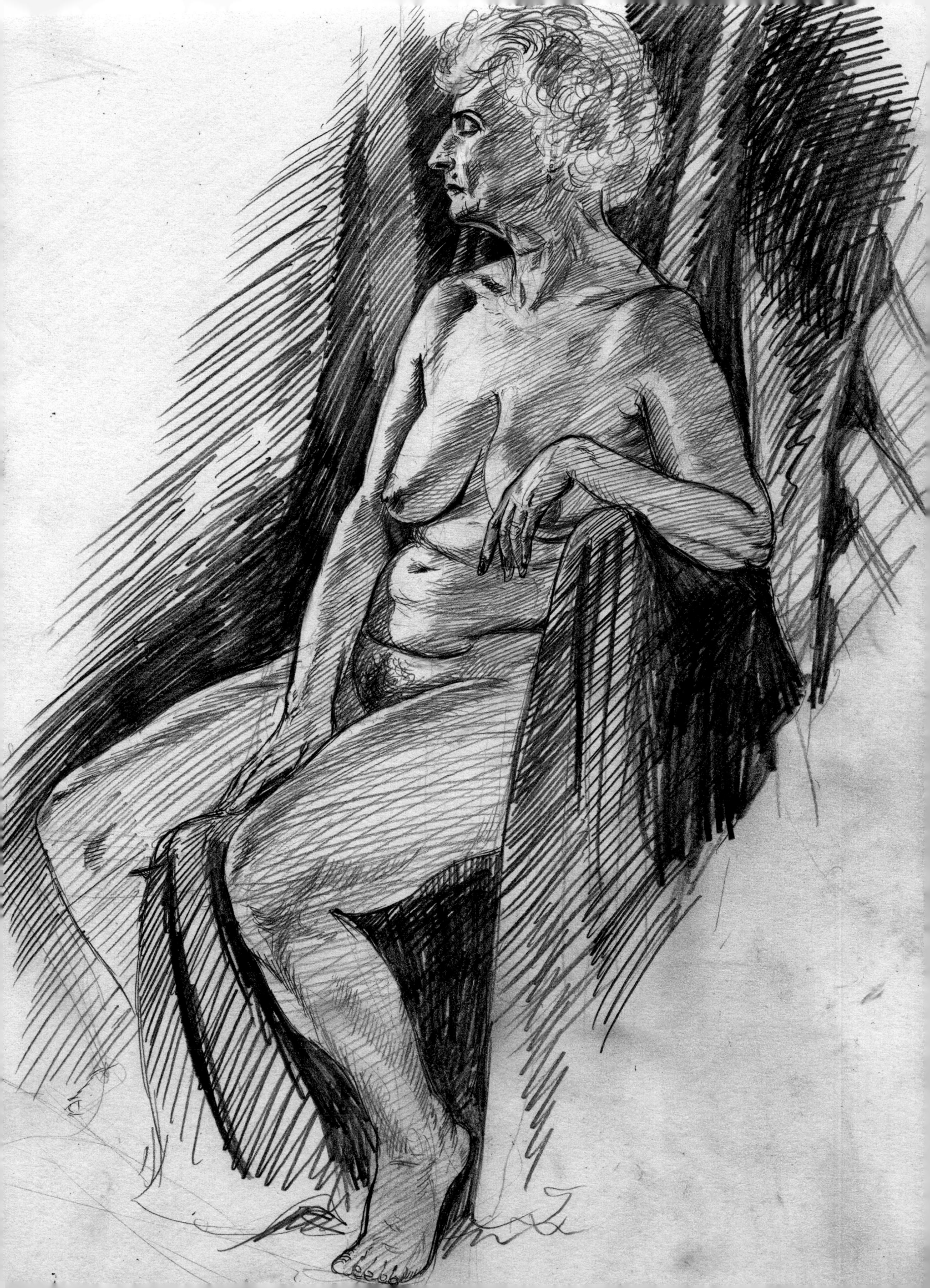

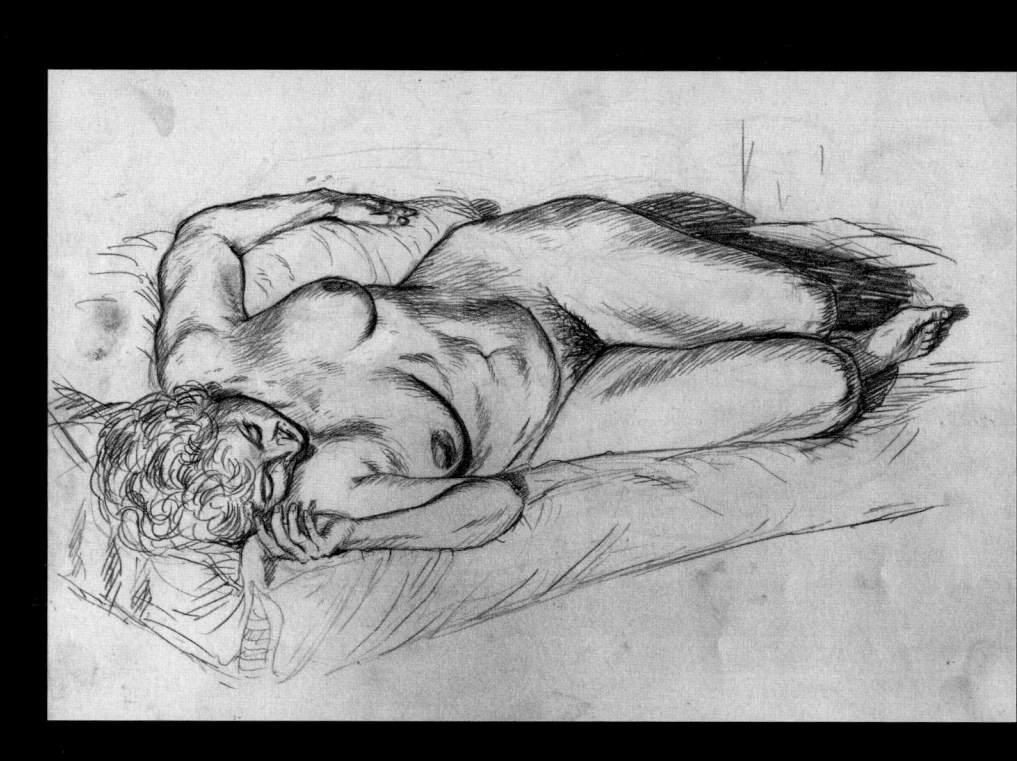

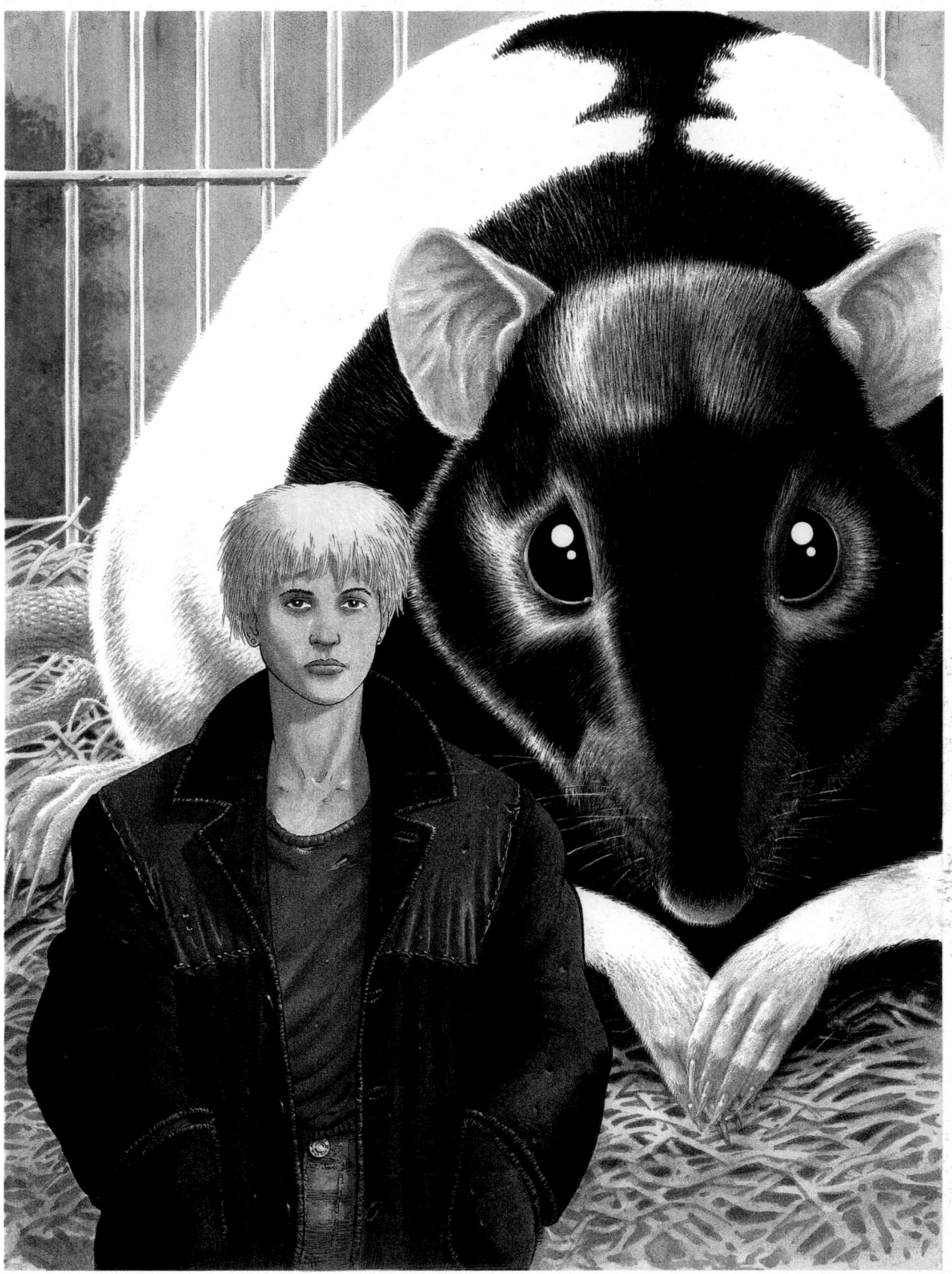

Above is the cover to the proposal for my graphic novel *The Tale of One Bad Rat*. I had about twenty copies of this made up and bound in a plastic folder and sent them to all the mainstream publishers of illustrated books in the UK. The publishers who did respond all turned it down and returned the proposal, mostly unread. I could tell because the pages were still sticking together. They presumably hit the word "comic" in the covering letter and cut off. This was in 1991. Watercolors and inks. Unpublished.

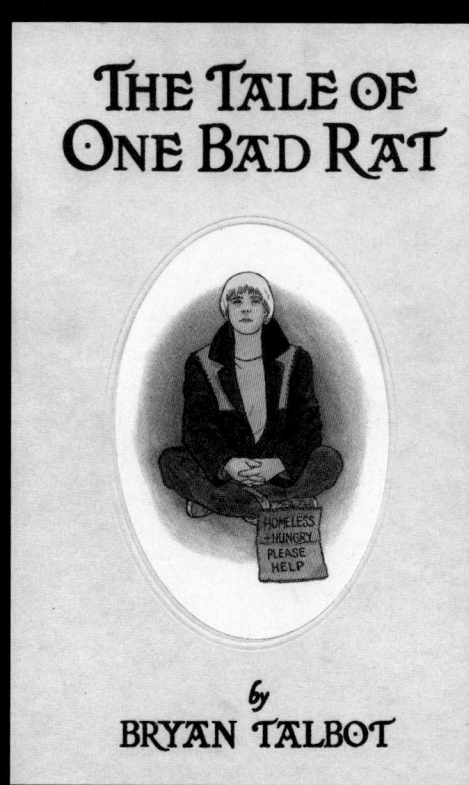

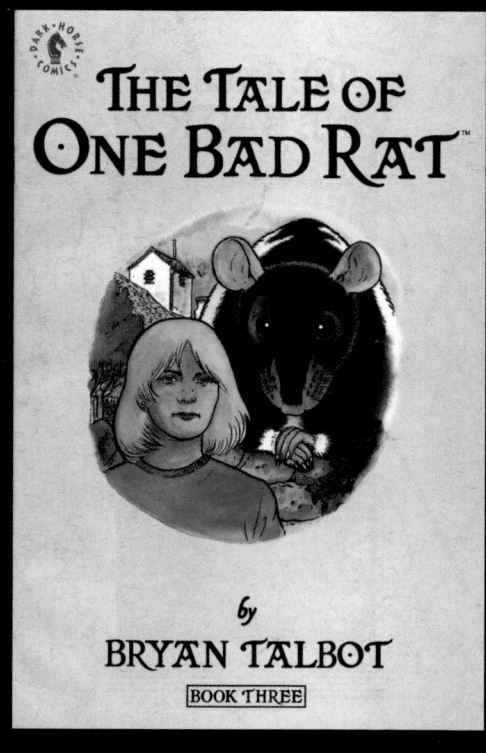

Fortunately, I found a publisher in the form of Mike Richardson's Dark Horse Comics. Mike took what was, at the time, something of a financial risk publishing a comic about child sexual abuse.

Of my comic work, Bad Rat is the book of which I'm most proud. Not only for the art and storytelling (of which I'm inordinately proud) but for the subject matter. I never set out to write a book about child abuse: it was one of those cases where the story took over and led me somewhere I'd never thought of going. Judging from the very positive responses I've had since then, and still get, from abuse survivors, I seem to have got it right.

The book is now in its fifth printing and has been published in twelve countries, with more to come this year.

Top left is the limited edition hardcover. Bottom left, the third cover to the original Dark Horse comic series. Below are covers to Italian, German and Danish editions.

Opposite is the original for the cover of the graphic novel. Sepia ink line and watercolors. 1994.

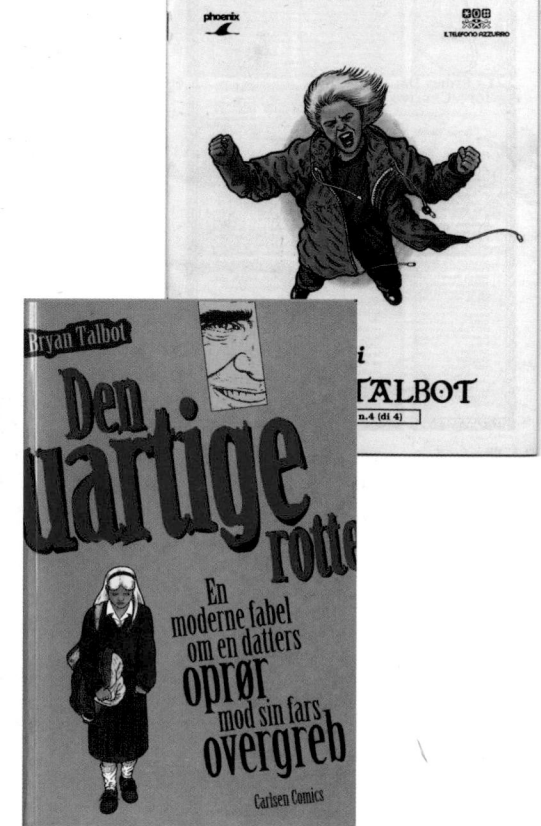

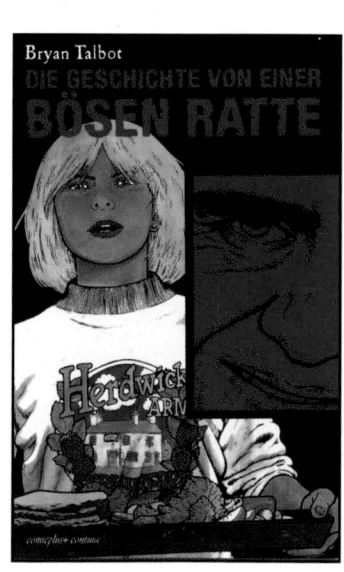

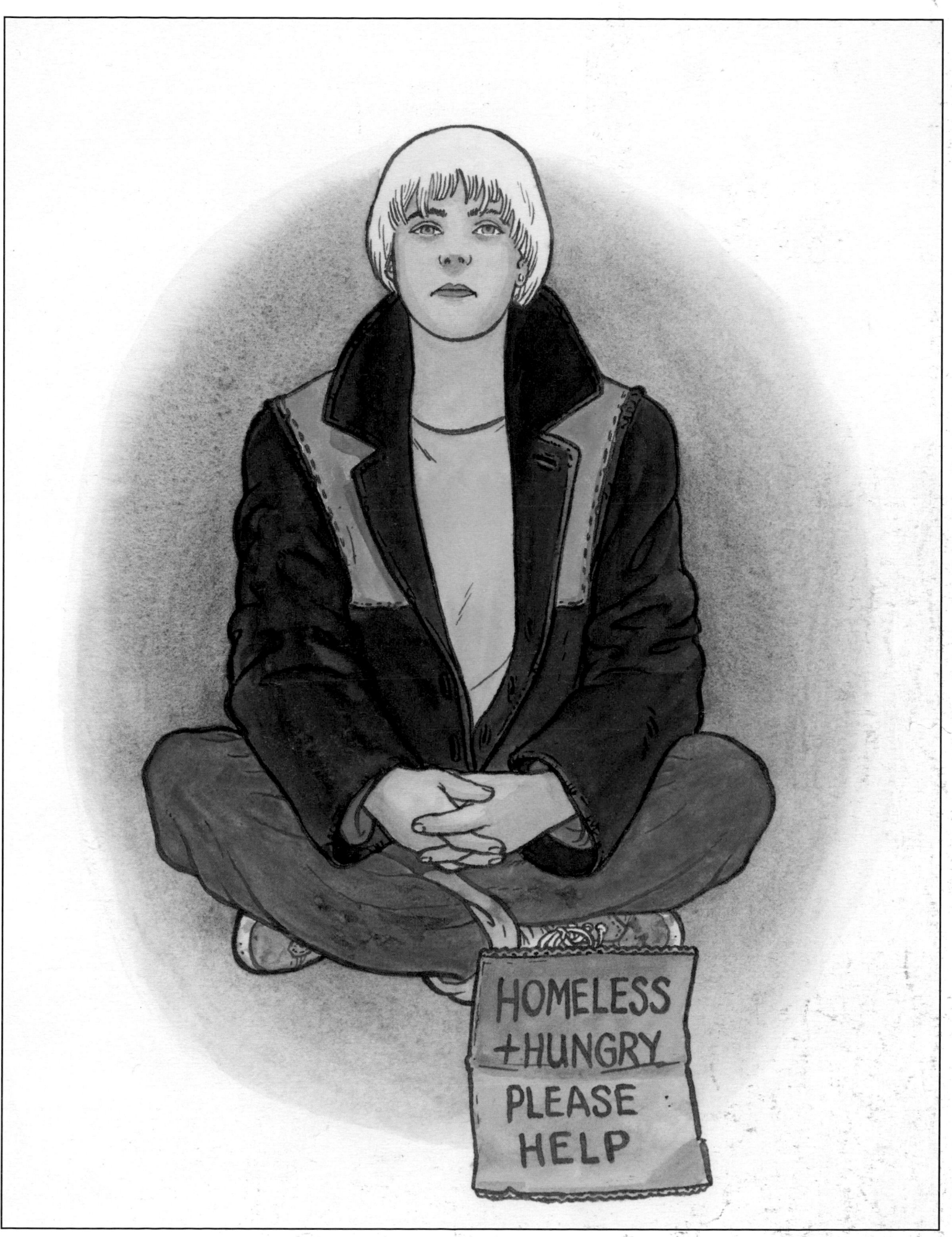

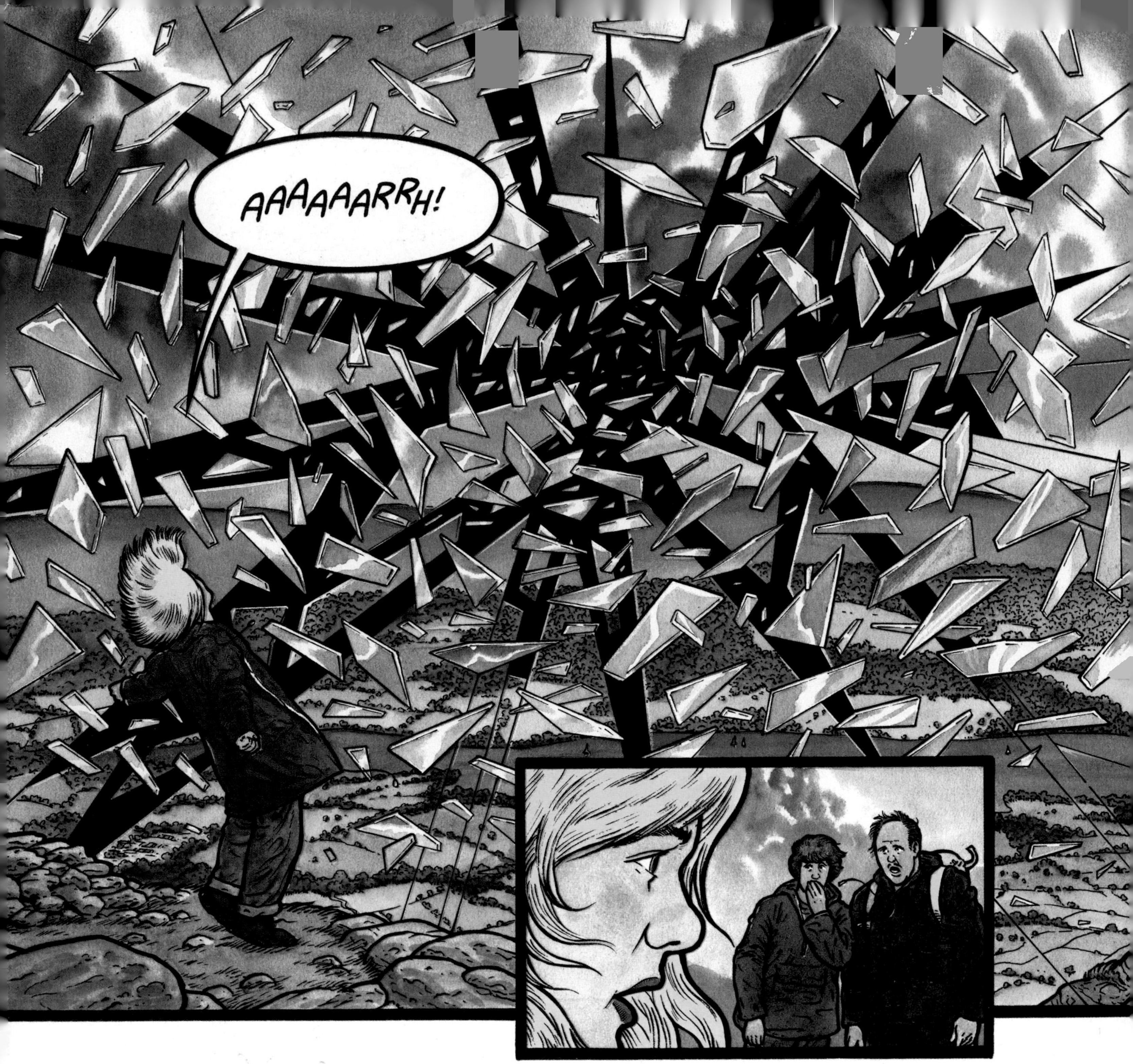

The comic pages were colored using *blue-line technique*: the black inks kept as separate line plates and the colors painted on watercolor board. The colors were then separated into magenta, yellow and cyan and screened for tonal gradation, then printed in halftone. The linework was printed over the top of them, resulting in a nice crisp line over the screened colors.

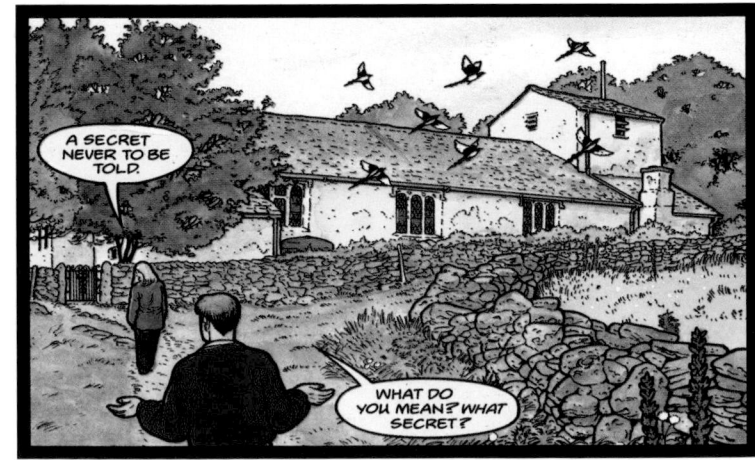

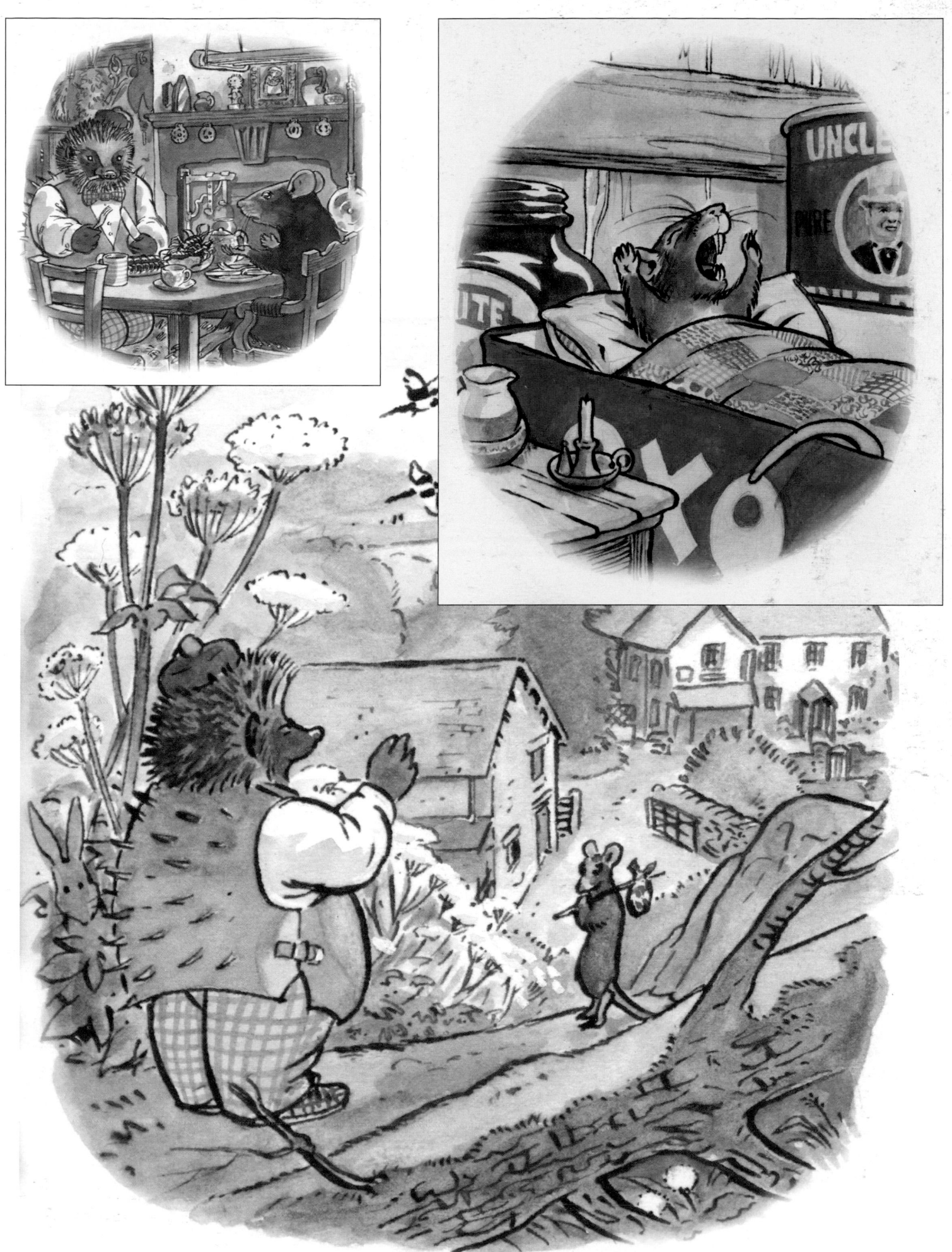

The end of Bad Rat featured a pastiche, paralleling the tale of the protagonist, Helen Potter, told in the style of Beatrix Potter. For the twenty illustrations I used the same nib and the same brand of French sepia ink used by Potter, still made at the same art supplies shop that she used, Cornellison's in Great Russell Street, London. Watercolors over line. 1994.

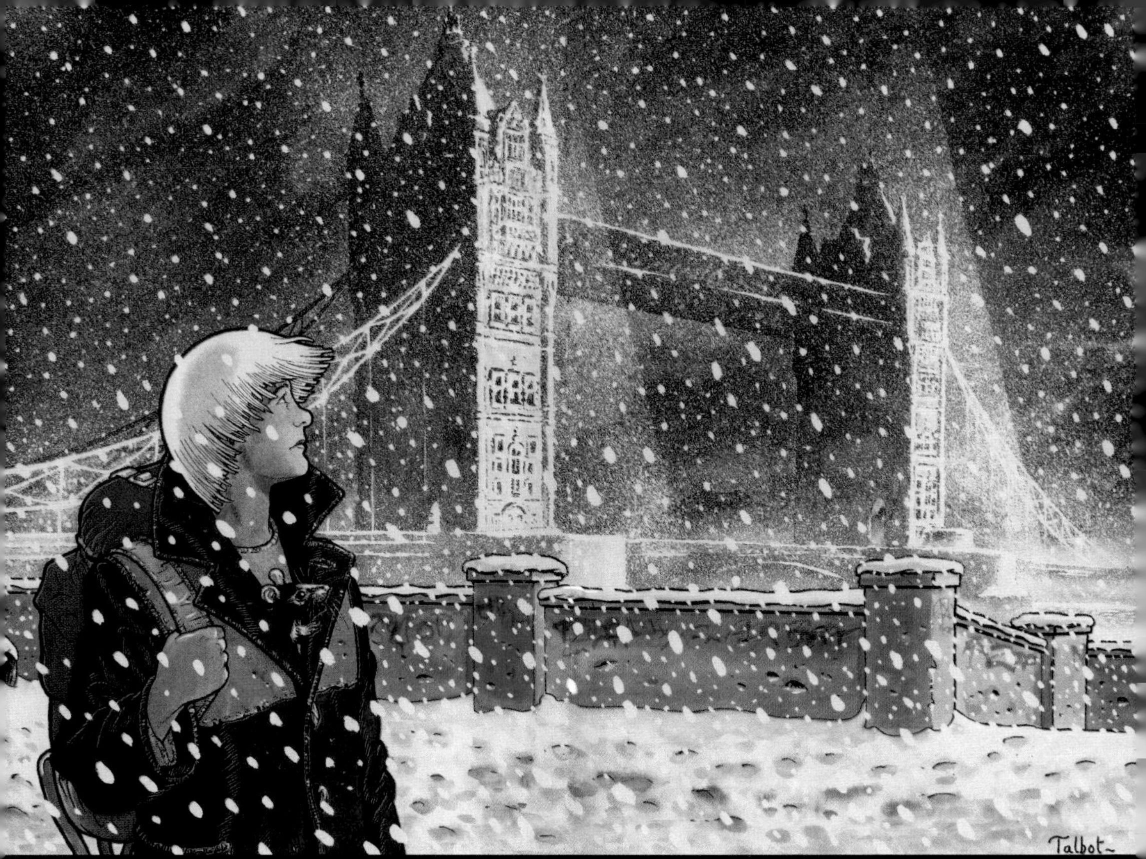

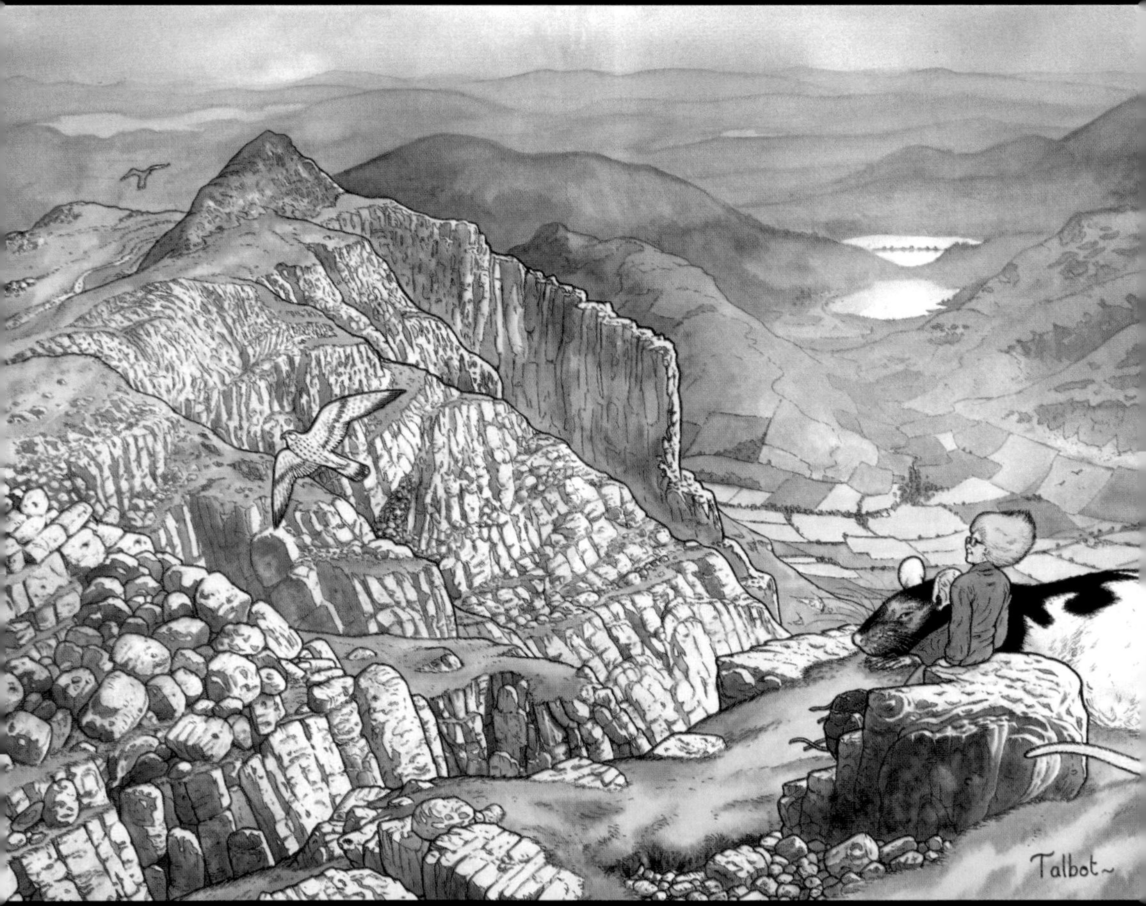

The limited edition hardback had two specially produced endpapers. The opening endpapers above (inks, 1995) set just before the start of the story and the closing ones below (line and watercolor 1995) after the end. I had in mind the wonderful endpapers painted by Alfred E. Bestall for his *Rupert the Bear* annuals and signed them in imitation of his signature.

Facing is probably my favourite page from the book. Line over watercolor wash, 1995.

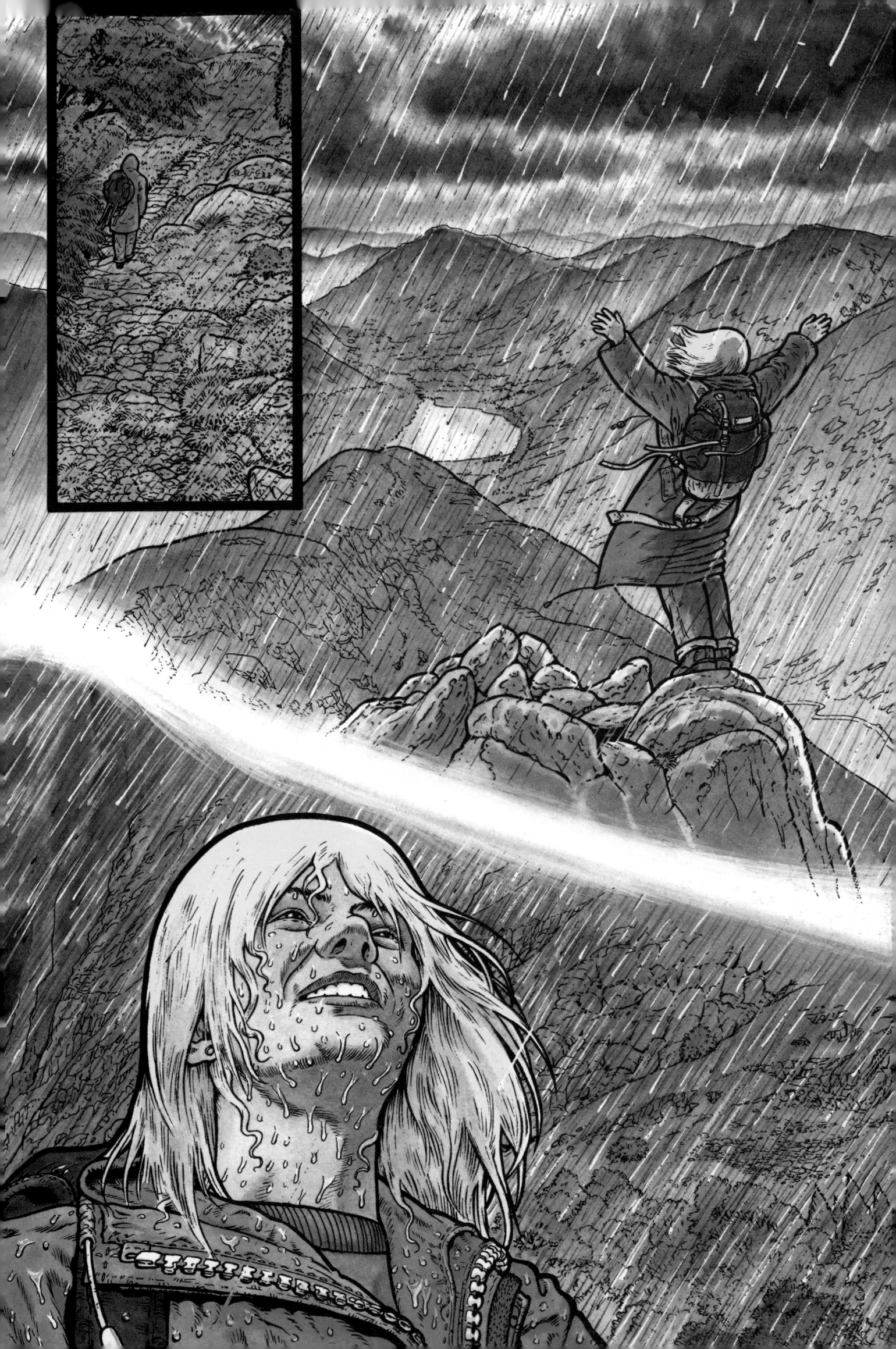

Right: private commission, a pastiche of *American Gothic* by Grant Wood. Watercolors. Unpublished.1998.

Below: first two frames of *Celtic Warrior*, written by Lucy Swan, 1994.

Facing page: the original linework for the cover of *Neil Gaiman's Teknophage*, issue six, published by Tekno Comix. 1996.

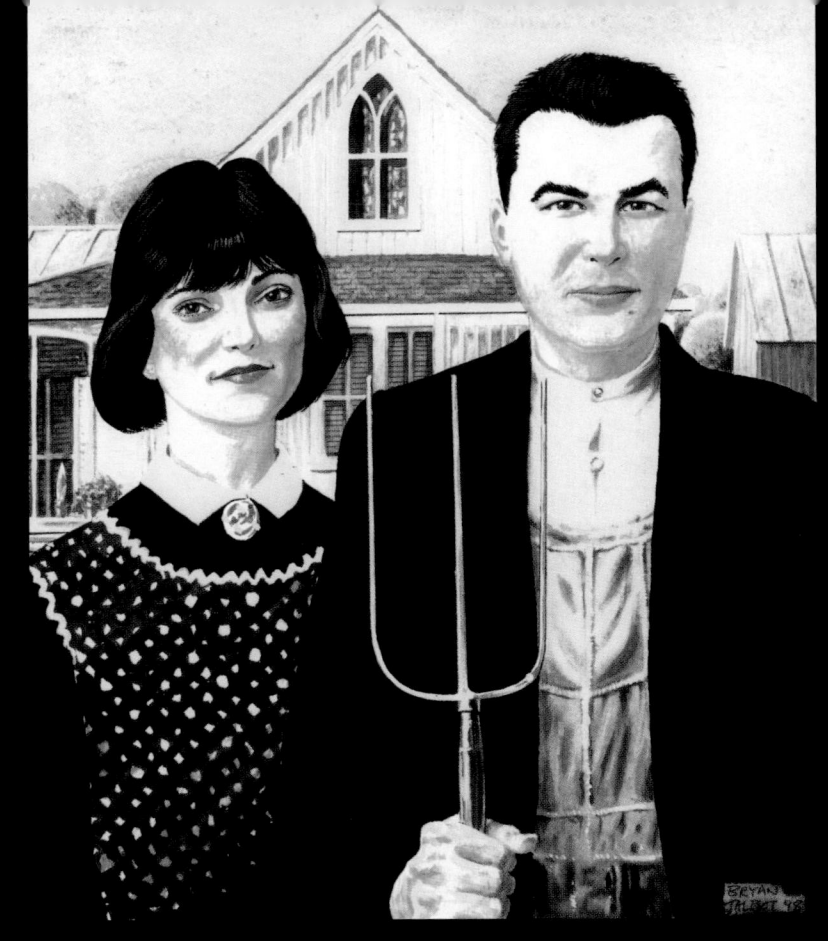

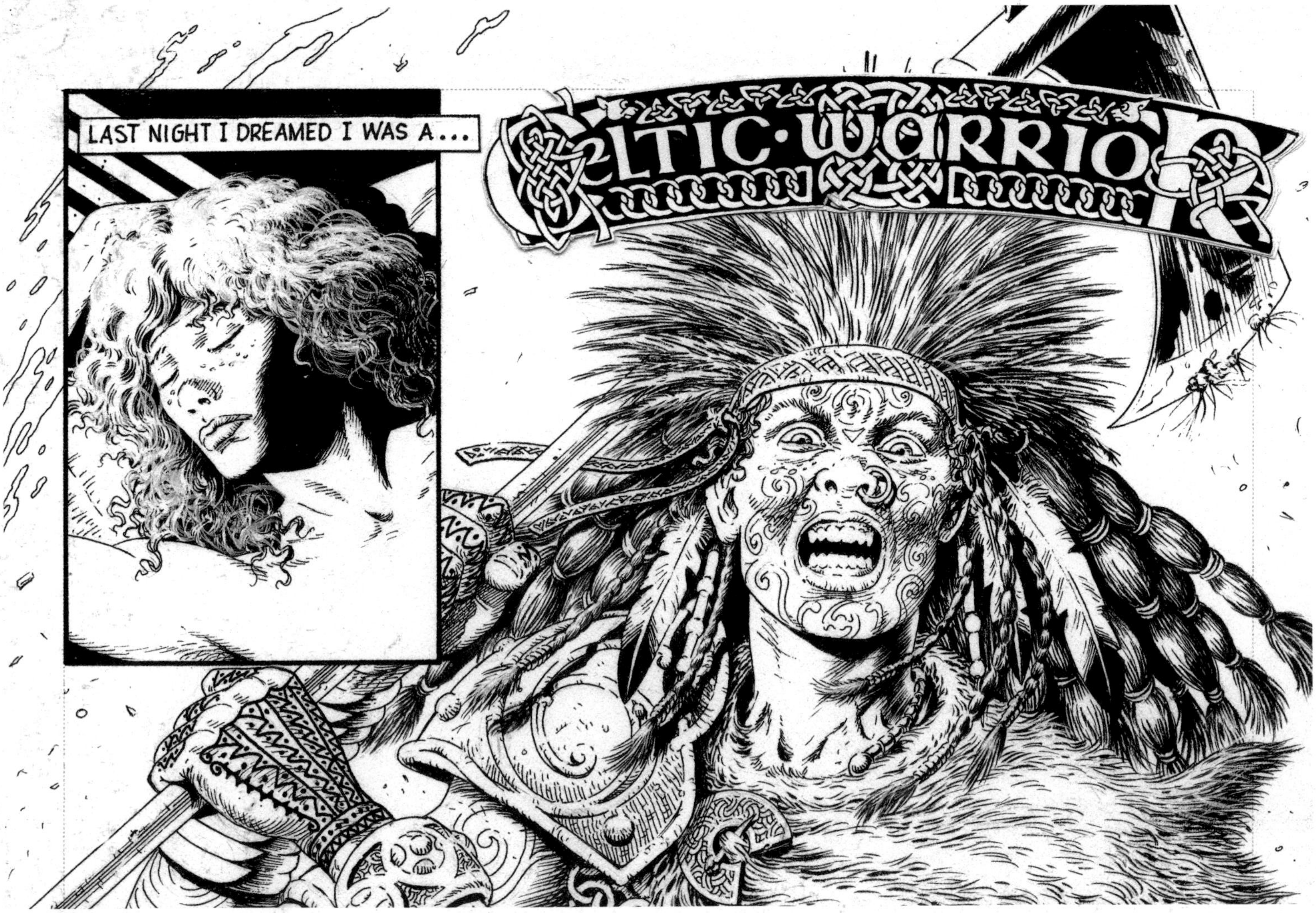

LAST NIGHT I DREAMED I WAS A...

CELTIC·WARRIOR

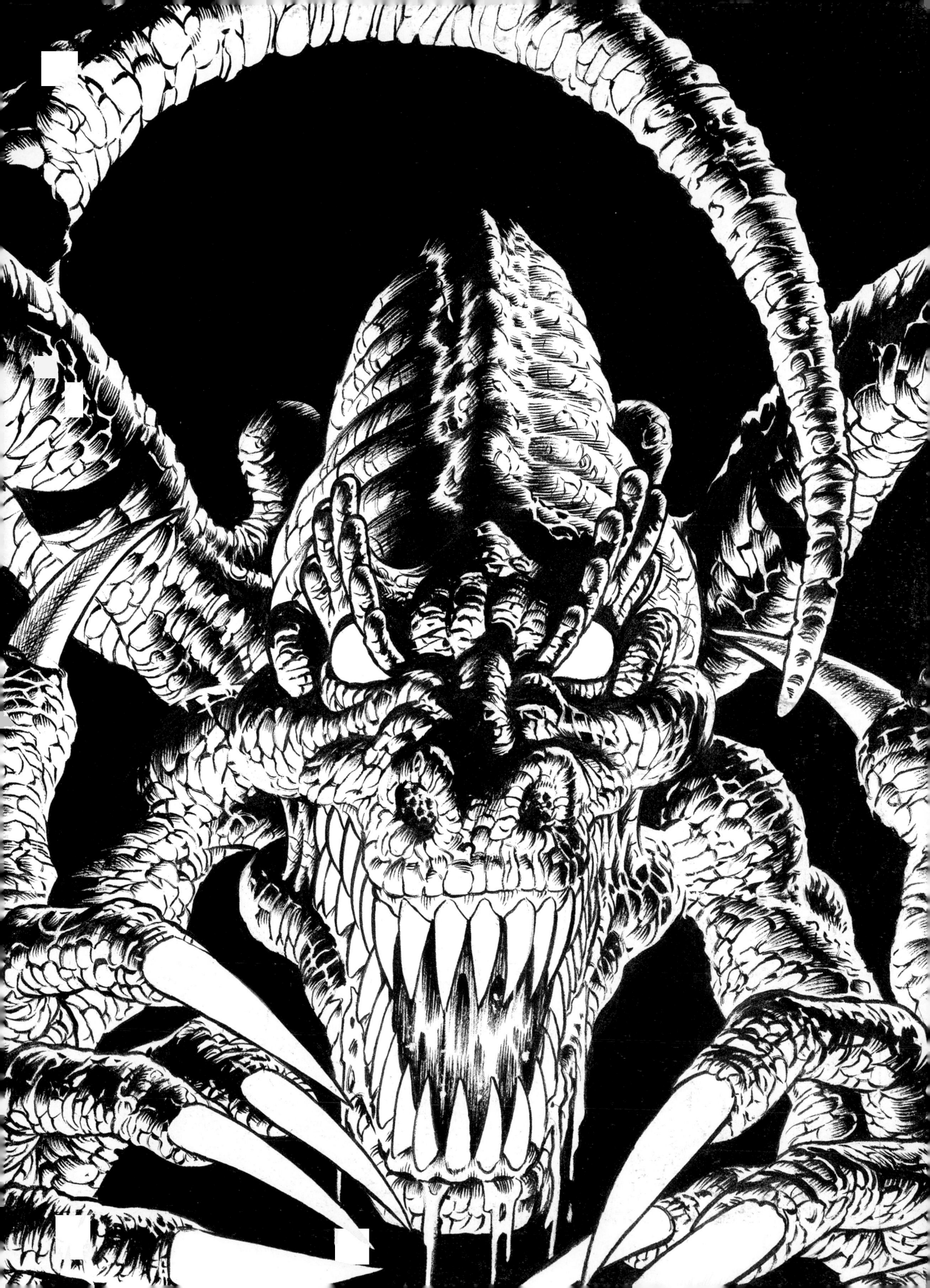

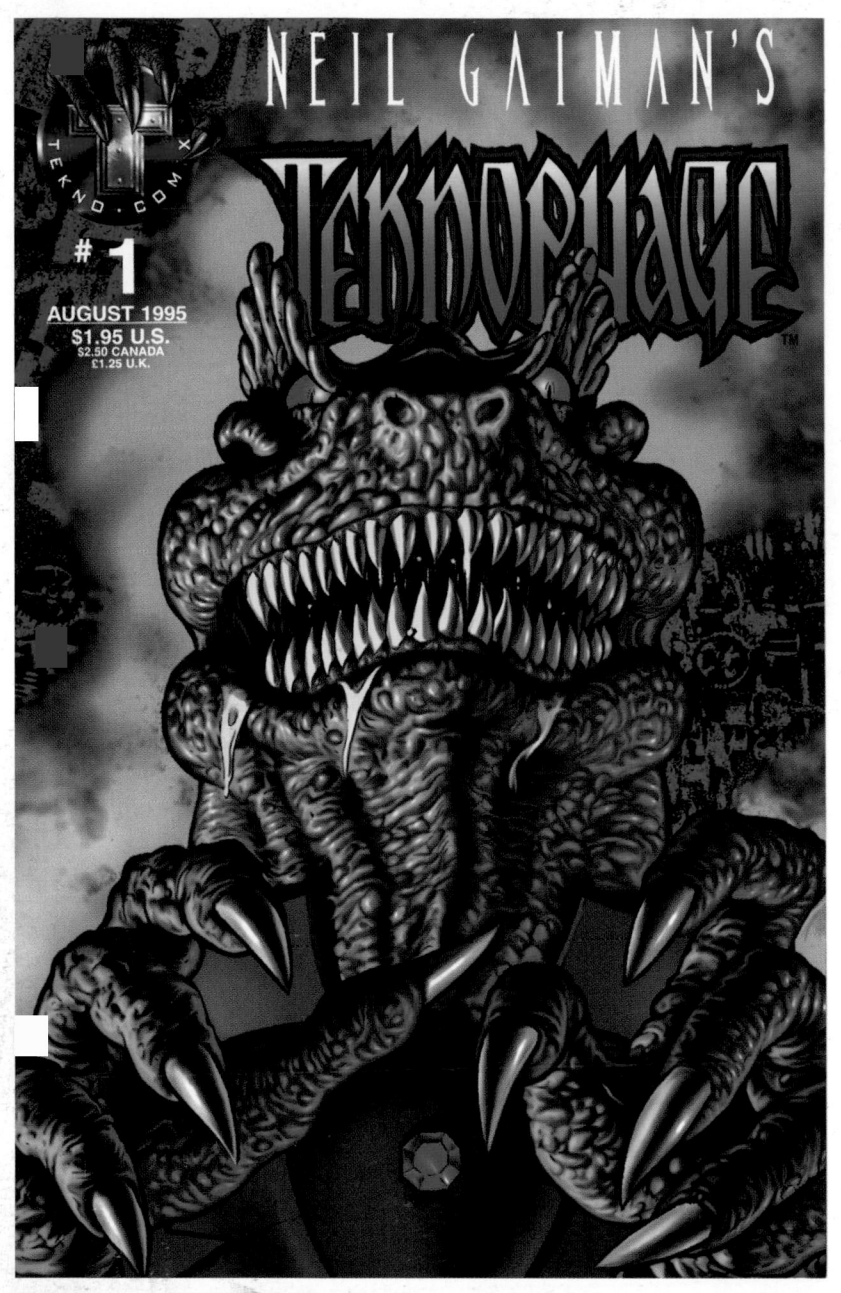

I drew the first six-issue story arc, written by Rick Veitch, and all the covers for the ten-issue series and the six-issue Teknophage spin-off, *Shadowdeath* (which I also wrote). All colored on computer by Angus McKie. 1995-96.

Opposite: the pencils for a splash page in the first issue of Teknophage. 1995.

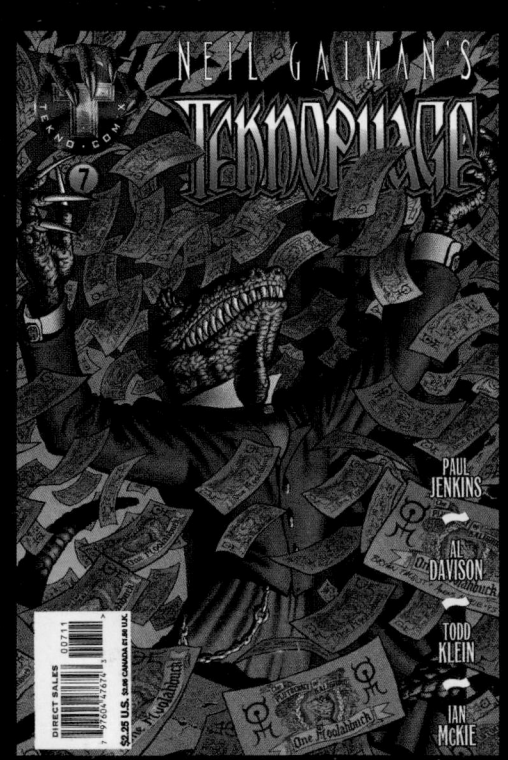

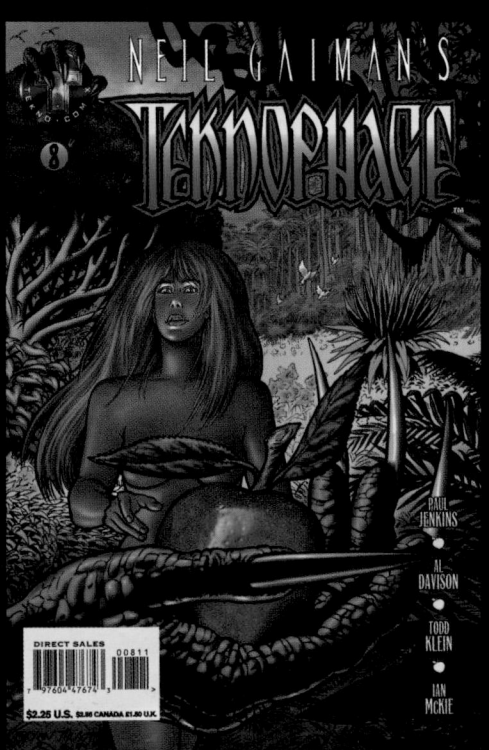

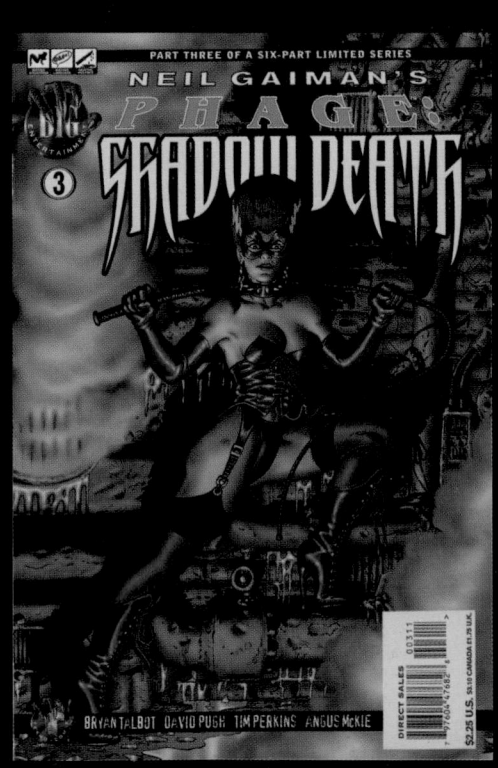

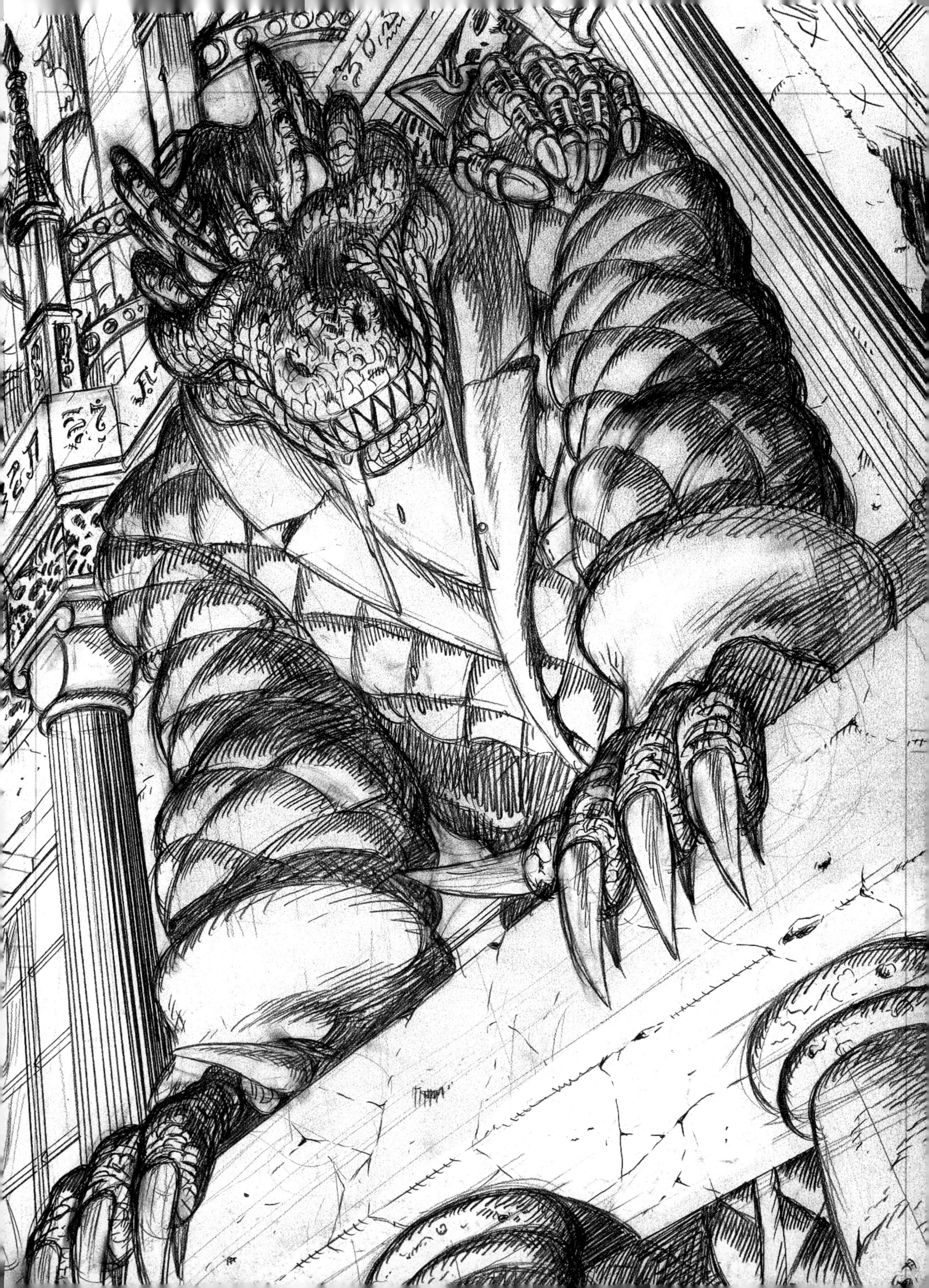

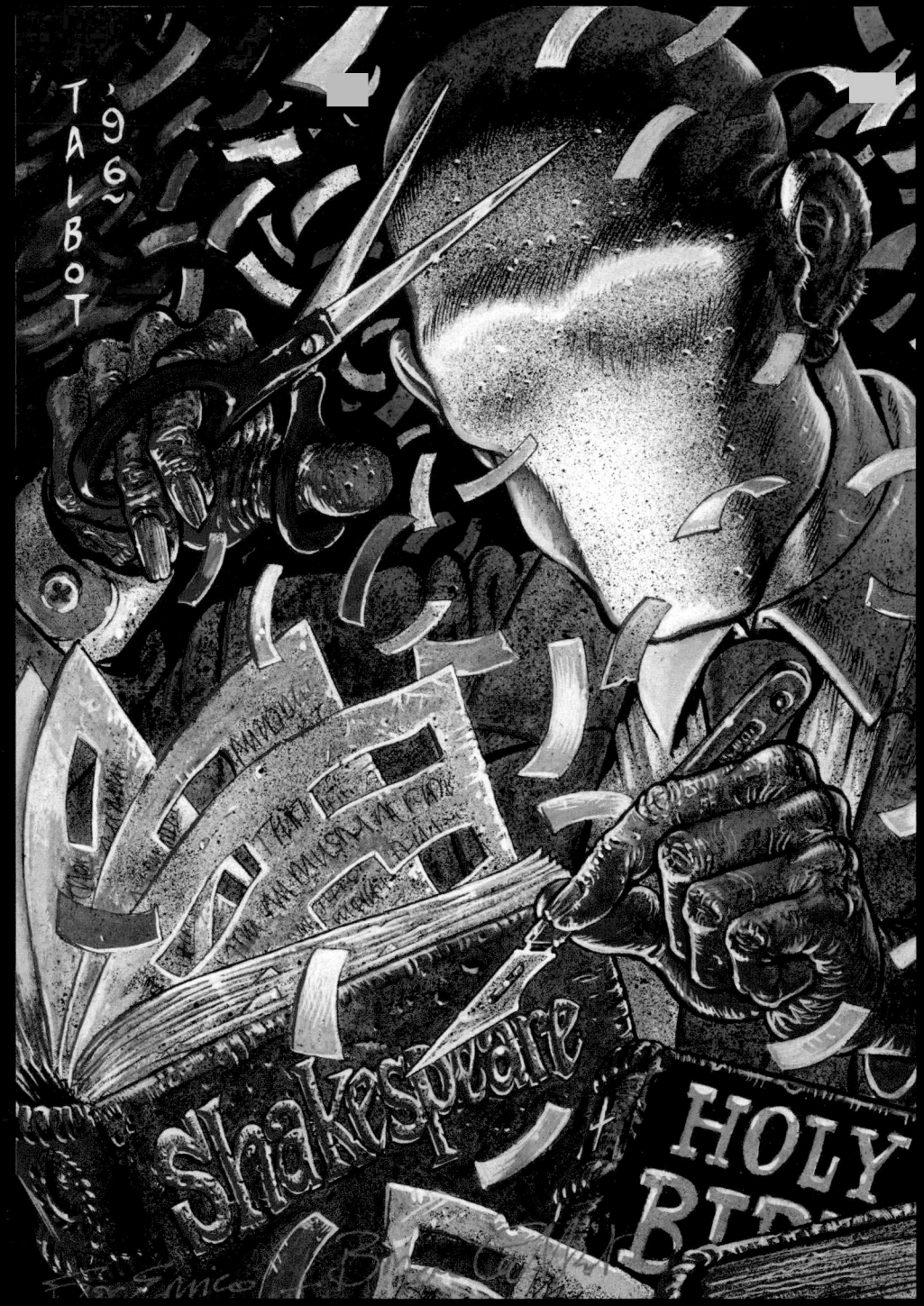

Above: *The Censor*, painted for *Visions of Freedom*, a trading card set produced to raise money for the *Comic Book Legal Defence Fund*. Later used as the cover for *What Right?* by Arsenal Pulp Press. Inks. 1997

Facing: *Omaha the Cat Dancer*, produced for the Reed Waller benefit book *Images of Omaha #2*. I was very embarrassed when I saw it in print - I'd forgotten to draw her tail! 1992.

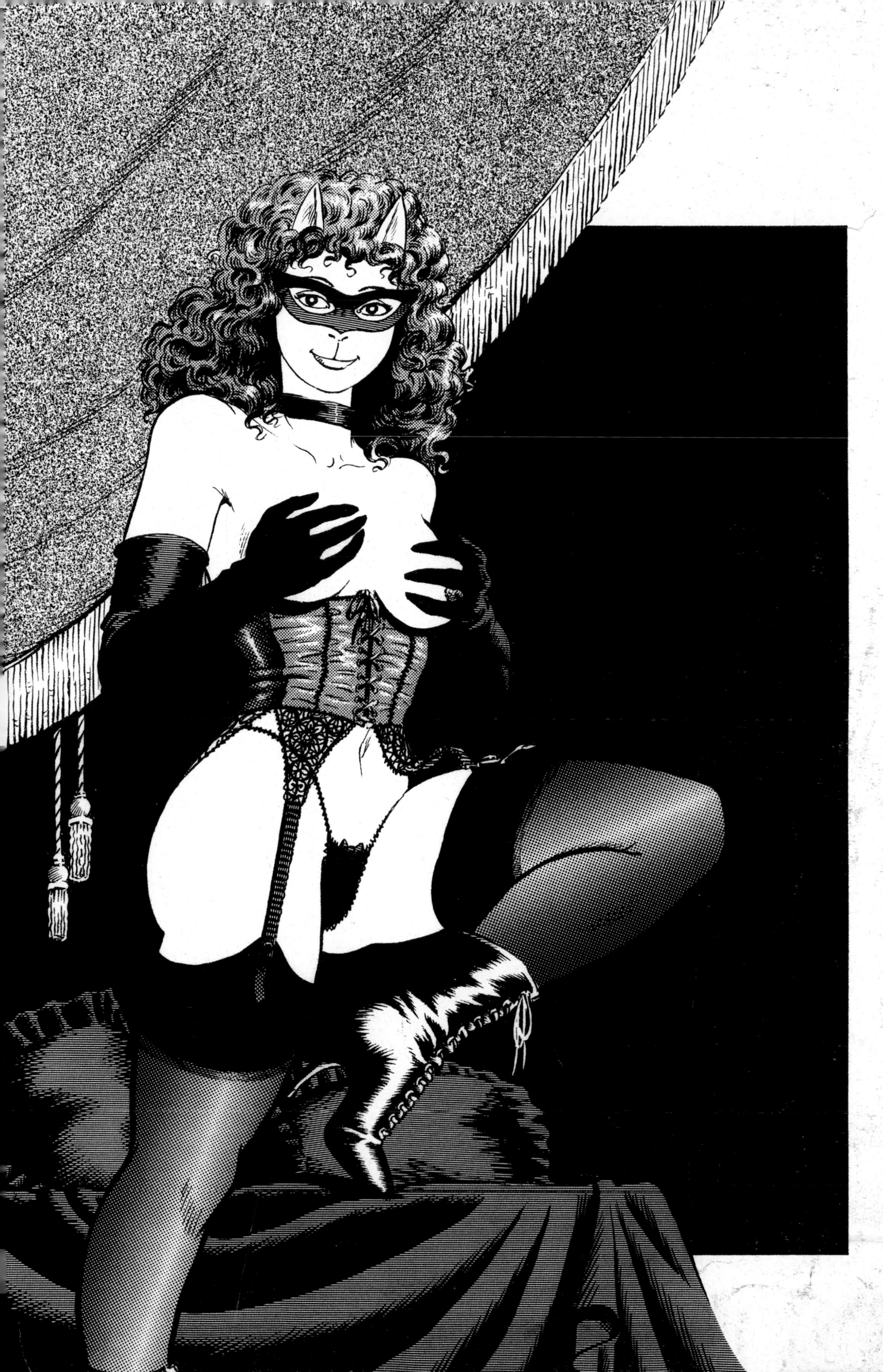

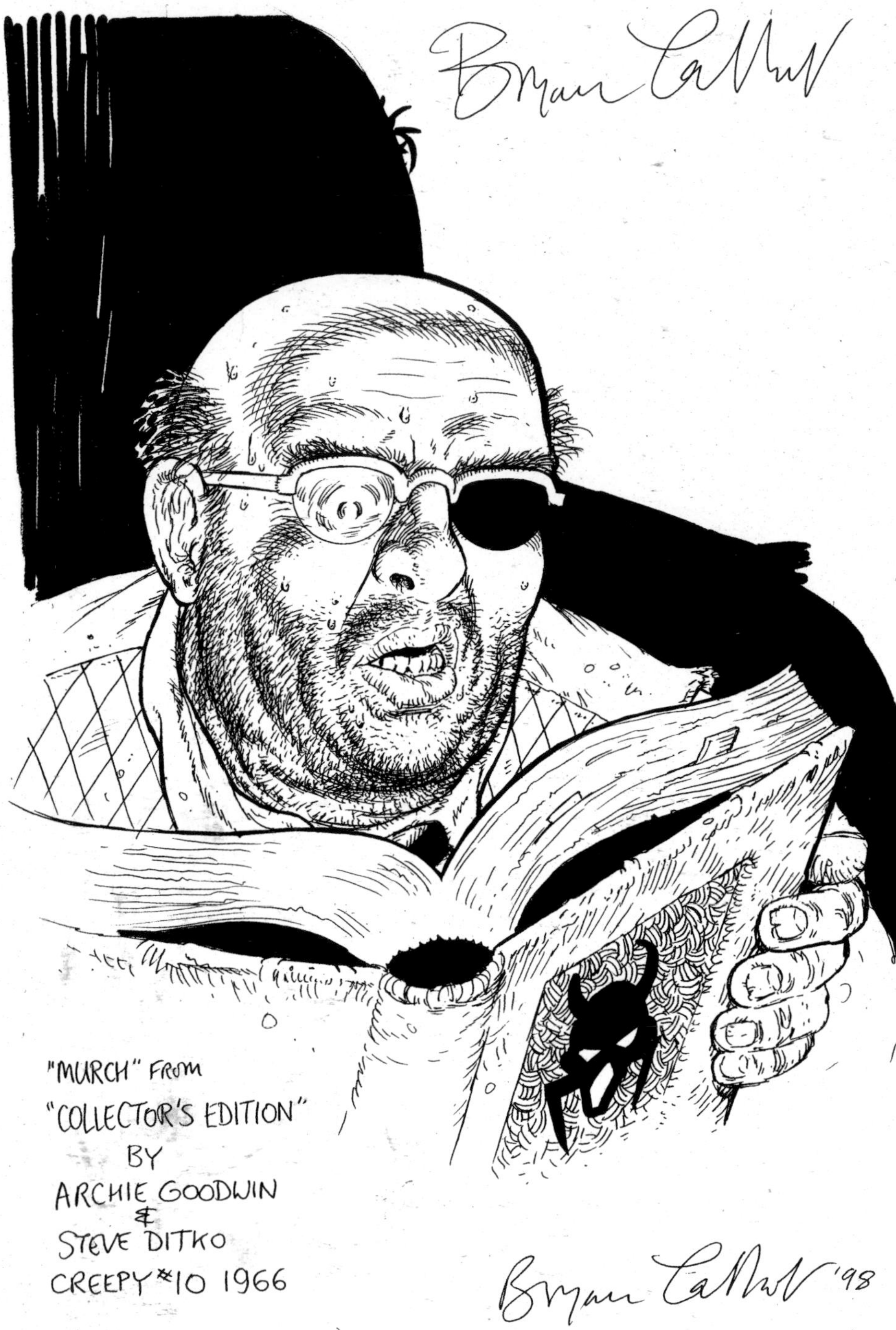

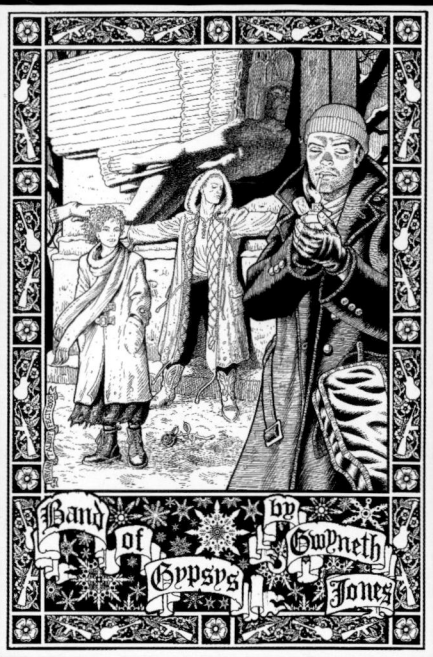

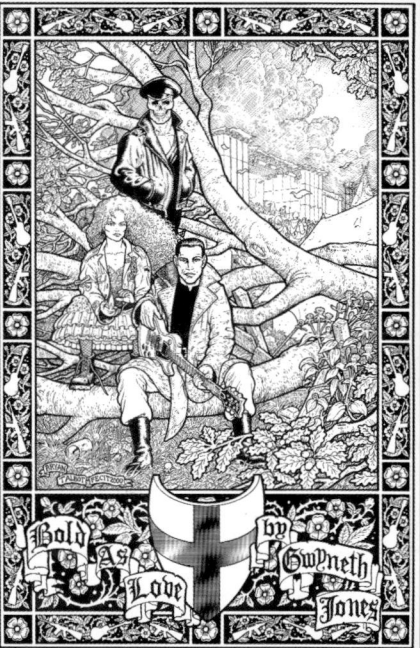

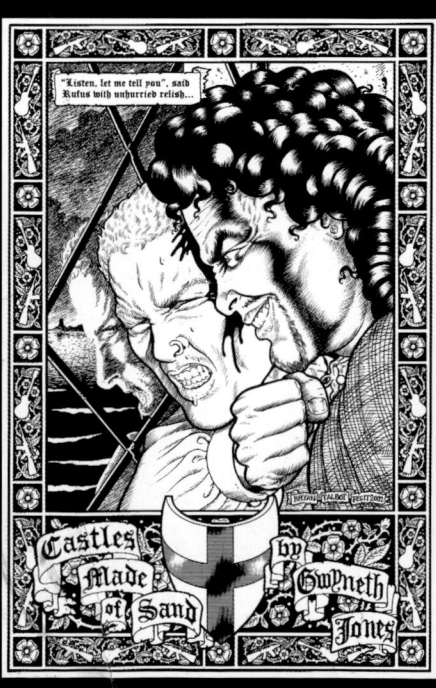

"MURCH" FROM
"COLLECTOR'S EDITION"
BY
ARCHIE GOODWIN
&
STEVE DITKO
CREEPY #10 1966

Bryan Talbot

Bryan Talbot '98

Above is a sketch of Murch, a character from *Collector's Edition*, a strip written by Archie Goodwin and drawn by Steve Ditko for *Creepy* #10, 1966, and one that had a big influence on my perception of comic storytelling. I contributed this to a memorial portfolio dedicated to Archie's work. 1998.

Right bar: I did the frontispieces to Gwynneth Jones' excellent *Bold as Love* series of rock SF novels. She made me jump through hoops to get the characters as close as possible to how she saw them in her mind. 2000–2005.

Facing page: Uncommon Mona, produced for the tee-shirt for the *Uncommoncon* convention, Dallas. Unpublished. Ink line, computer colored. 2000.

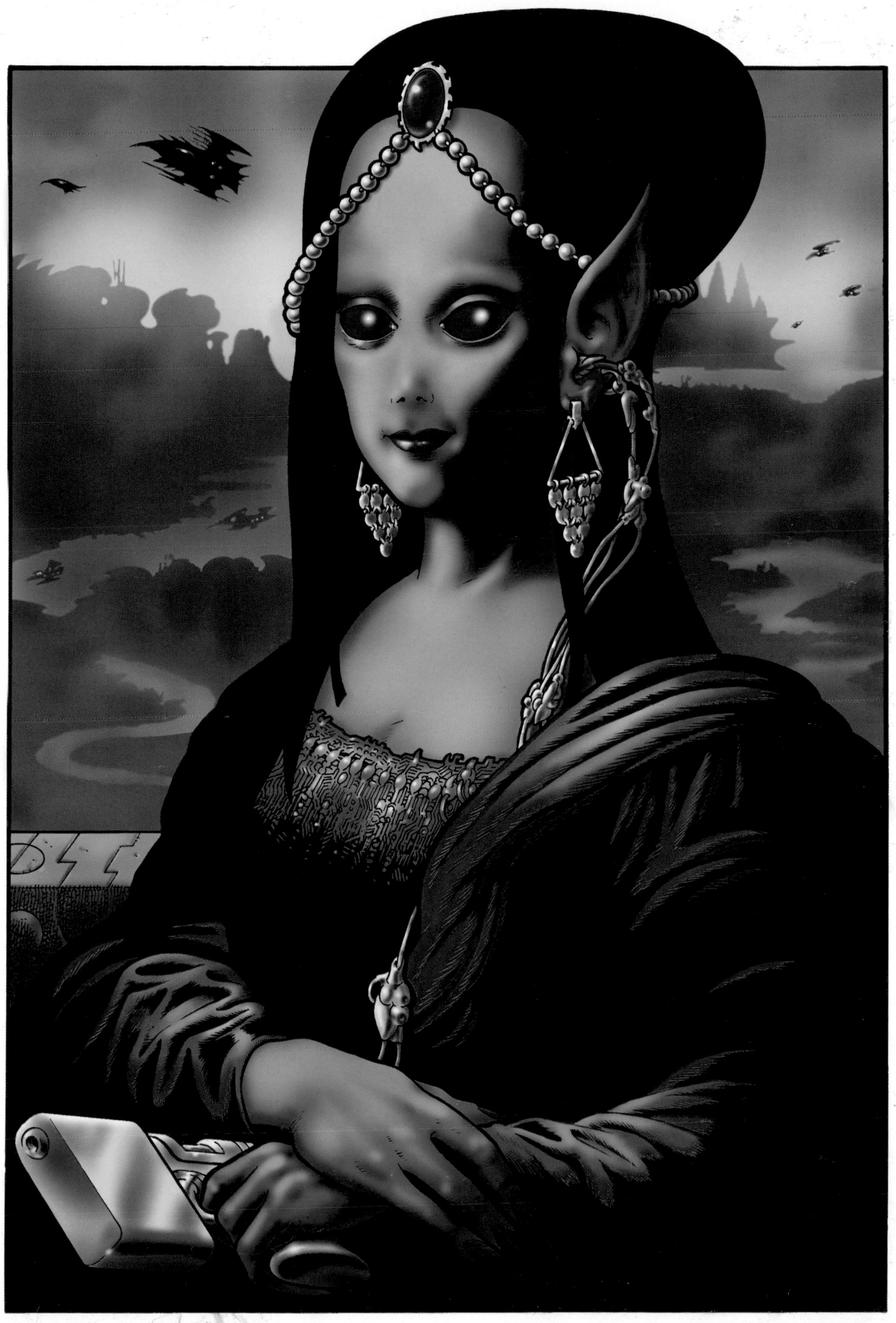

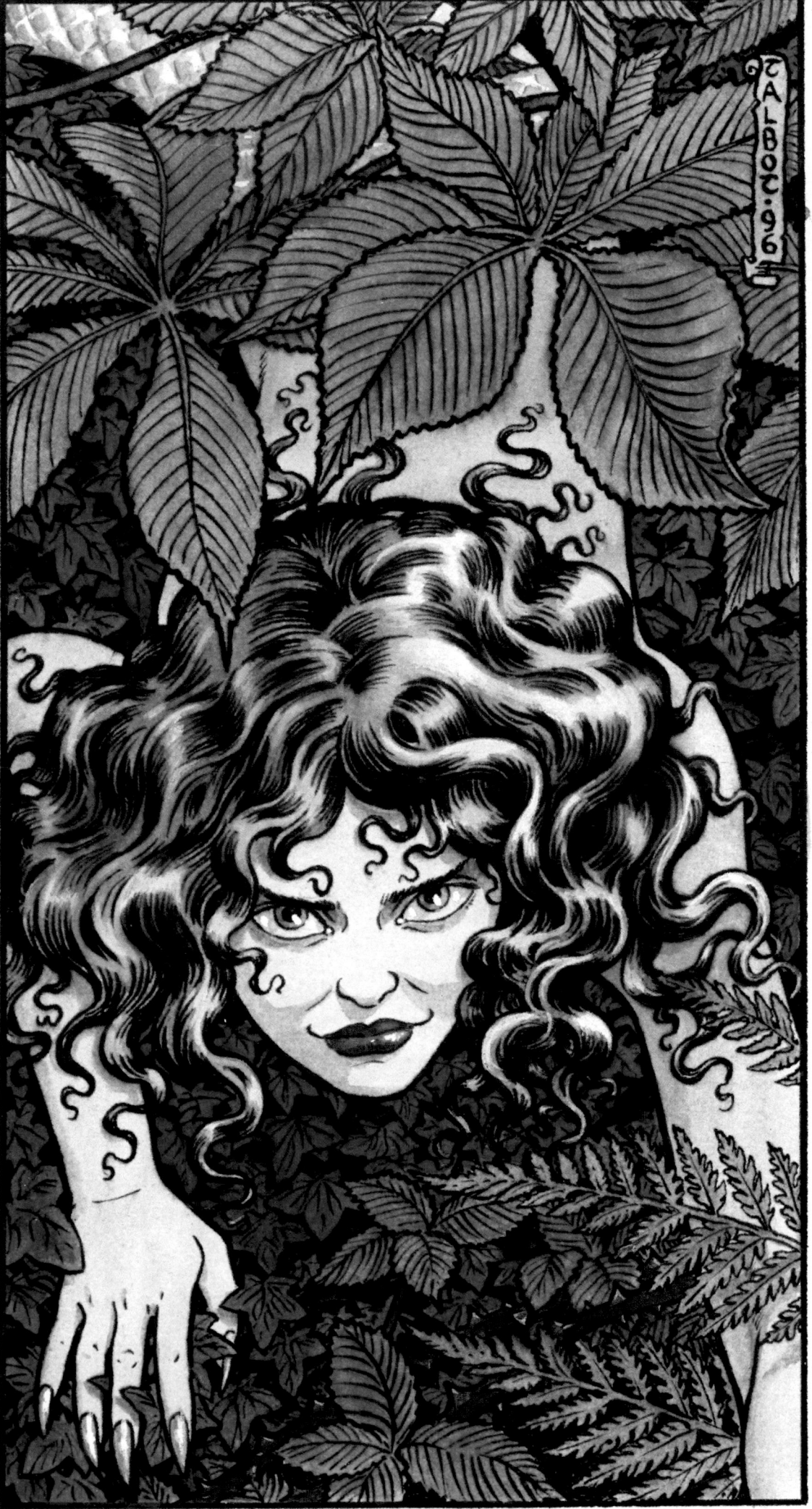

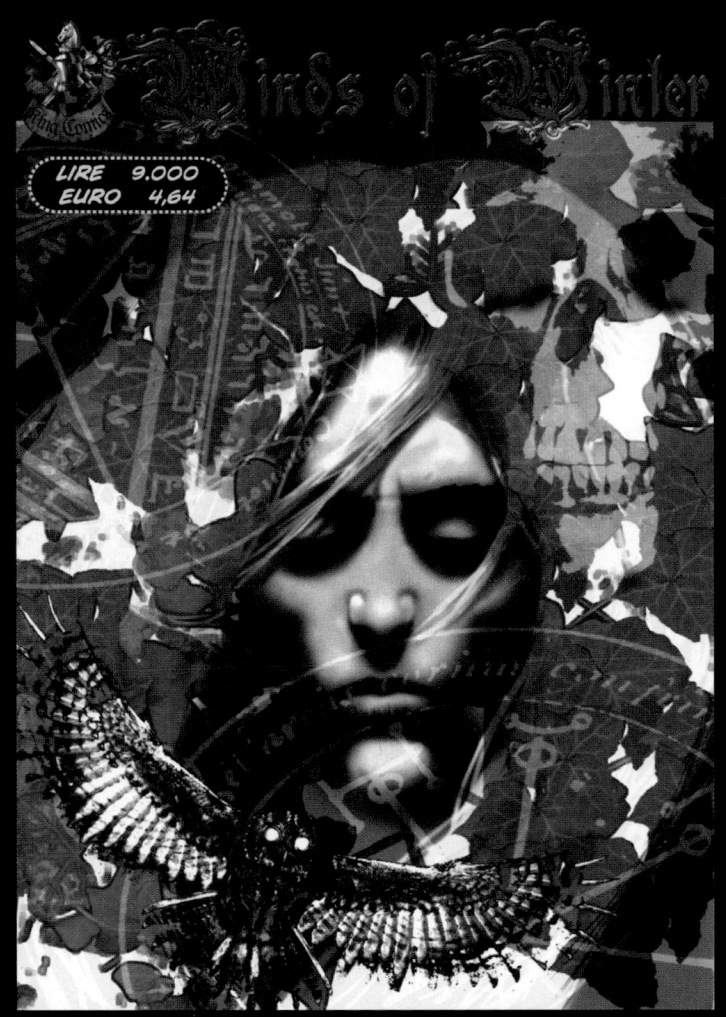

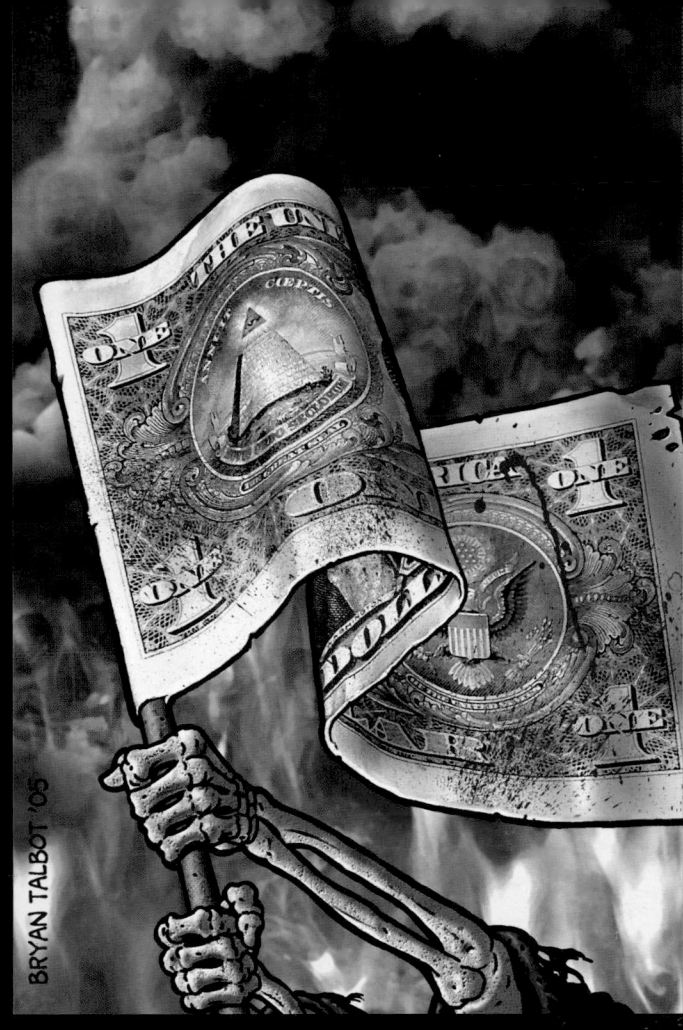

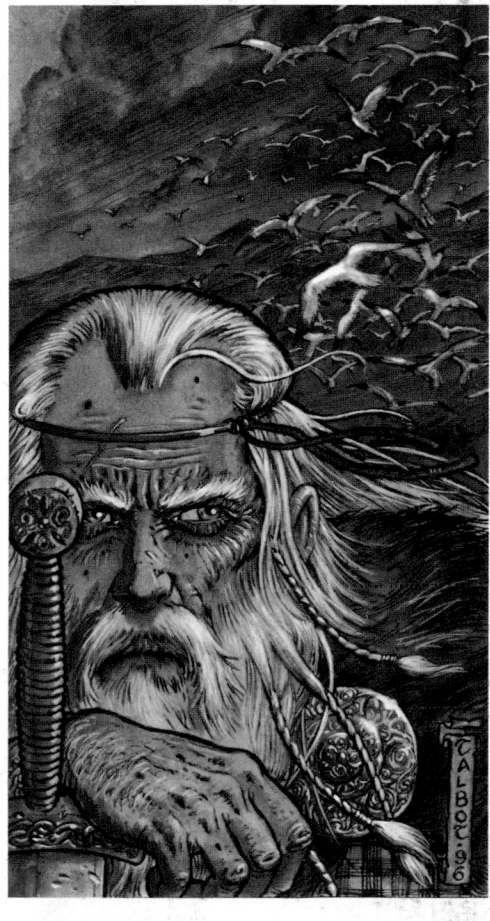

Opposite: *Melusine*, the half-woman half-serpent of European folklore, for The Radio Times to accompany an adaptation of the tale on Radio 4 (UK). Watercolors and inks. 1996.

Top left: the first illustration I created using a computer: the cover to Gianluca Piredda's *Winds of Winter*. First published in Italy. 2000.

Top right: cover illustration for an Italian comic series, *The Great Seals*. Ink line, computer colored. 2005.

Right: another *Radio Times* illustration, this time for *The Seafarer*, the story of a Viking explorer, set in the Dark Ages. Ink line and watercolors. 1996.

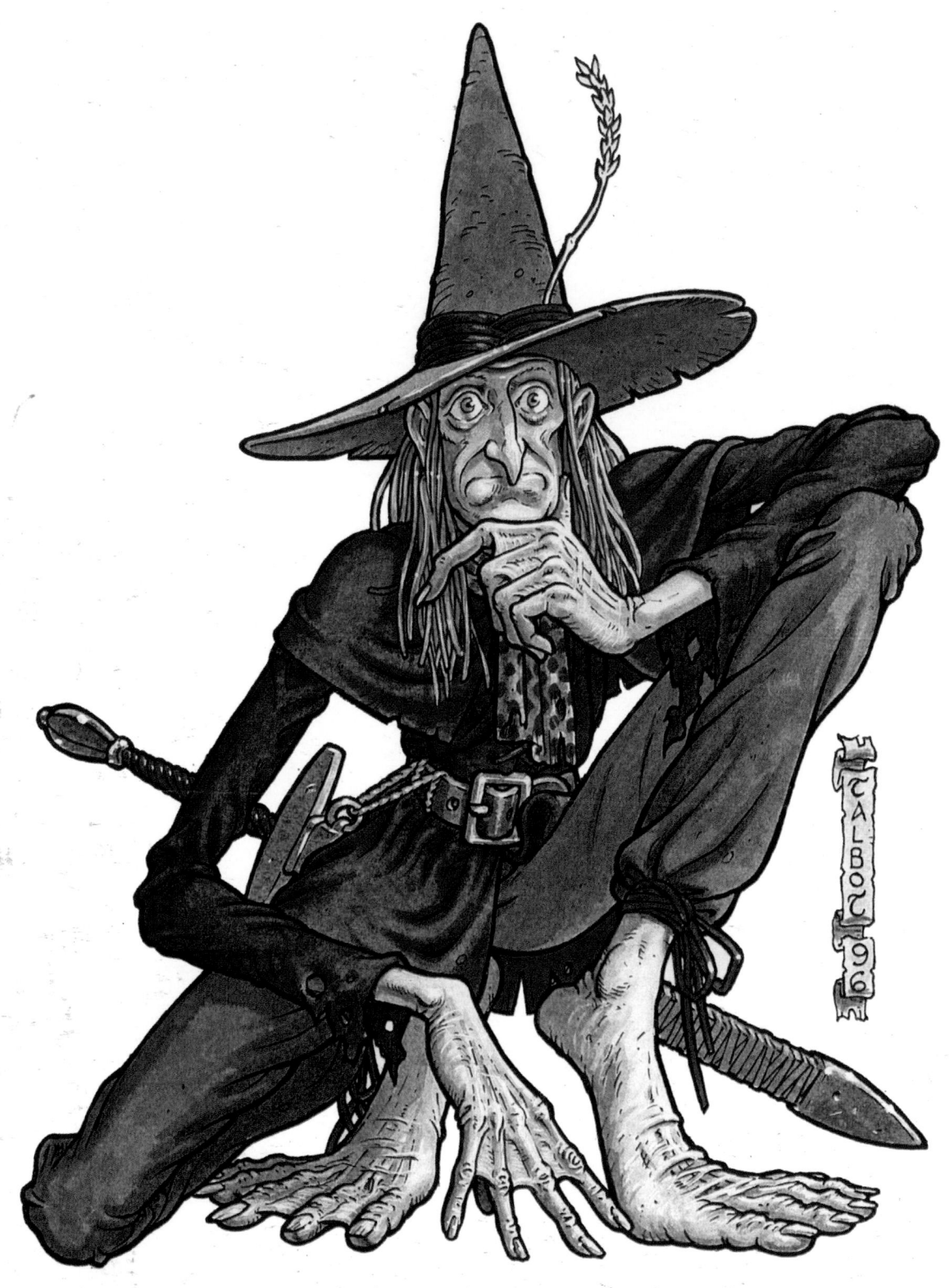

I like to think that this is the definitive depiction of *Puddleglum*, the *Marsh-wiggle* from *The Silver Chair*, the fourth book of *The Chronicles of Narnia* series. A favourite character of mine when a teenager, it was a delight to draw him for the Radio Times to accompany the Radio 4 serialisation. It was adapted from CS Lewis's original story by Brian Sibley, who bought the original artwork. 1996.

Facing is *The Fairy Caravan*, my contribution to the *Stardust* benefit portfolio for Charles Vess's wife Karen, who was badly injured in a road accident. Colored on computer by Eric Olive. 1998.

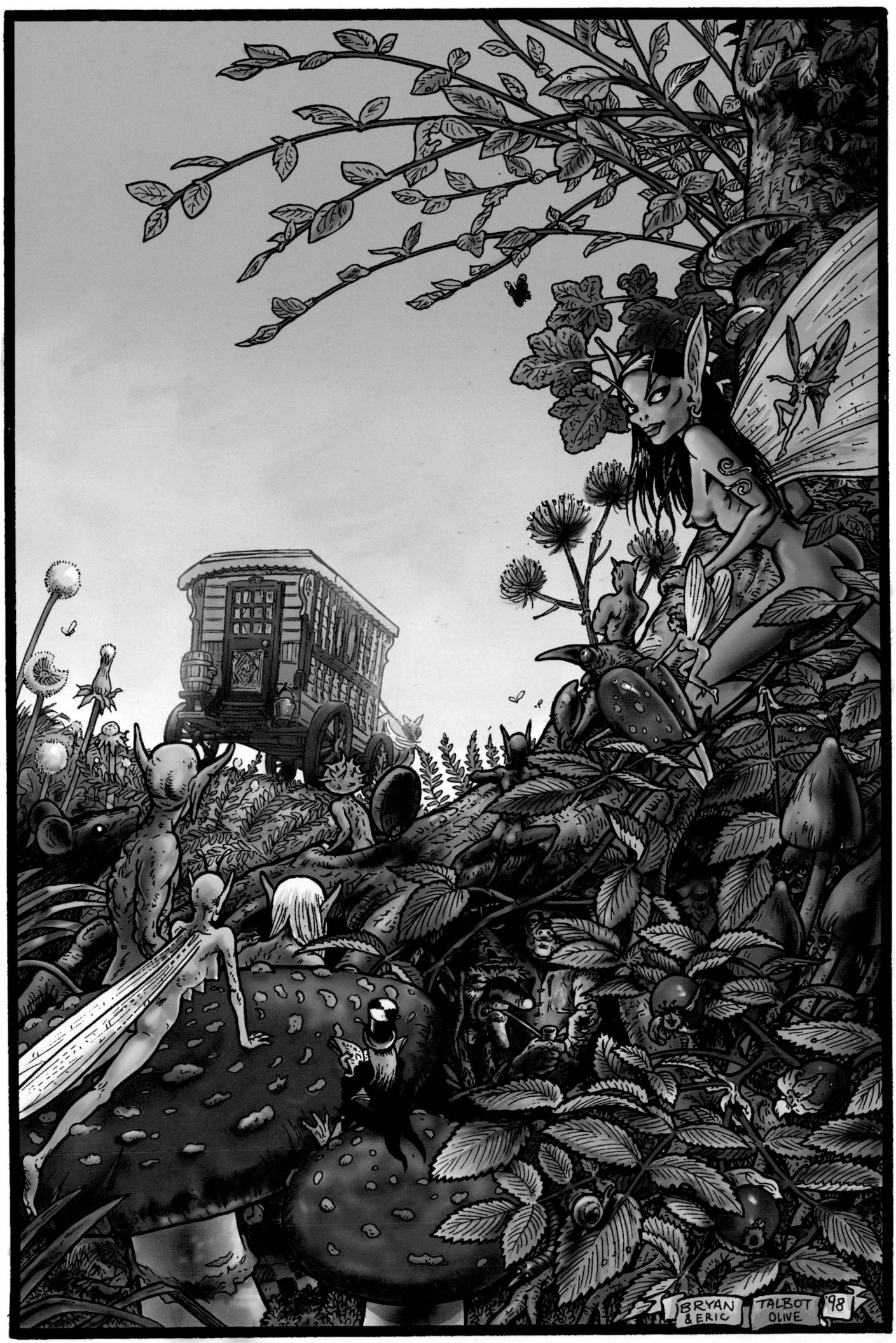

Heart of Empire, the sequel to *The Adventures of Luther Arkwright* was published in nine monthly issues by Dark Horse Comics, 1999 – 2000 and in book form in 2001. The 284-page story was set twenty-three years later and featured daughter Victoria as the protagonist, rather than Arkwright.

Facing page: Victoria seeks solitude in the Imperial Palace grounds. The book was colored on computer by Angus McKie.

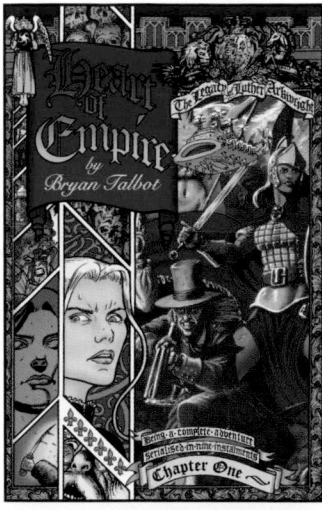

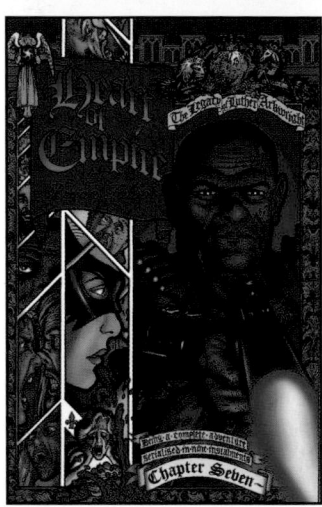

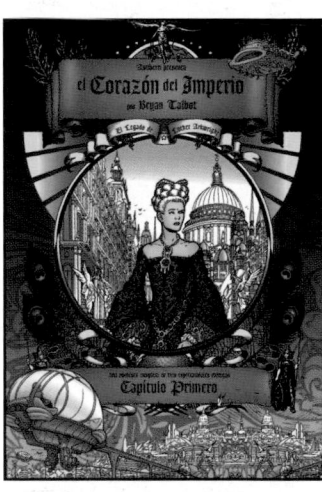

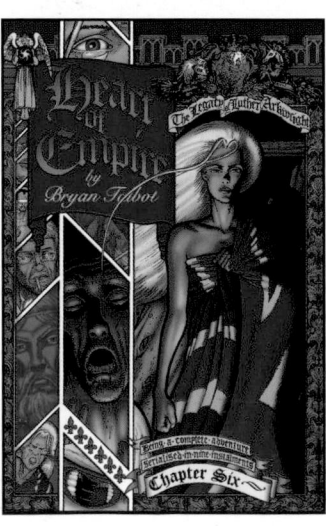

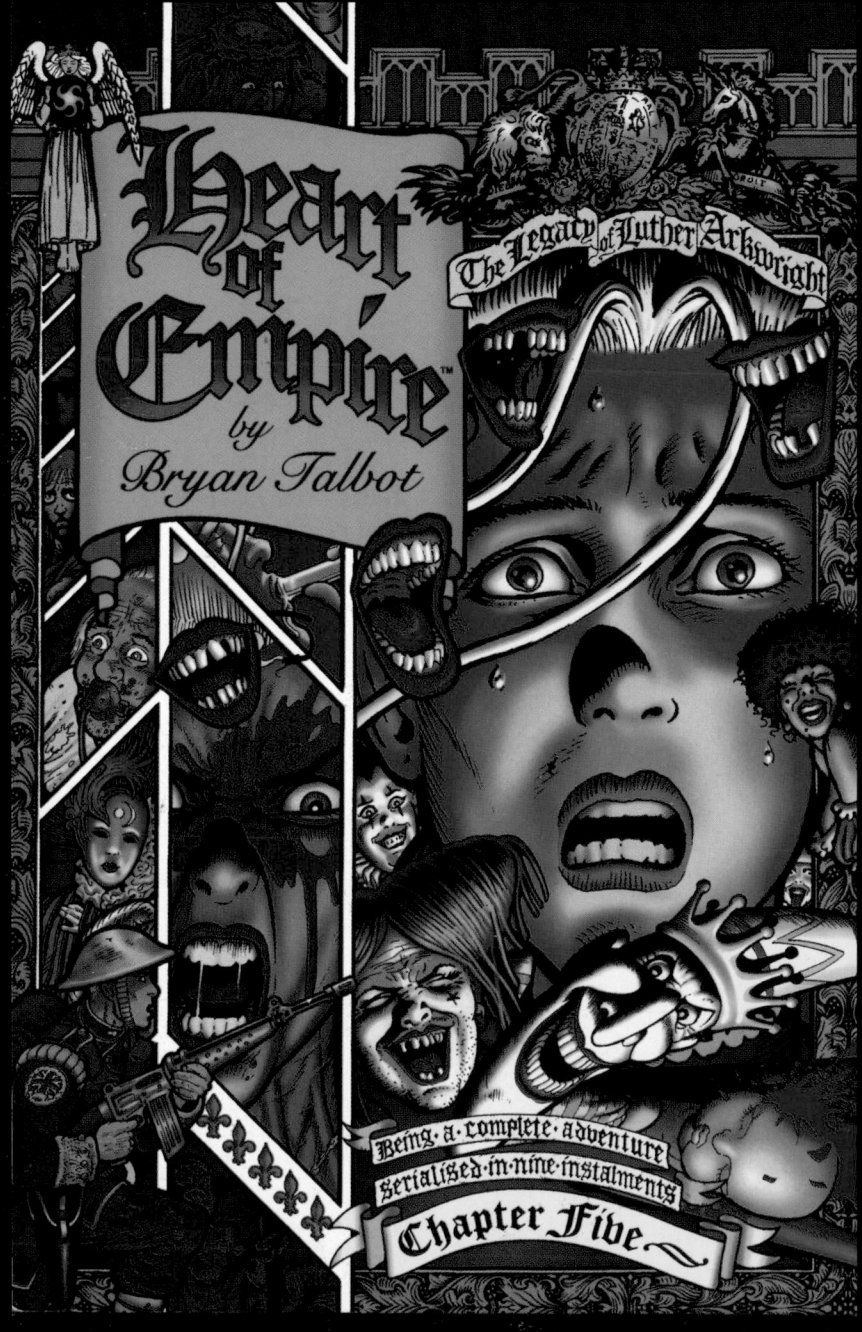

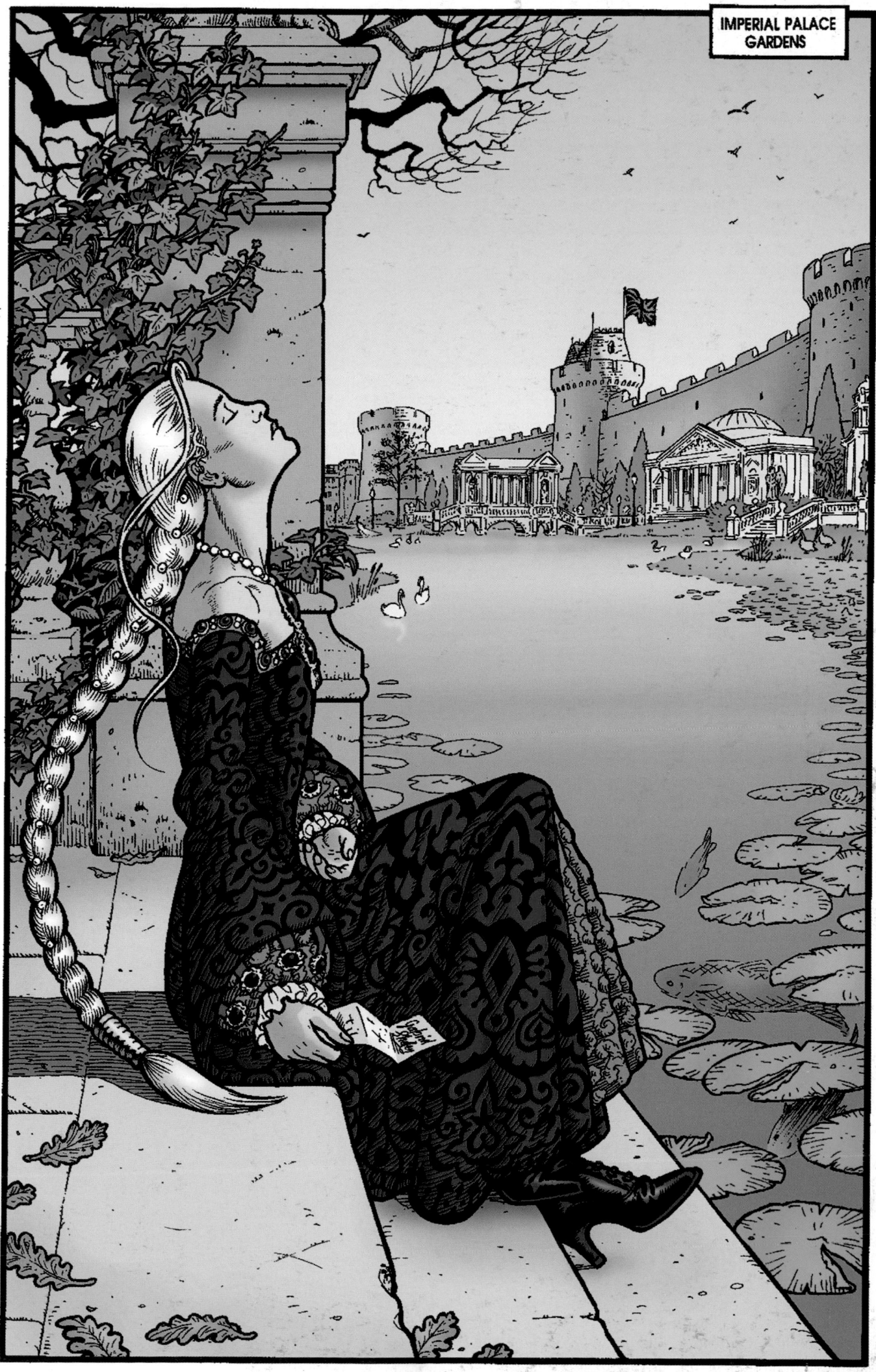

IMPERIAL PALACE GARDENS

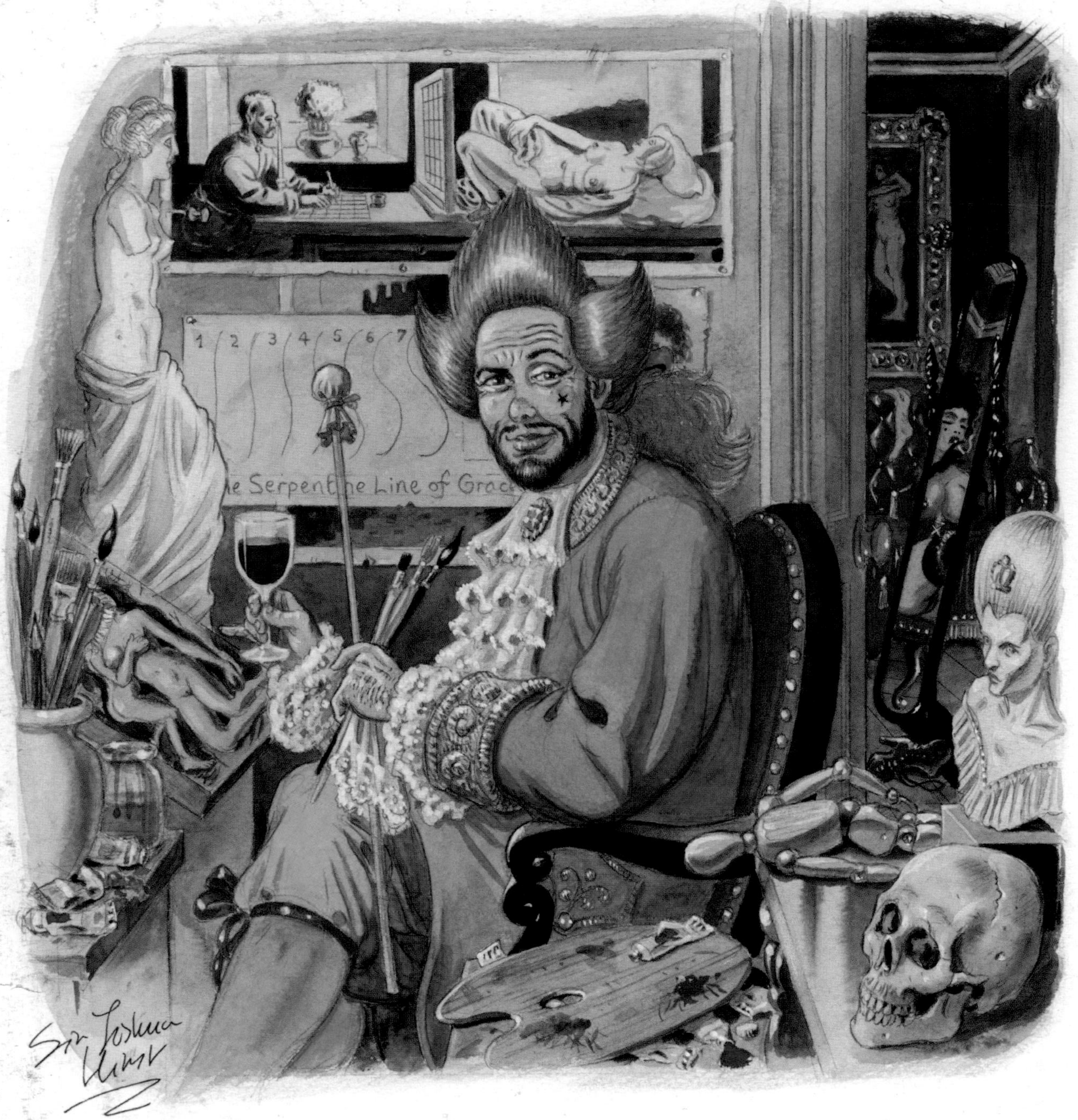

Each back cover of the comic series was a spoof advertisement, poster or magazine cover. This painting of court artist Sir Joshua Hirst (a parallel Damian Hirst) was on the back cover of issue two: a parody of the 1960/70s "We're looking for people who like to draw" ad for the *Famous Artists' School*, with Hirst taking the place of Norman Rockwell. I took it as an excuse to do a perspective exercise of the sort done by the Dutch Masters. You can see into the back room and around the corner, via the mirror, where a prostitute is visible. On the wall behind Hirst, there's Albrecht Dürer's drawing of a perspective grid and William Hogarth's *Serpentine Line of Grace*. Watercolors. 1999.

On the right is the back cover for issue five, based on the World War One recruitment poster of Lord Kitchener.

Facing: Queen Anne, Empress of the World.

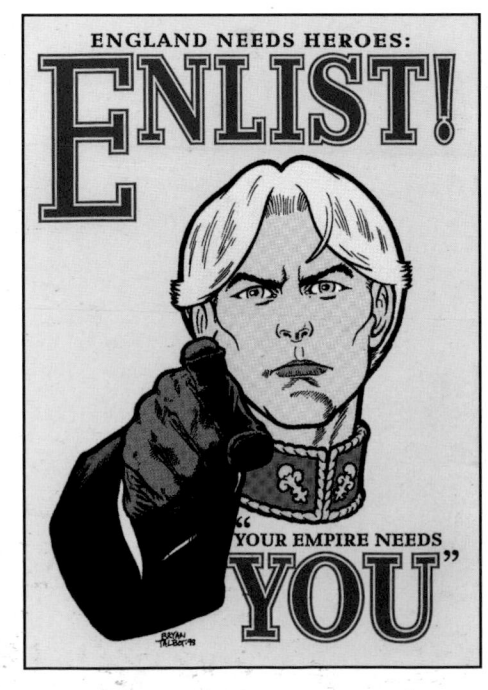

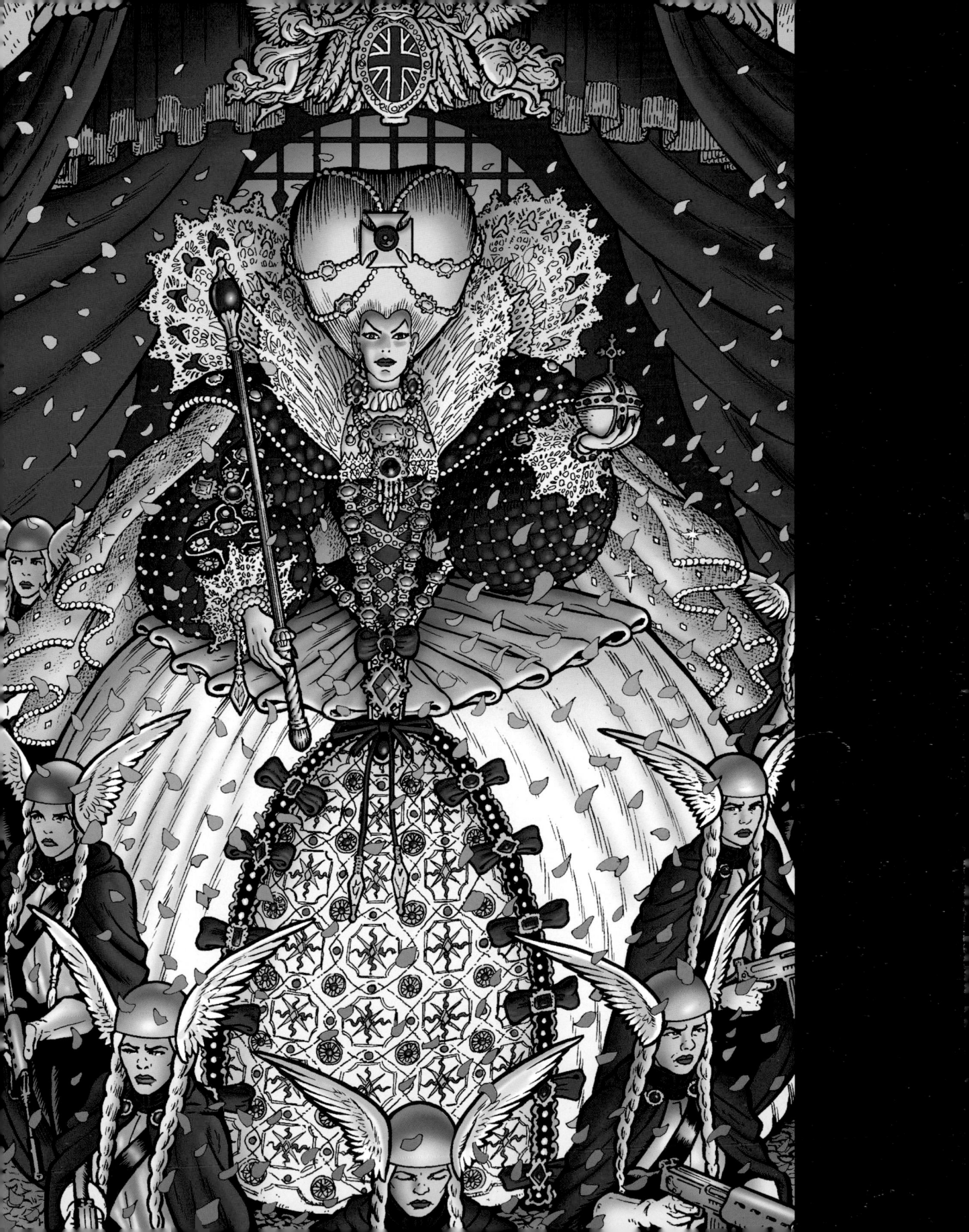

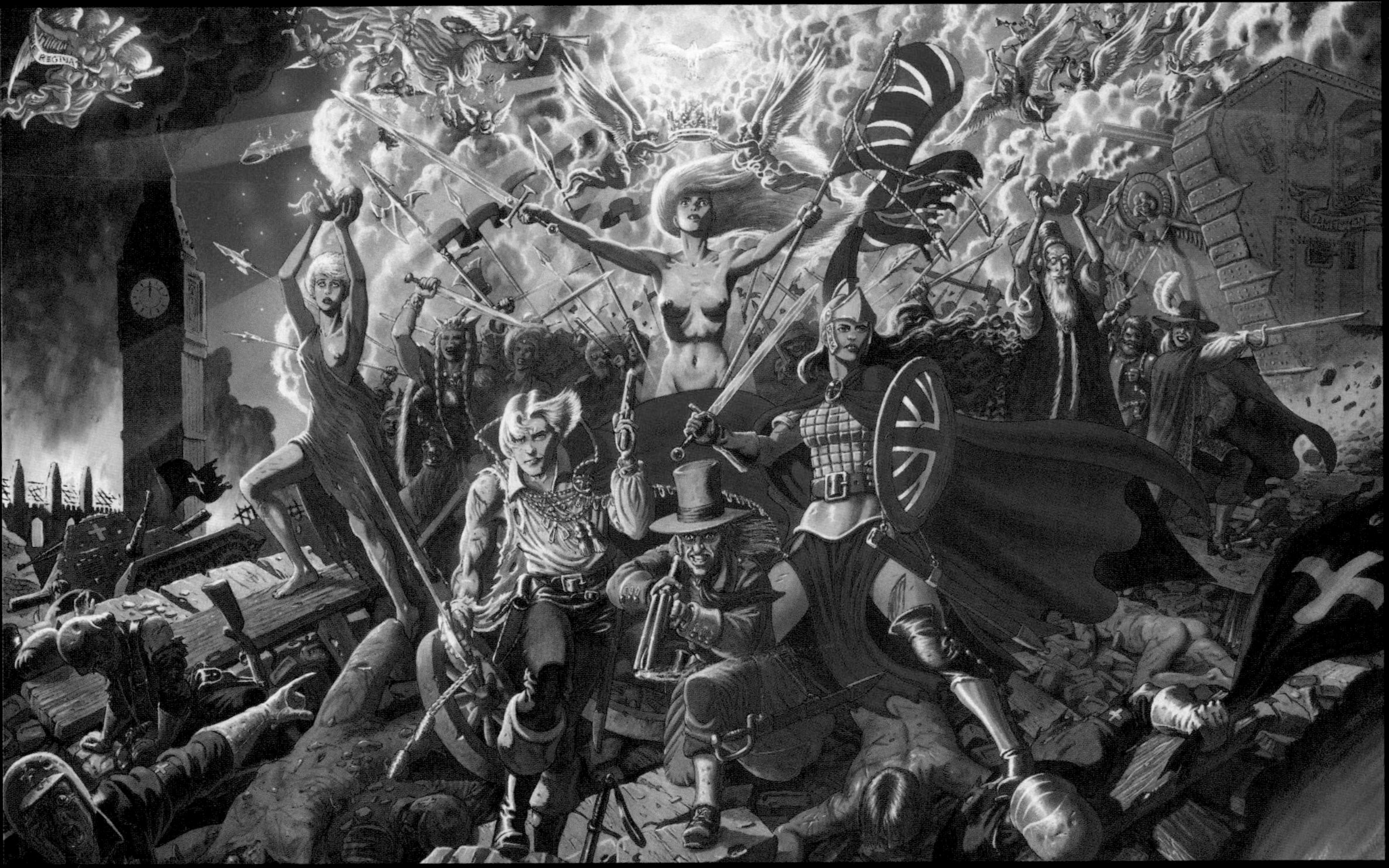

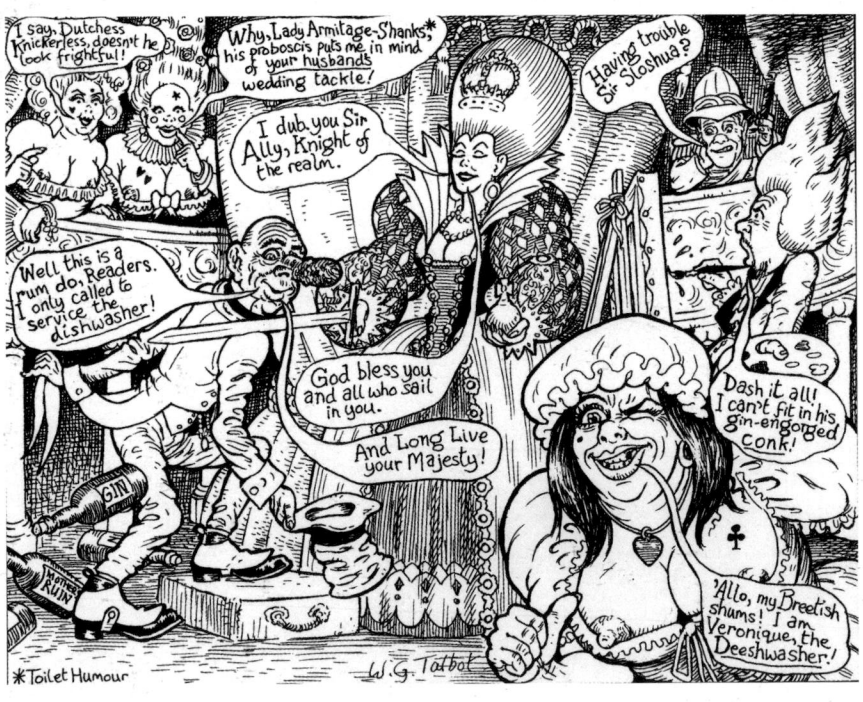

In the Imperial Palace is a large painting of *The Battle of London*, a romanticised version of the revolt at the end of *Luther Arkwright*: historical events recreated as legend. I wanted to produce a tableau of the kind seen in the Louvre, such as Delacroix's *Liberty Leading the People*. The composition is based around *Golden Section* divisions, radiating diagonals and concentric circles. It also appeared as an art print and was used as the limited edition hardback's endpapers. Watercolors. 1998.

Below that is a cartoon that appeared as part of the spoof of a Victorian comic, *Ally Sloper's Half-Holiday*, on the back cover of issue seven. Sloper was the UK's first continuing comic character. 2000.

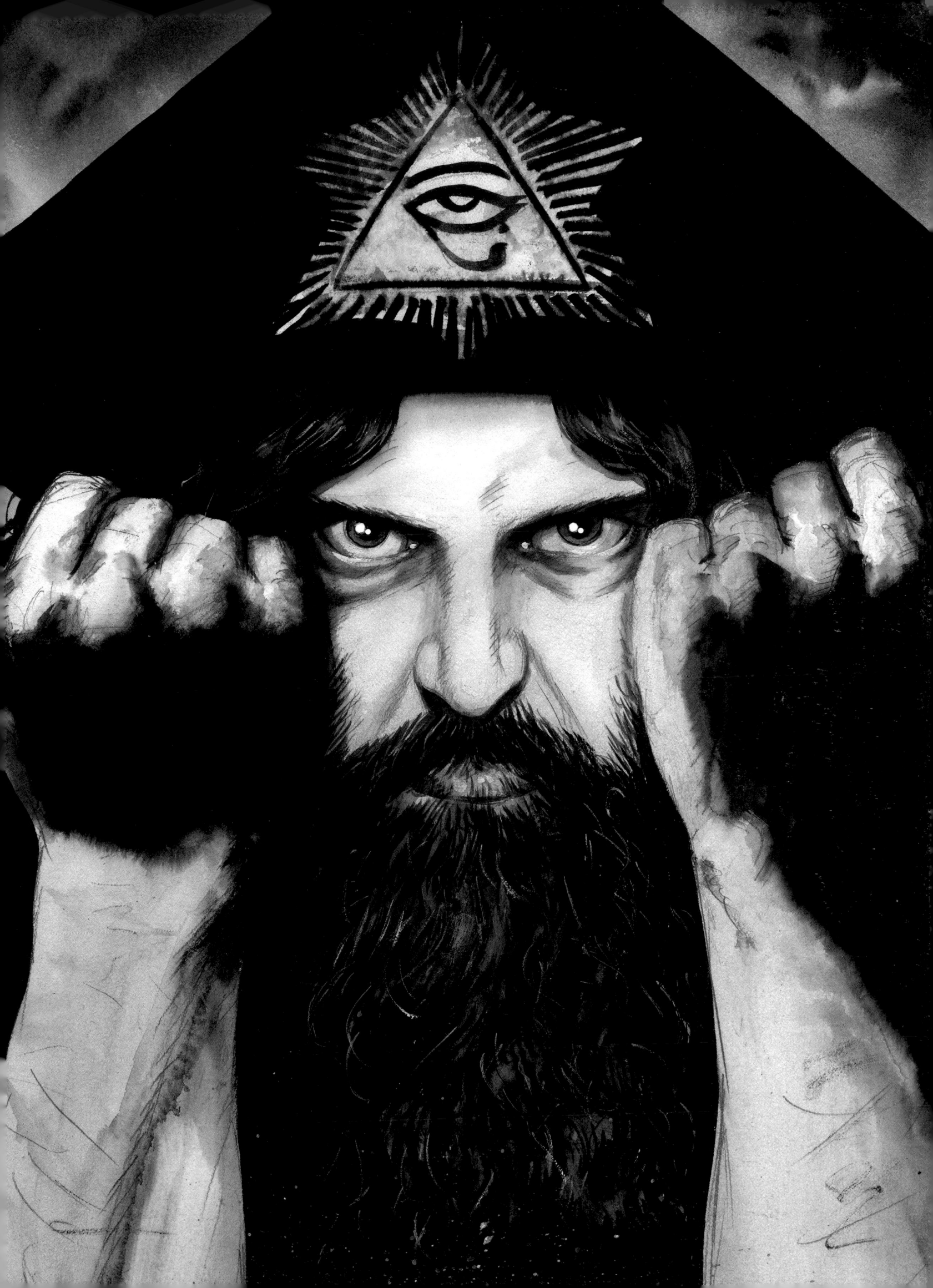

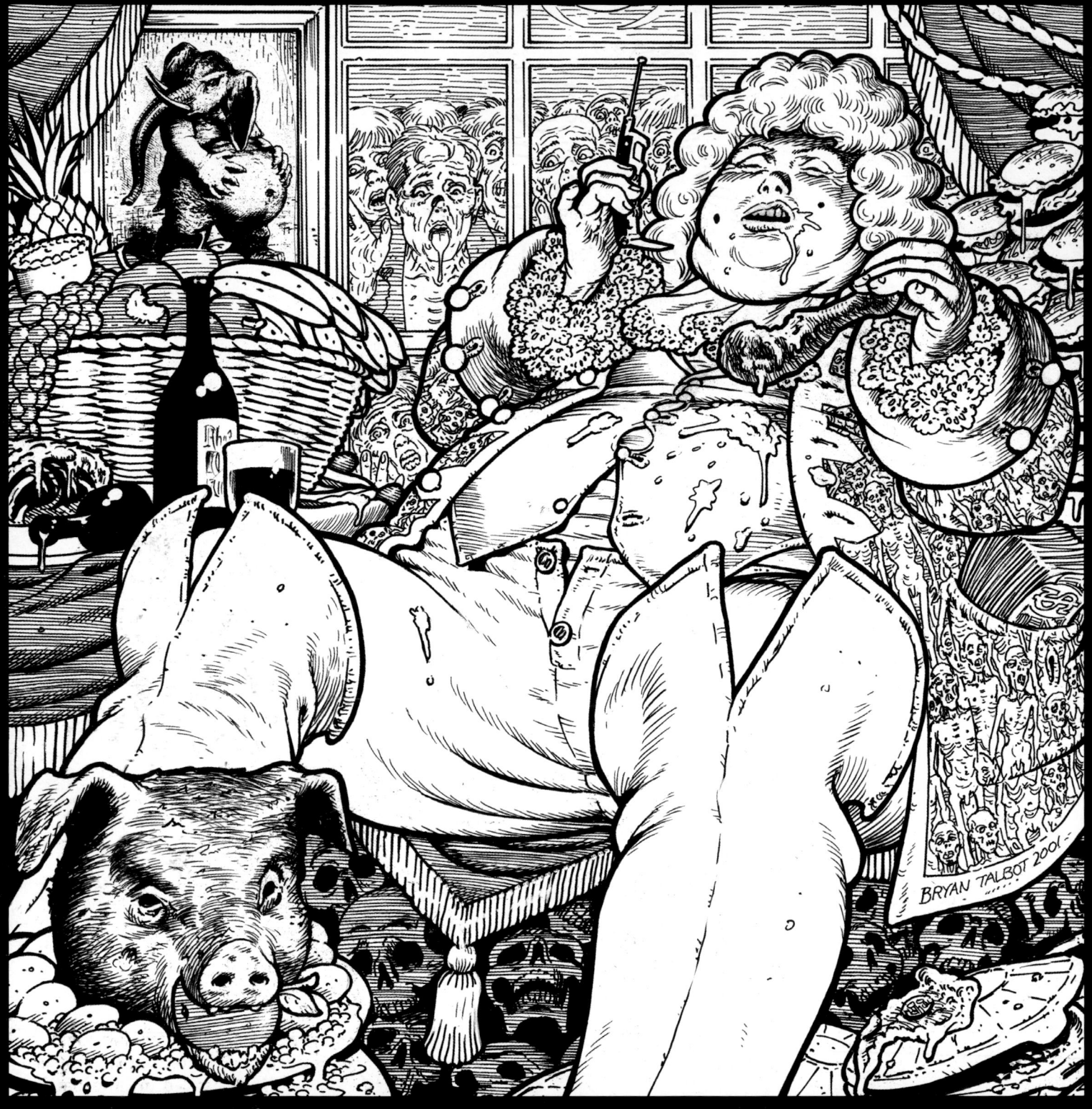

Previous page: Comic genius Alan Moore, my contribution to the charity hagiography *Portrait of an Extraordinary Gentleman* by Abiogenesis Press. It's based on a famous photograph of "the Great Beast" Alistair Crowley, one of Alan's heroes. Pencil and water-color. 2003.

Above is *Gluttony Demanding Repayment of Third World Debt* from the sophisticated role-playing game Nobilis by Hogshead Games. These three ink illustrations are all from the book, which also had work by Al Davison, Charles Vess, Michael Kaluta and others. As well as archetypical figures from mythology and folklore, anthropomorphic representations of abstract concepts were characters in the game. On the wall in the background is an eighteenth-century illustration of the *Demon of Greed*. 2001.

At the top of the facing page is a tree sprite. Below left is *Honesty*. 2001.

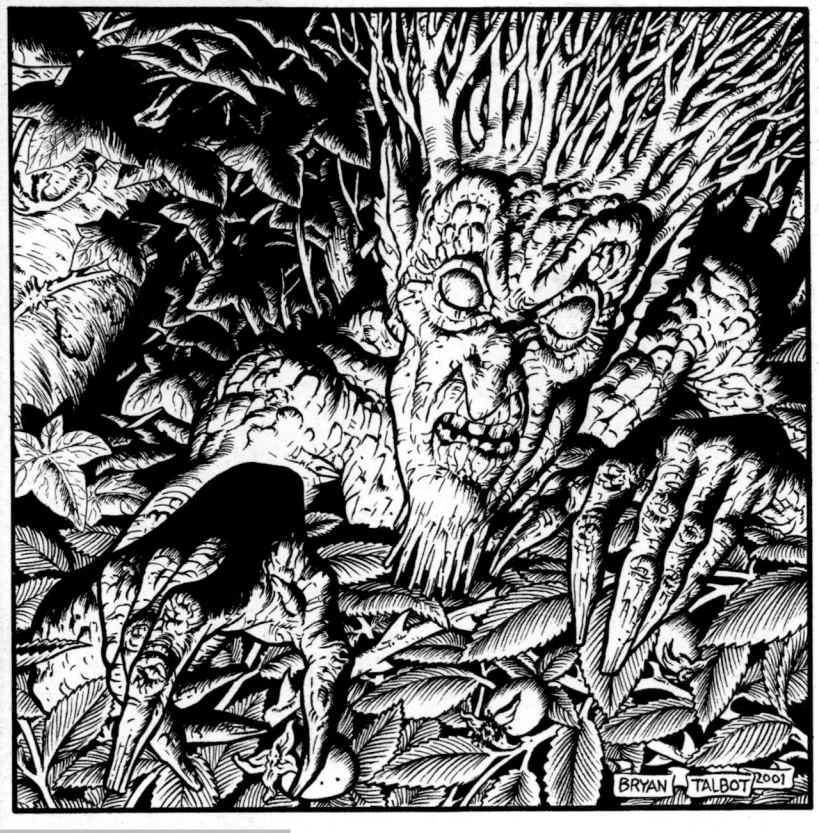

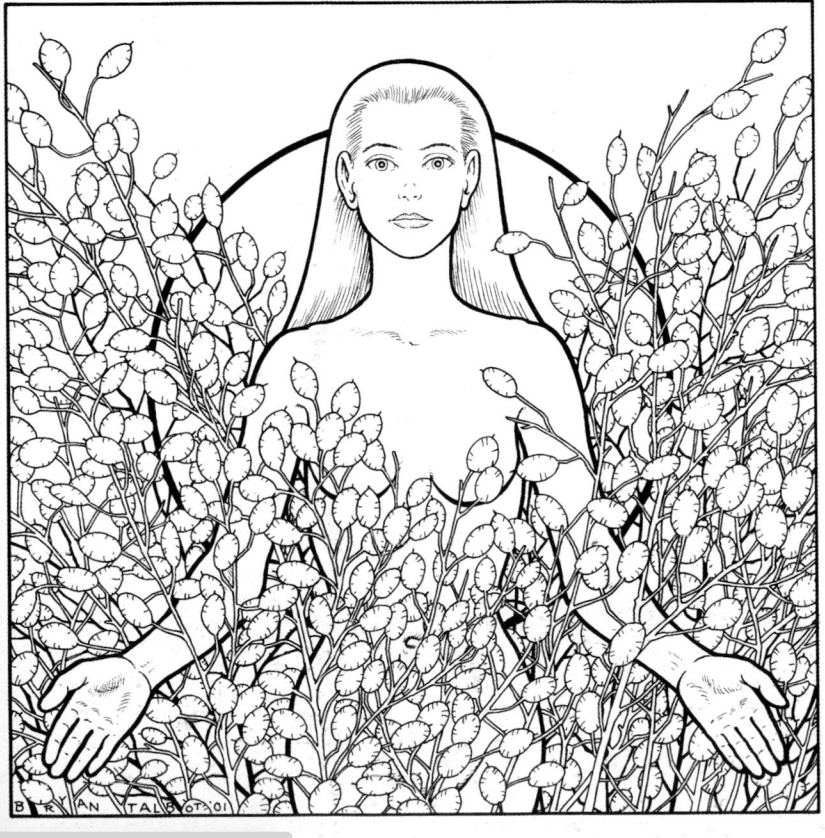

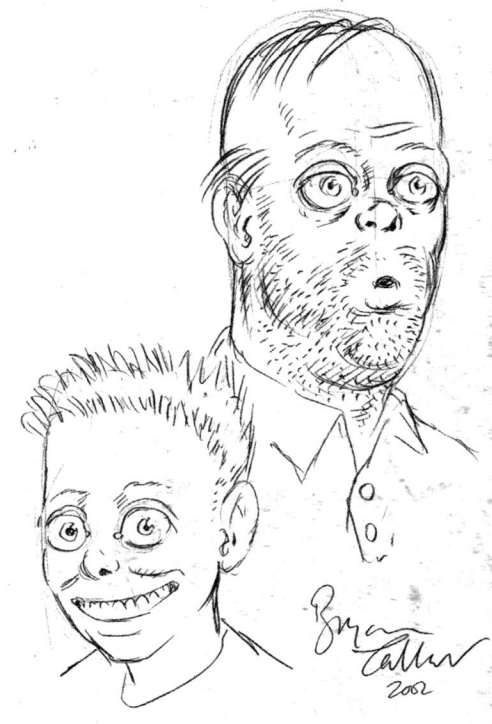

Arkwright fan Jesse McCann, a regular writer of *The Simpsons* comic, submitted a plot proposal wherein Bart and Homer ended up in a parallel world under a fascist dictatorship. The idea was that the framing sequence would be drawn by a regular Simpsons artist, while I drew the alternative, slightly more realistic world. The above was my concept sketch of what they'd look like there. The idea was turned down on the grounds that it would be "too disturbing". Unpublished. 2002.

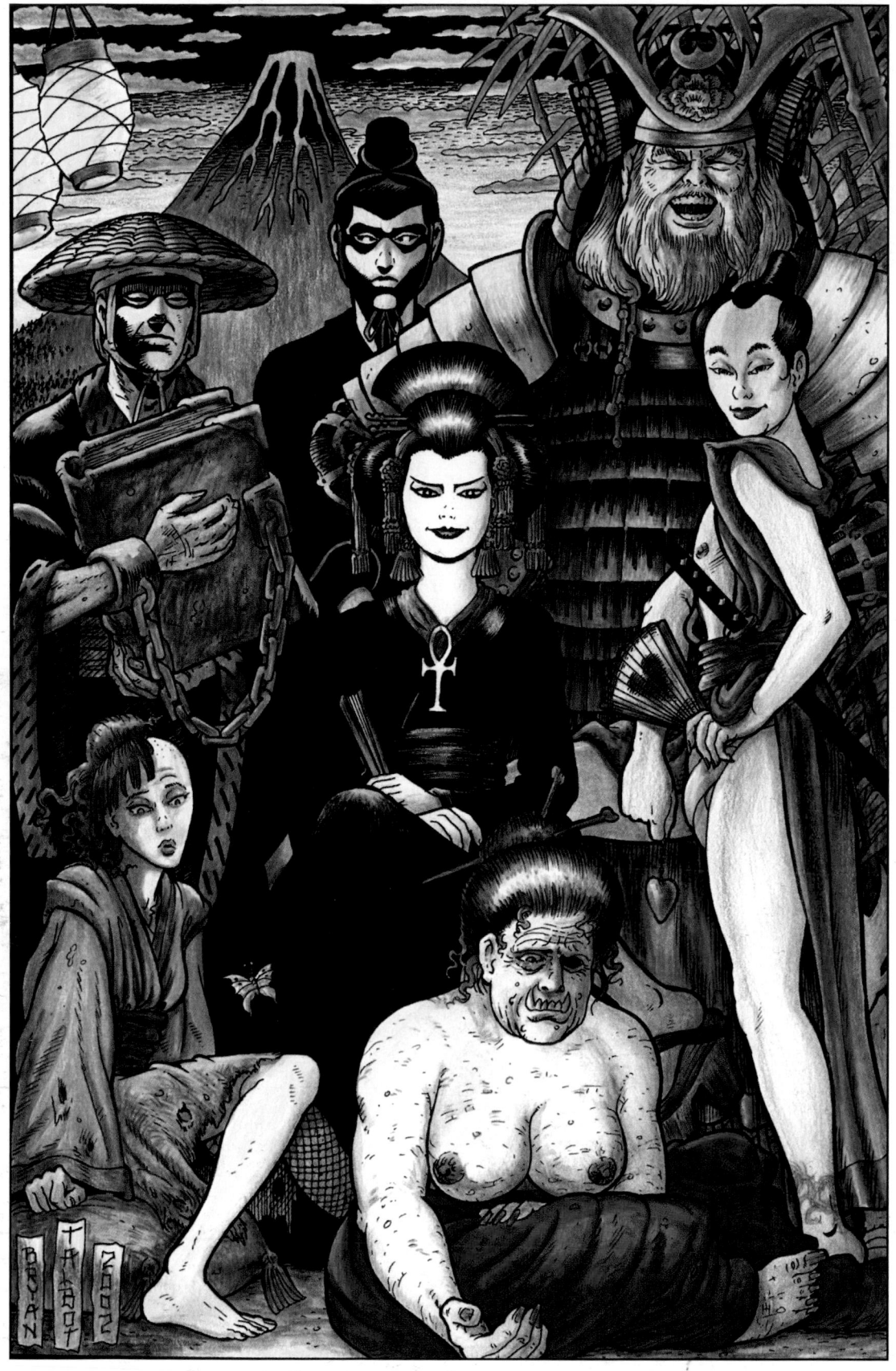

I drew several of Neil Gaiman's groundbreaking *Sandman* stories. The above was done as a private commission. 2002. Coloured by Steve Oliff in 2007.

The newspaper strip character Nemi by Lise Myhre is massive in Scandinavia and is also popular in other countries in Europe, appearing in the UK in the daily *Metro* newspapers. Every edition of the glossy monthly *Nemi* magazines in Norway and Sweden is a big event. Each issue has a theme. The illustration facing was the frontispiece to an issue with the theme of fairies. Ink line, colored on computer. 2005.

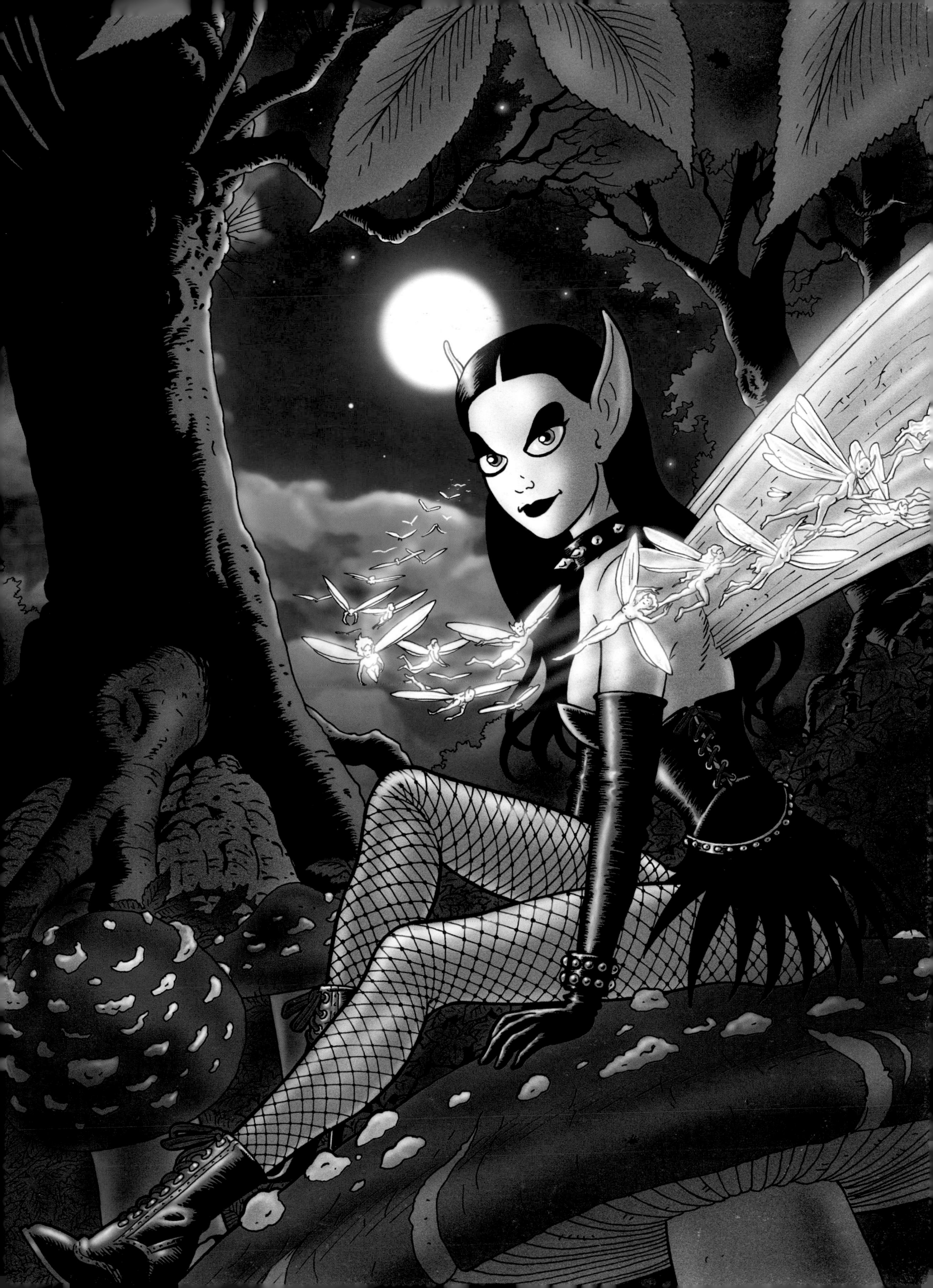

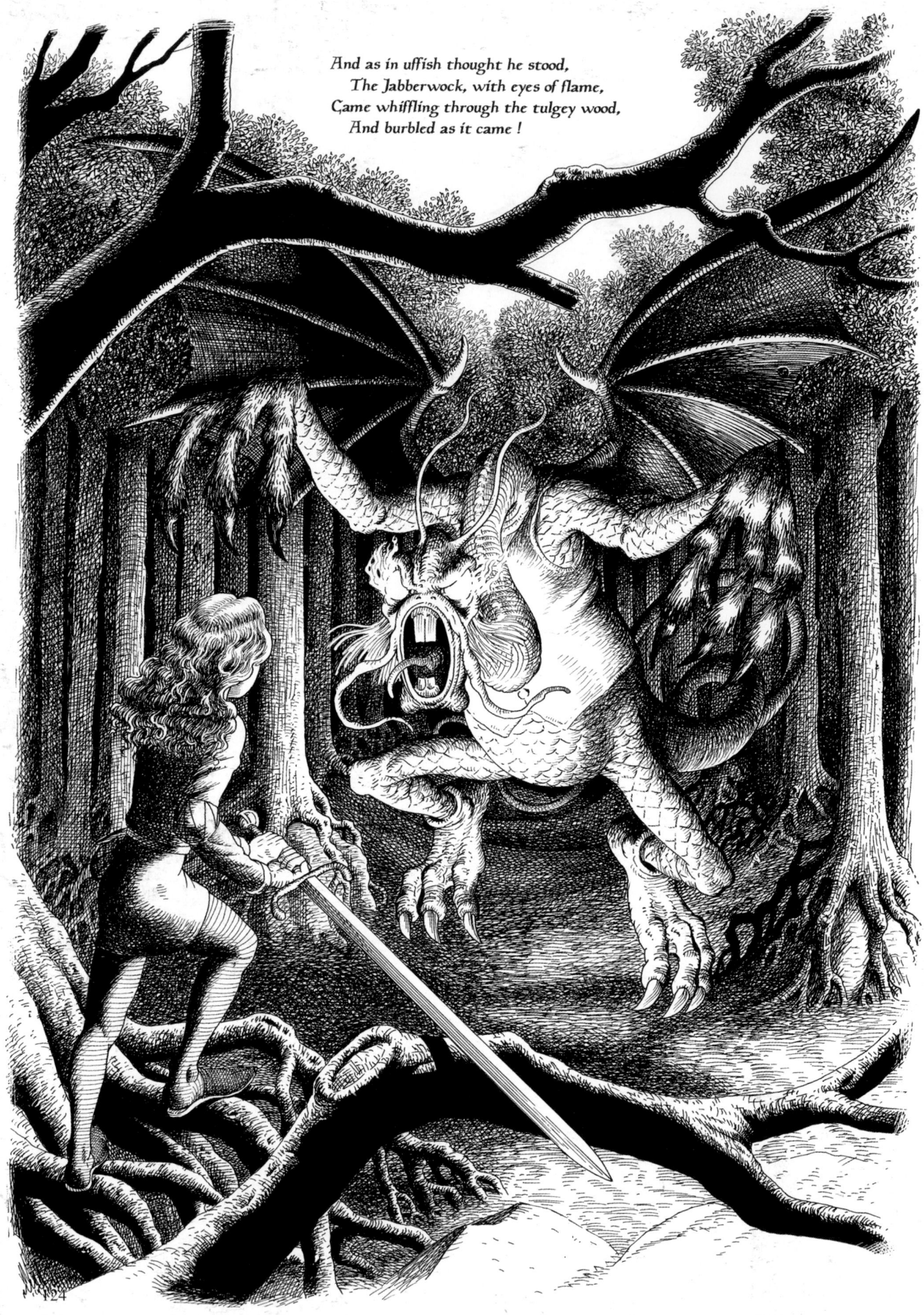

And as in uffish thought he stood,
The Jabberwock, with eyes of flame,
Came whiffling through the tulgey wood,
And burbled as it came !

Here's one page from my new graphic novel *Alice in Sunderland*. It's not really representative of the book as each sequence in it is done in a style I thought appropriate, but I like this one. It's from a three-page adaptation of *Jabberwocky* by Lewis Carroll and is designed to evoke the original *Alice* illustrator John Tenniel. 2007.

Facing is a depiction of Detective-Inspector LeBrock of Scotland Yard, the protagonist of Grandville, my graphic novel work-in-progress. Ink line, colored on computer. 2006.

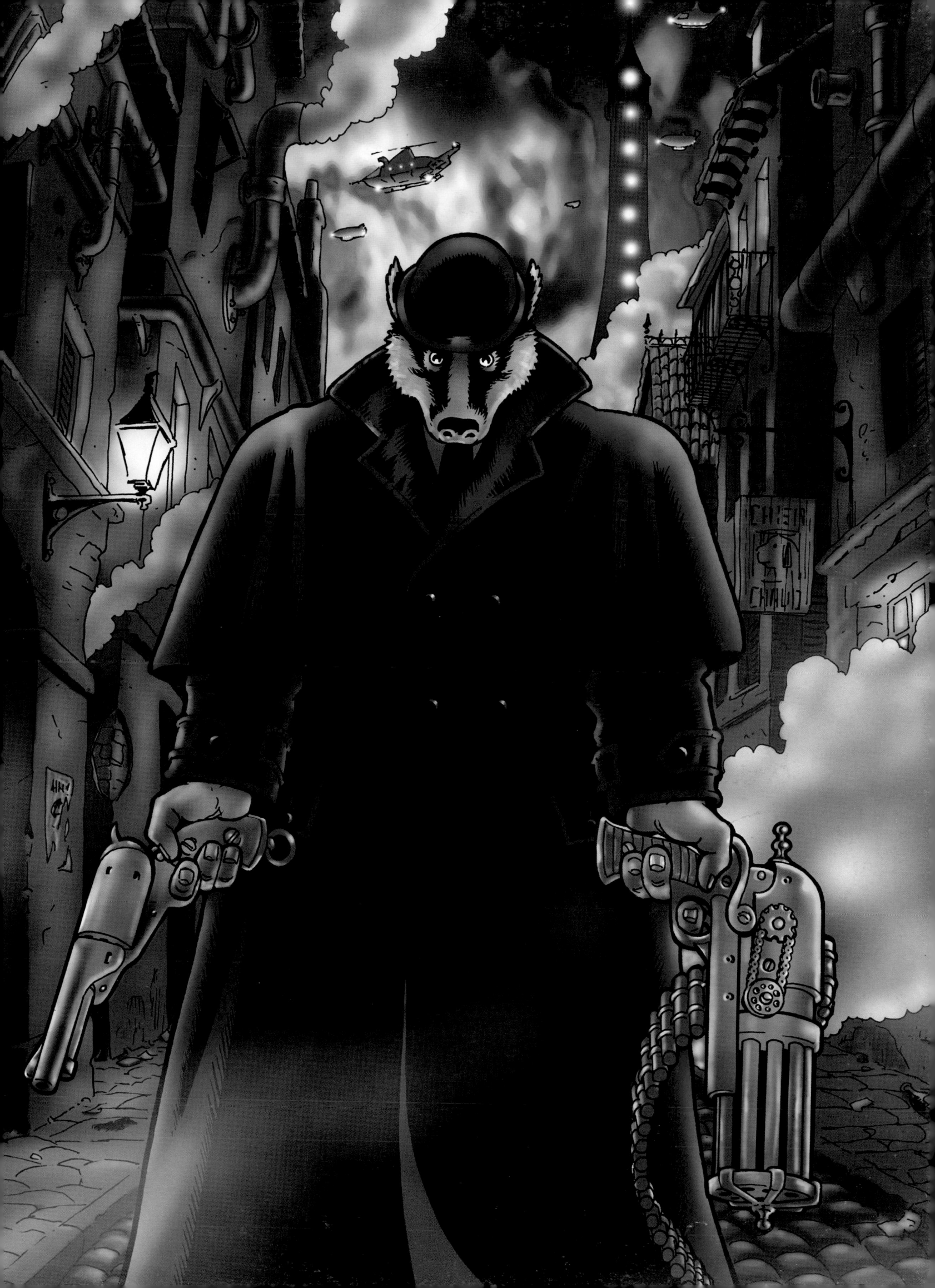

THE BRYAN TALBOT STRIPOGRAPHY

...does not include covers, illustrated stories or single illustrations. All strips written, pencilled and inked by Bryan Talbot unless otherwise stated. Only short strips have page counts and foreign language reprints are omitted. Strips are in black and white unless colouring is indicated.

Superharris (Ongoing jam with Bonk in Hac, Harris College (aka Preston Polytechnic) student newspaper 1971-1972)
Collected in one self-published litho edition (10 of which had laminated covers) in 1978 as Bog Standard Comix

CHESTER P. HACKENBUSH, THE PSYCHEDELIC ALCHEMIST
Out of the Crucible (in Brainstorm Comix 2, 1975, Alchemy)
From Here to Infinity (in Brainstorm Comix 2, 1976, Alchemy)
A Streetcar Named Delirium (in Brainstorm Comix 4, 1977, Alchemy)
All reprinted in one volume in 1982 and in 1999 with added material as BRAINSTORM! Alchemy.

The Influence of Hassab-I-Sabbah, 1 page (in Seed v5/5, 1976)
Reprinted in Ex-Directory – the Secret Files of Bryan Talbot, 1997, Knockabout Comics and in BRAINSTORM! 1999, Alchemy,

THE PAPIST AFFAIR, 7 pages (in The Mixed Bunch 1, 1976, first Luther Arkwright story), Alchemy.
Reprinted in The Crystal Palace Exhibition of 1991, 1991, Propaganda Comix and in BRAINSTORM! 1999, Alchemy

Komix Comics, 2 pages (in Streetcomix 3, 1977 Street Press)
Reprinted in Adult Comics by Roger Sabin, Routledge 1993 and in BRAINSTORM! 1999 Alchemy,

Claude Cloud, 1 page, manual seperation colour (in Brainstorm Comix 4, 1977 Alchemy)

The World Heavyweight Roboxing Championship, 3 Pages (jam with Bonk, Brainstorm Fantasy Comix 1, 1977 Alchemy)

Committed, 2 pages (in Kak Comics 2, 1977 Street Comics)

Komicsscimok, 2 pages (in Kak Comics 2, 1977 Street Comics)

Interlude, 1 page (in Home Grown 1, 1977, Alchemy)
Reprinted in BRAINSTORM! 1999 Alchemy

The Omega Report (in Amazing Rock'n'Roll Adventures, Brainstorm Comix 6, 1978 Alchemy)
Reprinted in BRAINSTORM! 1999 Alchemy

LUTHER ARKWRIGHT
Serialised in Near Myths 1-5, 1978–1980 Galaxy Media and Pssst! 2-10, 1982 Never Ltd. (reprints Near Myths and new material.)
Collected as The Adventures of Luther Arkwright Volume 1, 1982 Never Ltd. Reprinted with new cover 1987.

For A Few Gallons More, 4 page Arkwright and Ogoth the Barbarian strip (jam with Chris Welch, in Moon Comics 3, 1979 Street Comics)
Reprinted in Sideshow Comics 1, 1988 Pan Graphics

The Fire Opal of Set, 2 pages (in Imagine 14, 1984 TSR UK Ltd.)

THE ADVENTURES OF LUTHER ARKWRIGHT 1-9, Valkyrie Press, 1987-1989: reprints Near Myths and Pssst! plus new material to complete the story: reprinted as The Adventures of Luther Arkwright 1-9, Dark Horse, March 1990 - January 1991.
Material not in Volume 1, with the exception of For A Few Gallons More and The Fire Opal of Set, collected in The Adventures of Luther Arkwright Volumes 2 1987, Valkyrie & Volume 3, 1989, Proutt.
The whole reprinted in one volume, Dark Horse 1997

FRANK FAZAKERLY, SPACE ACE OF THE FUTURE (in Ad Astra 1 –17, October 1978-September 1981, by BT)
Serialised in The Manchester Flash, circa 1983. Reprinted in one volume, Frank Fazakerly, Space Ace of the Future, 1991 Kimota Publishing

Ghost Train, 1 page (in Comics Plus 5, 1979, Fanzine)

Smokey Bears (2 pages, manual seperation colour in Home Grown #5 1979, 1 page in #6, 1980, 1 page in #8, 1980, 3 pages in #10, 1981/82 Alchemy, the last strip reprinted in Ex-Directory – the Secret Files of Bryan Talbot, 1997, Knockabout Comics)

Spaced out in Amsterdam, 3 pages (in Home Grown 7, 1980 Alchemy)
Reprinted in Ex-Directory – the Secret Files of Bryan Talbot, 1997 Knockabout Comics

Arnold Gets Cross, 4 pages (in Knockabout Comics 2, 1981 Knockabout Comics co-plotted by Rick Jakimowicz)
Reprinted in Ex-Directory – the Secret Files of Bryan Talbot 1997, Knockabout Comics

The Wages of Sin (in 2000ad, Prog 257, 1982, IPC Written by Alan Moore).
Reprinted in The Best of 2000ad Monthly 1986 Fleetway, Alan Moore's Shocking Futures, 1986, Titan Books and Time Twisters, 1987, Quality

Ro-Busters: Old Red Eyes is Back, 7 pages (in 2000ad Annual 1983 IPC Written by Alan Moore)
Reprinted and crudely re-edited into 5 pages in The Very Best of 2000ad Special Edition, circa 1990, Fleetway

Scumworld (in Sounds, weekly 1983–1984, written by The Crabs from Uranus – BT Pseudonym)

NEMESIS (written by Pat Mills)
The Gothic Empire (in 2000ad Prog 389-406, 1984–1985, IPC)
Reprinted in one Volume as Nemesis Book 3, 1985 Titan Books
Reprinted in The Complete Nemesis the Warlock: Book One. 2006, Rebellion

The Vengeance of Thoth (in 2000ad Prog 435-445, 1985, IPC)
Reprinted in one Volume as Nemesis Book 4, 1986, Titan Books

Torquemurder (in 2000ad Prog 482-487, 500-504, 1986–1987 IPC)
Reprinted in one Volume as Nemesis Book 6, 1987, Titan Books.
These Nemesis stories were also serialised in Spellbinders 1987–88, Quality Comics and also reprinted in The Best of 2000ad Monthly circa 1989, Fleetway

Torquemada: The Garden of Alien Delights, 20 pages (in Diceman 3, 1986, IPC)
Reprinted in Nemesis Book 7, 1987, Titan Books

Cold Snap, 4 pages (in Food for Thought Ethiopian benefit comic 1985, Flying Pig Enterprises, written by Alan Moore).
Reprinted in International Times circa 1987, Slow Death, 1992, Last Gasp and Ex-Directory – the Secret Files of Bryan Talbot, 1997 Knockabout Comics

Slaine, 7 pages (Inks only, in 2000ad Prog 431, 1985, IPC, written by Pat Mills, pencils by Glen Fabry)

JUDGE DREDD
House of Death, 20 pages (in Diceman 1, 1986, IPC, written by Pat Mills).
Reprinted in 2000ad Extreme Edition 1, Autumn 2003, Rebellion

The Last Voyage of the Flying Dutchman, 7 pages (in 2000ad Prog 459, 1986, IPC, written by Alan Grant & John Wagner).
Reprinted in Judge Dredd's Rough Justice, 1990, Titan

Judge Dredd and the Seven Dwarves, 7 pages. Fully painted colour (in Judge Dredd Annual 1987, 1986, IPC, written by Alan Grant & John Wagner).
Reprinted in Judge Dredd's Crime File, 1998, Titan

Ladies Night, 8 pages. Fully painted colour (in 2000ad Annual 1987 IPC by Alan Grant & John Wagner).
Reprinted in Judge Dredd's Hardcase Papers 4, 1991, Fleetway

Untitled **Judge Dredd,** 1 page. Fully painted colour (in Info. 1993, Dept. of Trade: free teenage consumer guide circulated to all the schools in the UK. Written by publisher)

Enemy Alien, 4 pages (Inks only, in 2000ad Sci-Fi Special, 1986, IPC, written and pencilled by Mike Matthews)

Spill it! 1 page (in Heartbreak Hotel 2, 1988, Willyprods/Small Time Ink).
Reprinted in Ex-Directory – the Secret Files of Bryan Talbot, 1997 Knockabout Comics

From Homogenous to Honey, 4 pages (in AARGH! 1988, Mad Love, written by Neil Gaiman, inks by Mark Buckingham)

Sloth, 7 pages (in Seven Deadly Sins, 1989, Knockabout Comics, written by Neil Gaiman)
Reprinted in Ex-Directory – the Secret Files of Bryan Talbot, 1997 Knockabout Comics

The Bloody Saint (in Hellblazer Annual 1, 1989, DC Comics, written by Jamie Delano, coloured by Lovern Kindzierski)

Mr X: Windows, 1/4 page panel of 7 page jam, various artists. (in A1 #2, 1989, Atomika Press)

THE NAZZ (in The Nazz 1-4, 1990-1991, DC Comics, written by Tom Veitch, coloured by Steve Whittaker (1) and Les Dorscheid (2-4)

Africa, 3 pages (in The Comic Relief Comic, 1991, Comic Relief, written by Igor Goldkind, fully rendered colour by Al Davison, benefit comic)

SANDMAN (Written by Neil Gaiman)

August (in Sandman 30, 1991, DC Comics, inks by Stan Woch, coloured by Daniel Vozzo)

The Song of Orpheus (in Sandman Special 1, 1991, DC Comics, inks by Mark Buckingham, coloured by Daniel Vozzo).
Both reprinted in Fables and Reflections (hardback 1993, trade paperback, 1993, DC Comics)

A Game of You: Over The Sea to Sky, 16 pages (in Sandman 36, 1992, DC Comics, inks by Stan Woch, coloured by Daniel Vozzo)
Reprinted in A Game of You (hardback 1993, trade paperback 1993, DC Comics)

Worlds End, 34 1/2 pages, (framing sequences in Sandman 51-56 1993, DC Comics, inked by Mark Buckingham (51–55) and Mark Buckingham, Dick Giordano, BT and Steve Leialoha (56), coloured by Daniel Vozzo).
Reprinted in Worlds End (hardback, 1994, trade paperback, 1994, DC Comics)

The Tempest, 7 pages (in Sandman 75, 1996, DC Comics, inked by Charles Vess, coloured by Daniel Vozzo).
Reprinted in The Wake (hardback, 1997, trade paperback, 1997, DC Comics)

NB: In the case of A Game of You and The Tempest, Bryan was called in for pencilling chores at the last minute to meet deadlines, hence the small page count.

All the above Sandman stories have since been re-issued in a set of standard format trade paperback editions and also as individual comics in the **Essential Vertigo series by DC Comics.**

────────────────

Shade the Changing Man: The Sante Fe Trail (in Shade the Changing Man 14, August, 1991, DC Comics, written by Peter Milligan, inks by Mark Pennington, coloured by Daniel Vozzo)

Brainworms, 10 pages, fully painted colour (in Xpresso Special 2, December, 1991, Fleetway, written by Matthias Schultheiss)

Mask in Legends of the Dark Knight, 39–40, 1992, DC Comics (coloured by Olyoptics).
Reprinted in Dark Legends, 1996, DC Comics (US) Titan Books (UK)

Celtic Warrior, 4 pages (in Dark Horse Presents, 1994, Dark Horse Comics, written by Lucy Swan).
Reprinted in Ex-Directory – the Secret Files of Bryan Talbot, 1997, Knockabout Comics

An Honest Answer, 4 pages (in the UK SF Eastercon souvenir booklet, 1995, written by Neil Gaiman).
Reprinted in Ex-Directory – the Secret Files of Bryan Talbot, 1997, Knockabout Comics and Unknown Quantities, benefit comic by Funny Valentine Press (US) 2000.

Last Refuge, 2 pages in Kimota 2, Preston SF Group, 1995, (from unpublished IPC kids' horror comic, 1983), rescripted by Graeme Hurry

Nativity on Ice 1, page in Kimota 3, Preston SF Group, 1995, Written by Alan Moore (unpublished Sounds strip from 1883)

Evolution, 2 pages (in the UK SF Eastercon souvenir booklet, 1996).
Reprinted in Ex-Directory – the Secret Files of Bryan Talbot, 1997, Knockabout Comics

The Tale of One Bad Rat 1-4, ink line with fully painted colour (1994-1995, Dark Horse comics).
Trade paperback edition, 1995 (US: Dark Horse comics, UK: Titan Books)
Limited edition hardback, 1996 (Dark Horse comics)

TEKNOPHAGE
Neil Gaiman's Mr Hero 1, 6 pages, pencils and inks (1995, Tekno Comix, written by Rick Veitch, coloured by Angus McKie)

Neil Gaiman's Mr Hero 2, 5 pages, inked by Angus McKie (1995, Tekno Comix, written by Rick Veitch, coloured by Angus McKie)

Neil Gaiman's Wheel of Worlds One shot, 11 pages (1995, Tekno Comix Written by Rick Veitch, coloured by Angus McKie)

Neil Gaiman's Teknophage 1–6 (1995–1996, Tekno Comix Written by Rick Veitch, inked and coloured by Angus McKie, #6 inked by John Coulthart)

ShadowDeath 1–6 (1996, Tekno Comix, written by BT, pencilled by David Pugh, inked by Tim Perkins, coloured by Angus McKie)

BIG BOOKS

The Cannabis Conspiracy, 4 pages (in The Big book of Conspiracies 1995, Paradox Press, written by Doug Moench).
Reprinted in Tales of Reefer Madness, 1999, Zephyr (unauthorised bootleg)

The Ten-in-One, 4 pages (in The Big book of Freaks, 1996, Paradox Press, written by Ricky Jay)

Sore Losers, 2 pages (in The Big book of Losers, 1997, Paradox Press, written by Paul Kirchner)

The King and Mrs Simpson, 2 pages (in The Big book of Scandal, 1997, Paradox Press, written by Jonathan Vankin)

Weird Romance (in The Dreaming 9–12, 1997, DC Comics, written by BT, pencilled and inked by Dave Taylor (9) and pencilled by Peter Dougherty, inked by Tayyar Ozkan (10-12), coloured by Daniel Vozzo)

The Worm (trade paperback version of The Longest Comic Strip in the World charity project, 2 panels, 1999, Slab O' Concrete, written by Alan Moore and others and drawn by "a galaxy of greats")

HEART OF EMPIRE, or the Legacy of Luther Arkwright 1–9, (1999, Dark Horse comics, coloured by Angus McKie)

Trade paperback edition, 2001 (Dark Horse comics)
Limited edition hardback, 2001 (Dark Horse comics)

Sire, 4 pages, fully painted colour (in Vampires, 2001, Editions Carabas, France, written by Jérôme Martineau)

The Dead Boy Detectives and the Secret of Immortality 1– 4 (2001, DC Comics, written by Ed Brubaker, inked by Steve Leialoha, coloured by Danny Vozzo)

Memento, 12 page "silent" strip, fully painted/computer colour (in 2000AD Prog 2002, Rebellion 2001)

9/11, 2 pages, Sept. 11th benefit book, 2002

Real Life Rock Tales, 1 page full colour, written by Nick Cave (Spin magazine, USA, Jan. 2003)

Bag o'Bones, 22 pages (Fables #11, DC Comics, 2003, written by Bill Willingham, coloured by Danny Vozzo)

Nightjar, 8 pages (Yuggoth Cultures #1, Avatar Comics, 2003, written by Alan Moore)

Alice in Sunderland, 320 page graphic novel (US: Dark Horse, UK: Jonathan Cape, March 2007)

The History of British Comics, 3 pages, computer composed (The Guardian Guide Newspaper supplement, September 2007)

Cherubs! Graphic Novel (Desperado, November 2007, drawn by Mark Stafford)

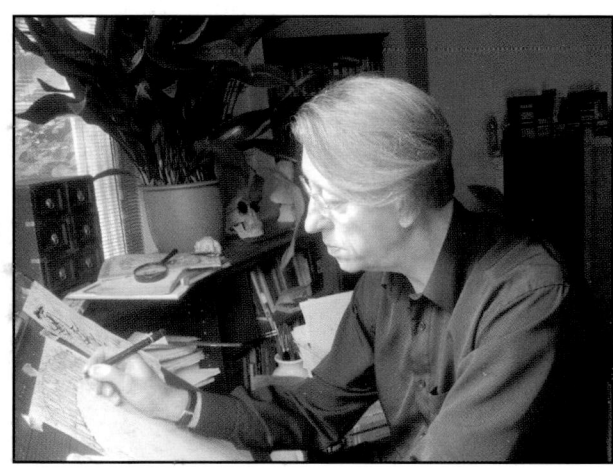

Other Books in print by Bryan Talbot

BRAINSTORM!
THE ADVENTURES OF LUTHER ARKWRIGHT
HEART OF EMPIRE: THE LEGACY OF LUTHER ARKWRIGHT
THE TALE OF ONE BAD RAT
ALICE IN SUNDERLAND
THE NAKED ARTIST (Prose)

Also contributions to:

DARK LEGENDS
THE COMPLETE NEMESIS THE WARLOCK Vol 1
SANDMAN: FABLES AND REFLECTIONS
SANDMAN: A GAME OF YOU
SANDMAN: WORLDS END
FABLES: STORYBOOK LOVE
SEVEN DEADLY SINS